THE STELLAR MAN

THE STELLAR MAN

Hermetic Philosophy, Book Two

By

JOHN BAINES

SECOND EDITION

Edited by the Editorial
Staff of the John Baines Institute, Inc.

2002

Published by
JOHN BAINES INSTITUTE, INC.
Box 8556 • F.D.R. Station • New York, New York • 10150
jbi@bway.net

THE STELLAR MAN
(Originally published as "El Hombre Estelar")
By John Baines

Translated from Spanish by Margaret L. Nunez.
Formerly Edited by Judith Hipskind
(First Edition published by Llewellyn Publications,
formerly ISBN 0-87542-026-5)

ISBN 1-882692-04-7
Library of Congress Control Number: 00-093458

First Edition, 1985
Second Edition, 2002

CONTENTS

Notes from the Author vii

    I   Message from ISIS 1

   II The Antichrist 5

  III Dissection of *Sapiens* 25

  IV The Collective Soul of the Species 41

   V To Be or Not to Be? 67

  VI The Illusion of True Knowledge 87

 VII The Illusion of Freedom 107

VIII Hermeticism 121

  IX The Seekers 131

The Road to Olympus

   X The Seven Keys of Wisdom 147

  XI The Disciples 193

 XII True Initiation 207

XIII The Ordeals 237

XIV The Obstacles 247

 XV Initiatic Practices 251

XVI The "Volitive I" 257

XVII The Life and Powers of the Stellar Man 279

XVIII General Overview 297

NOTES FROM THE AUTHOR

Whoever reads this book expecting to find an informative essay on "sugar-coated" commercial esotericism will be greatly disappointed.

The Stellar Man is about a science more elevated than any now known, and what it can do for mankind.

This wisdom, the true origin of all knowledge, represents the highest treasure that the human being can ever succeed in possessing in this or any other century, on the planet Earth or anywhere else in the far reaches of the Universe. It is the *arte magnum*, the perfect vision of the essential reality of Nature, which encompasses developing the capacity to see oneself objectively, and evaluating the true level of development of one's own instrument of knowledge, the mind. All knowledge, in order to be true, has to be based on man's internal reality, and has to be integrated into a wise, just, omnipresent, immortal, and eternal nature.

The ability to see reality is not a congenital capacity. The human being is only able to observe the map that he himself created from a subjective, limited, and rationalized interpretation.

This process creates a personalized pseudo-reality, of which there are as many as there are inhabitants of this planet. I call this imaginative creation "social reality," since in practice, the individual is a mere cultural resonator and an appendage of the collective psyche of humanity. This is why people live "half-way" and are a mixture of good and bad; why they are a little asleep and a little awake; why they are insignificant even with all their delusions of grandeur. In other words, they do not live profoundly and cannot even grasp the overwhelming significance of this fact. They just graze the surface of the planet and the epidermis of knowledge.

According to tradition, more than twenty centuries ago, the greatest sage of all lived on our planet; Hermes Trismegistus, the three times great. His Teaching, being of extraterrestrial origin, was called *Hermeticism*. Its objective is the profound knowledge of oneself and of the Universe. According to Hermes, the microcosmos and the macrocosmos are analogous, which is why the conscious penetration into one's own Universe will also lead the student to universal wisdom. The characteristic of this knowledge is that it transcends time and space, and corresponds to the secret anatomy of Nature, which like God, has neither beginning nor end.

When Hermes wanted to transmit his teachings to a chosen few, he found himself faced with the problem of the limitations of language, which is descriptive and informationally based. This inherent disability made human language inadequate to meet the desired end, since all authentic wisdom is "meaningful" and not "informational." It can only be comprehended at the level of BEING, and not through merely intellectual faculties. For this reason, an unknown language had to be used, different from the language of people and nations. It is a "language of meaning," that emanates exclusively from a potent mind at the level of higher consciousness, and which far exceeds the habitual condition of man. The "language of the gods" was the only means that could assure the comprehension of that sublime teaching.

Hermes started to transmit his Teaching in great secrecy, choosing only the most prepared as his students, due to the great difficulty that such a *magnum opus* entailed. In time, he succeeded in forming a few inheritors and continuers, Masters who formed an Initiatic School. They formed an occult fraternity that fulfilled its work behind the scenes and in silence. They knew that there were many neophytes who were guided by greed and ambition to obtain unlimited personal power to satisfy sordid passions, rather than a genuine spiritual or philosophical restlessness.

Many of those who gained admission into this School failed in their tests and their twisted intention and absolute lack of ethics became evident over time. The possession of ethics was an indispensable condition to be chosen to receive the highest level of instruction.

The limited and superficial information that these pretenders thus obtained became the basis for the birth of a false and spurious esotericism. It was based on speculation and superstition, and its dissemination is the foundation of the immense majority of what today is erroneously known as "magic," "occultism," and so forth. True and sacred occultism was the knowledge of Hermes, hidden from those who have not succeeded in mastering the language of the gods, and from those who, owing to their own limitations, pride, and pettiness, were not concerned with developing their higher consciousness.

What is certain is that despite the time and difficulties, a few Masters with the necessary power and wisdom to confer *Hermetic initiation* have existed in every epoch. This initiation is a mystical and transcendental event that offers the individual a certain opportunity to cross the threshold that leads to the path towards spiritual perfection and cosmic wisdom. If the individual triumphs in such an undertaking, he becomes a *Stellar Man*. This represents the highest goal that *Homo sapiens* can aspire to, and which corresponds to the culmination of the evolutionary process, but which the species would reach only after many thousands of years of successful development. Making this ascending leap leads the individual to completely overcome his animal condition, thereby moving him up one step on the evolutionary scale in the Universe. The path of self-perfection is long and arduous. There can be no other way than to pursue the attainment of authentic power over oneself and one's own existence, and to pursue the possession of a state of consciousness in which disharmony, destructiveness, ugliness, aggression, and unhappiness no longer exist. The real Hermetic Initiate acquires the capacity to transcend such petty realities, to instead place himself in the unlimited and infinite context of absolute reality; that which transcends time and space. From that moment on, he will never again be defeated by hesitation, loneliness, or doubt. He will have united himself harmoniously with that unique and powerful force which is a creator and maintainer of life, what Hermes called "MIND."

The Hermetic Principle says: "The ALL is MIND; The Universe is Mental." This means that only one class of essential energy exists in the cosmos. This energy, this higher conscious and intelligent force, is divided, and projects itself into infinite vibrations and forms of life, thus maintaining the balance of creation and life of all animate and inanimate species.

The occult anatomy of the cosmos is the mechanics of Nature, whose forces reciprocally feed from and nourish man, influencing everything in his life. Knowledge, and the use of these forces, is what permits the genuine Hermeticist to act with his mind in different vital situations in order to ensure the achievement of his goals. Fate does not exist; everything has a cause and effect; nothing happens by chance. True magic bears no resemblance whatsoever to superstition and witchcraft. The true magus, is a KING of his internal world which by analogy can influence the external world. "As it is above, so it is below." "As it is within, so it is without."

Guided by voraciousness and greed, there are many who believe that it is possible to steal the secret and usurp the magic power, supposing that it is based on the development of parapsychological faculties. Nothing is further from reality. Magic is the path of the mutant. It is the supreme art, which leads to one's own liberation and spiritual perfection. It is the ascending evolutionary spiral that leads the individual to the only true heaven—the one gained through one's own merit and through internal discipline—it is the legacy of Hermes. It is not possible to reach this goal without having first dominated oneself. Nature makes the candidate for immortality undergo various tests. The will and character of the candidate have to be tempered silently in the forge of daily experience, until he cleanses his heart of all impurities. It is not possible to approach Isis, the mistress of the mysteries of Nature, without having first achieved a state of inner transparency. If this were not so, the candidate would end as the butterfly burned by the flame of a candle, for supreme truth blinds or burns the evildoer and the impure as much as it elevates the just and perfect.

The noble figure of Hermes, the envoy of the gods, rises out of the remote past showing us the correct path.

You who read this book are free to make your own decision.

THE AUTHOR
Written for the 2nd edition

NOTE: The use of the masculine pronoun "he" is used throughout this book, (other than in cases that specifically refer to the masculine gender) to refer to both men and women. This was done with the aim of simplifying the sentence structure.

I

MESSAGE FROM ISIS

"I, ISIS, mistress of the mysteries of Nature, speak to you.

You, novice who seeks to go through the gates of initiation, and you, layman who will read with idle curiosity, calm your spirit, clear your mind, calm your emotions. Get away from worldly noises, and look for shelter under the mantle of your own SELF so you may cross the threshold that leads to the abode of the magicians with no danger. Cast away your prejudices; shed your egotism; flee from personalism and rashness for an instant; analyze with serene eyes.

Do not fear aught but yourself; do not doubt but that which you analyze superficially; do not deny before meditating. Separate yourself from the multitude that obscures your ideas; be yourself and think for yourself; do not limit yourself.

You, seeker of wonder, you, candidate for initiation, do not look into the distance. Gather all your energy within yourself. Forget about India and Tibet. Do not cry out for God, Allah, or Jesus.

What you look for is right where you are at this moment. Yes, stop looking toward the outside and bury your sight deeply within yourself. Tune your perceptions, sharpen your senses, and there in the center of your being are you, your "I," your real essence, the truth behind lies, the immortal energy that gives life to the clay that is you. Look with devotion and reverence because there is light . . . and the light that blinds you is God. Listen to how it decrees: 'I am the road and the life.'

But . . . beware! You cannot contemplate God face to face without dying. Are you willing to continue? I can grant you a great gift. I offer you . . . death! Do not tremble, this death is the gift of the immortals; it is the gift of the phoenix that is gloriously reborn from its own ashes. To be, one must not be; to be born and to be, one must first die. If you achieve this, you will be called the twice born. Do not scorn my offer; consider it carefully. It is better to die now than to live awaiting death. Do not believe that if you reject me you will be able to continue your path unharmed. On the contrary, all paths lead to me; ignore me and you will be like an orphan who does not know its parents. You only have two paths; either I devour you or you unite with me. Yours, and only yours, is the choice.

If you decide to be devoured, fully dedicate your life to enjoyment; drink the last drop from the cup of pleasure. Close your mind to the voice of your spirit, abandon yourself to the beast and enjoy the sensual pleasure of matter. Thus, when you are least aware, the moment of final cannibalism will arrive. Do you really believe I will take pity on you? You deceive yourself; I have no feelings. I am beyond pleasure and pain, beyond right and wrong. I am like the sun that rises in the morning to light everything equally. After your death, you will become only remains and a relic. Afterwards . . . not even that.

If you desire to marry me, you must be ready to suffer the death of initiation. You must pass the trials the terrible Sphinx will send to you without mercy in order to judge your spiritual courage and the quality of your nature. I surrender myself only to he who has reached the stage of crucifixion, resisting the attacks of the four elements. I love only those who have drunk from the cup of bitterness, of betrayal, of ridicule and mockery, of persecutions, of slander, and of defamation. I love the initiates who have persisted with courage, suffering the loneliness of the spirit in the midst of a world of animals. You come to me after experiencing slander and defamation, which are the specific trials of the element of air; after blows and persecution, the trials of the element of earth; after sensual temptations and vices, which are trials of the element of water; and after dominating uncontrolled ambitions, which are the trials of fire.

This quaternary corresponds to each of the ends of the cross to which one who came to me was nailed . . . Jesus Christ. Nevertheless, others even greater have lived and live in secret; no one knows of their existence because it is better for their work.

Do not believe that in the world there exist only the once born and the twice born; unfortunately the once-and-a-half born and the aborted ones also exist. Beware not to be taken in by their convincing lies and machiavellian language. These beings live neither in this world nor the next. They are neither initiates nor laymen, but imitators of Masters, semi-sages, sowers with unclean hands, the followers of dead scrolls, and black magicians who covet me and boast of my love when they are not even worthy of my smile. Some may wear saris or tunics; others, collars and aprons; others, the

Rosicrucian attire; some proclaim themselves the only possessors of the truth, believing that they actually possess this monopoly. All of them claim my friendship, but are only beggars who plead to me for crumbs of wisdom. You do not achieve second birth by standing on your head or meditating, nor in the coffin of purely symbolic ceremonies, nor by good works or the grace of the Holy Spirit.

If you disdain me, receive my blessings and continue on your road, destined to be food for the gods. Not all can be men; some can only be animals, or worse, vegetables. If you come to me through curiosity, think twice. It is easy to be rash with what one does not know. If you are not brave enough, turn back; shield yourself with your vanity and your pride, content yourself to look down at the ground like your kin. If you are not prepared, do not aspire to see my face; unfortunate is he who, possessed by animal greed or misguided curiosity, contemplates only my reflection, as he will never forget me, and will die tormented by the desire to possess me.

If you are prepared, if you have eyes to see and ears to hear, if your intention is pure and noble, proceed without discouragement and know that from the moment you cross the threshold of the occult abode, I will be anxiously awaiting you like the young bride for her first love. This book can help you; it can be the guide that will take you to the hidden door, which so many seek and so few find. Seek and you will find; do not pray to the gods, fight for me. You will conquer me with the strength of your decision, not by praying."

II

THE ANTICHRIST

It is surprising how the human being knows so many things and understands so little. Just as in homeopathy, the noble product (knowledge) is infinitesimally diluted by man's inability to understand.

Homo sapiens dedicates his most important efforts to increasing his knowledge, but it is precisely in this persistence that he begins to lose himself more and more in a haze of uncertainty and disorientation. Afire with the thirst for knowledge, he tirelessly pursues any new thesis or theory that may beckon, but, like that of the mythological Tantalus, his thirst, far from being satiated, only increases.

A paradoxical destiny surrounds this deluded creature: to know more each day but to understand less. Inevitably, he extends himself daily up to the point of losing his own identity, constrained to draw away from himself to merge with the external. *Homo sapiens* has advanced with extraordinary speed in the conquest of science, and with the same momentum, he has lost himself in a world of phantoms born from the collective hallucinations of a world becoming daily more artificial, stereotyped, and programmed. In this world, the one who triumphs is usually the man of the masses who demonstrates perfect submission to the norms of the multitude, and who decides at an early age not to think for himself, but to act instead with the multitude's *collective mind*. This is an unfailing passport to material success, but the price paid is so much higher than the reward. The price is one's own individuality, the much-prized goal of the Delphic command, "know thyself." As it happens, one who knows himself well and therefore understands others is often harassed, disregarded, and ostracized. This is due to the fact that leadership usually belongs to the mediocre who glorify the golden calf and celebrate the empty stereotype of the programmed individual. The temple of Delphi and its ideals no longer exist. They have been replaced by the temple of the university, the temple of the law, the temple of religions, and the temple of political ideologies and economic systems, along with all their slogans and phrases. All these are united by a common denominator: "Do not recognize yourself; surrender yourself to the multitude and obey its designs."

Very few people are aware of this situation, but some feel it instinctively and try to rebel against the system, without knowing what really leads them to this reaction. Young people, for example, intuitively resist, although sometimes by mistaken paths, only to be absorbed by the collective entity. Later, as the years go by and their cerebral programming is strengthened, youth also yields to the strong influence of the collective mind.

A person who does not rapidly integrate collectively is believed to be antisocial, but he who merges easily and completely with the masses and loses his individuality is considered very valuable. This willingness to merge is considered the correct way to be and is seen as the mark of a *social conscience*. Here again *sapiens* has missed the point, for it is not possible to help or love others without first knowing oneself.

Two thousand years ago, *sapiens* basically had the same problems he does now; the same fears, desires, anxieties, ambitions, greed, lies, cowardice, complexes, internal conflicts, and confusions. His norms of behavior were no different in essence than those at present. On the other hand, his material conditions were dramatically different from today's circumstances, considering the astounding progress that can be observed up until the present day. The question arises whether this same progress has also occurred in the internal nature of *sapiens*. That is to say, is he a better human being today; does he have more quality as a person than in earlier times? The reply is clearly no. No appreciable change has taken place in the human quality of *sapiens* in two thousand years, nor even in five thousand years. He has only increased his intellectual capacity, due to the powerful and ever increasing demands of civilization.

Although the world has progressed from a barbaric state to civilization in the course of history, the *savage sapiens* is today basically as primitive as in the distant past, except that he is now covered with dozens of layers of cultural and educational varnish.

To break through the spiritual isolation of humanity, a superior being full of love and compassion came to the world one day: Christ. He wanted to give *sapiens* an opportunity to know a different world, a world without violence, hate, slavery, or contradiction, to show *sapiens* what he could achieve.

The collective mind of the multitude, programmed according to the dictum "an eye for an eye, a tooth for a tooth," violently rejected the Christian message and destroyed the Messiah, as had happened on other occasions when Christ had come to earth, manifested through other superior men.

This is how the multitudes serve as an instrument for the Antichrist, the blind monster, the headless beast that lies in wait for all those who want to achieve the conscious individuality which would allow them to stop being *sapiens* and convert them into *Stellar Men*. To be *Stellar Men* is the pinnacle of the evolution of *Homo sapiens*.

At some time, no one knows when, the false legend of the Antichrist was born. The legend is erroneous in imagining that a mythological being would be born into the world in order to destroy it through the perversion of Christian values, and that this being would incarnate into a man to undertake this ominous work.

The legend as it exists now might be a distortion of the original Hermetic term *Antechrist*. In Hermetic circles, the term *Antechrist* designated one who would act as *announcer of Christ*, preparing the way. In these terms, the only *Antechrist* was John the Baptist. Thus, we use the word

Antichrist to mean *contrary to Christ* and *Antechrist* to mean *before Christ*.

Unfortunately, today we cannot count on the spiritual impulse of Christ incarnated in a human body. Christ as a divine force, omnipresent in religious temples, is but a symbolic allegory that invites believers to follow a comforting example. No known individual currently possesses a real spiritual force which could be called *Christic*. The priests of different religions only try to imitate Christ, but unfortunately they do it with external and prefabricated spirituality, in accordance to the stereotypes established by the patriarchs of the church.

However, ignorance does not necessarily mean nonexistence. The truth is that the torch of spirituality is presently carried by only a few individuals who are unknown to the masses. Let us call them the *magicians*, in the dignified sense of this expression, which is usually employed in a vulgar manner. We are referring to the *great initiates, Masters, unknown superior beings, or occult sages of humanity*.

Why use the term "magicians?" Simply because the ignorant masses have always thus described those who possess strange qualities or powers unknown to them. Also, there was the Inquisition, which labeled these wise men as such in order to disparage and annul their unusual ideas. For this reason, it is time to adopt this term with pride, with the intention of eventually washing away its negative and superstitious stigma. Witchcraft, ignorance, and superstition belong exclusively to *sapiens*, and not to the *magicians*. Unfortunately, in the past, popular opinion has described *magicians* as those simple sorcerers who travel to "sabbaths," using low-class sorcery to satisfy their base passions.

Why do we designate Christ as the symbol of spirituality? Because Jesus was the most distinguished member of the *Magician's Fraternity*, prepared specifically for his mission to make Christ incarnate in himself. Jesus and Christ were two different persons; one human, the other, divine.

Christ is a superior being who is on an advanced level on the scale of evolution, which a human being could reach in perhaps millions of years of evolution. Let us conceive of him as an extraterrestrial spiritual power, which we could call an *Archangel*. This *Archangel*, due to his very lengthy evolution, possessed perfect and powerful spirituality. This is why Jesus went through a long preparation for this role, for he had to be able to withstand an extremely high vibration in his physical body. This vibration could only manifest itself for brief moments, as its intensity could destroy the nervous and cellular system of Jesus' body. Christ was the one who performed miracles through Jesus, who provided the matter for his manifestation.

The *Magician's Fraternity* remains well hidden, as it has a right to its own privacy, but some of its members have intermingled with ordinary people, motivated by the wish to show *sapiens* the road to a higher life. The magicians know, however, that knowledge of *The Hermetic Art* as an instrument to reach spiritual heights, is only for the "elite" and is not to be divulged. Nevertheless, the fraternity of initiates provides the opportunity for any person with sufficient merit to join the Hermetic elite of *Magicians* or *Stellar Men*, if the scope and intelligence of his efforts permits him to do so.

The science of the Magicians is called *Hermetic Art* in honor of Hermes Trismegistus. According to tradition, he arrived on earth from outer space approximately thirty thousand years ago, anointed as Supreme Grand Master of the Initiatic Fraternity.

Inspired by his light, Egypt became great and wise, and the sacred science of its priests was called *Hermeticism*. In those days, only by means of huge sacrifices and trials was it possible to belong to a Hermetic Initiatic School. The great majority who succeeded in entering such a school faltered along the way, lacking the moral and spiritual courage to overcome the multiple obstacles, temptations, and trials by which ISIS, mistress of the mysteries of Nature, evaluated the true worth of those who aspired to the supreme knowledge of the absolute truth.

It was in one of those schools that Jesus himself became a Hermeticist and reached the highest degrees of initiation.

Because the time is right, we will divulge the mystery of Jesus the Christ and the causes for the moral suffering of humanity, according to the teachings of the *Magician's Fraternity*. This moral mystery stems from the *adoration of the golden calf*; from the submission of the human being to the god of money. In honor of this god, he must give up or sacrifice his spiritual possibilities in order to be able to subsist. Those who possess adequate means of subsistence generally pervert their potential spiritual values in the foolish game of gaining social position on the consumer market. The spiritual or moral quality of an individual is worth very little, as the need for money leads him to lower and prostitute himself for the vile metal, which buys honor, respect, love, fame, and power. The money god is sitting above the world, and whoever wishes to enjoy his gifts must adore him. The real power of money is not only material, but it is principally a hidden force, as the coin is not worth anything in itself; it is only symbolic for human effort or work. By a strange paradox, although work is intrinsically noble, money, the result of this effort, is under the control or influence of a satanic or diabolic power.

We invite the reader to meditate on what he could do to corrupt human beings if he was Satan; what means or tools would he use to instigate crime, greed, war, fratricide, and decay of moral values? It would be difficult to imagine anything more perfectly suited for this than gold; neutral in its own condition, but diabolical when handled perversely.

Does Satan really exist, or is he only a myth created by the masses to explain certain things? If a person believes in the existence of God, then he must believe there is a devil or Satan as a counterpart of the Supreme Creator. Because absolute unity does not exist in life, the mere existence of something leads us to the affirmation that its opposite is also real. There is no light without darkness, no good without evil, no truth without falsehood. Death follows life, and life follows death.

God would thus be the supreme creative intelligence, and the "devil," the destructive intelligence. In the ancient Kabbalah, the devil has been symbolized as the shadow of God. Therefore, just as the Great Creator has his angelic hosts, the devil also has his infernal legion. William Blatty, in his book *The Exorcist*, refers to this legion when he presents the phenomenon of "demonic possession." After the following explanation we can continue our story.

The tradition transmitted by the great Hermetic Masters affirms that at a crucial moment in the history of humanity, a powerful *diabolic Archangel*, if we are allowed to call him thus, succeeded in penetrating the earth's occult defenses and entered its atmosphere, provoking extreme disturbances. To be able to imagine such a being, we suggest reading the book *The Lurker at the Threshold* by H. P. Lovecraft. According to Hermetic tradition, the direct, albeit unwilling cause of this catastrophe which affects us to this day, was Moses.

Everybody knows that Moses appeared floating in a basket down a river and was subsequently adopted, deceiving the Egyptian priests of the time. They took him for an Egyptian and initiated him into the mysteries of ritual magic, which is a method for making the key notes of Nature vibrate, and thus produce certain phenomena which the operator wishes to achieve. The study of atomic physics shows us that it is theoretically possible to produce changes or transmutations in matter; therefore, there is nothing miraculous about these mutations being achieved by means of secret procedures. In spite of his esoteric identification with Egyptian magic, Moses was always loyal to his ancestral blood. Thus, his most powerful wish was to make himself the leader who would free his people from enslavement, leading them to the promised land. Guided by this desire, and conscious of the powerful forces he had learned to control, Moses had a daring idea: to make a magic pact or alliance with an angel, a divine creature charged with the task of providing him with power and assistance from heaven to save his people.

After lengthy preparations done in deep solitude, he performed the ritual ceremony with magic words and corresponding invocations. In the midst of amazing atmospheric and terrestrial phenomena, an impressive being appeared, making Moses tremble with fear and panic, due to the tremendous force it projected. It will never be possible to know or even imagine the conditions under which the pact between man and heaven was made. The angel agreed to everything Moses requested and promised his help, demanding the strictest obedience in return. He revealed his name as Y., and requested that as a sign of union, all his followers should undergo a small ritual surgical operation, with a light discharge of blood. Every man who underwent this would come to be a son of Y. The blood that was shed sealed the pact.

From that day forward, Moses was invested with superhuman powers and started doing all kinds of magical feats, converting the Ark of the Covenant into the center of his power. Plagues and calamities fell over Egypt, and non-believers and rebels were struck down by the wrath of Y. In this manner, Moses' people started the Exodus that would last forty years.

Later, Y., the occult power behind the leader, suddenly started to change his procedures by formulating strange demands, all of which had the shedding of blood as the common denominator.

Moses was overcome with fear and started to become aware of the magnitude of the error he committed. He then understood that the *divine angel* was in truth an *angel of darkness*, the complete opposite of the luminous power he had intended to invoke.

This *infernal angel* was a member of the host of shadows. In order to maintain its power and strength, this vampire needed to feed on human blood, an essence charged with the vitality conferred by the divine spark. This is why all through the Exodus, so many blood-shedding incidents occurred, provoked by the occult dictator.

In reality, who was Y.? One could say he was a very ancient being whose evolutionary origin is unknown. Through long periods of cosmic time, this being kept his individuality, but unfortunately his evolution was directed toward negative, dark, and destructive aspects; much like a human being who grows bitter with the passing of time and adopts a negative and destructive concept of life.

Many beings similar to Y. exist in the Universe. Fortunately, the magnetic defenses of the planet constitute an impenetrable barrier against those beings. However, Moses' magic ritual opened a door and cleared a pathway through which Y. was able to penetrate into the Earth.

It is possible to see this as the most transcendental, but unfortunately harmful event in the occult history of humanity. To justify this statement, it is necessary to digress in order to clarify exactly what the planet Earth really is.

One can affirm, without fearing any sarcastic mockery from the ignorant or the semi-wise, that the planet Earth is a human being. It is not something equivalent to a human being, but a man in all aspects of the word.

Hermetic philosophy upholds the truth of reincarnation,

but affirms that this takes place only with some people who possess, or have developed within themselves some qualities or characteristics apart from the physical body, which are capable of resisting death. The term "people" refers to human beings, even if these beings may present physical characteristics different from terrestrial man. Regarding reincarnation, Hermeticism teaches that a Hermetic initiate of a high degree can achieve the power to reincarnate consciously, that is, changing physical bodies while maintaining his individuality and a certain degree of memory. Gradually, in the course of successive lives, the initiate grows in spiritual power. His essence or divine spark grows successively more powerful.

In this way, the moment will come when the body of man, in the dimension and shape we are familiar with, is no longer capable of containing or supporting such a vast and powerful essence. For this reason, such a spirit or super-developed essence must seek an adequate physical body that corresponds to his tremendous energetic force. Thus he *reincarnates* in the body of a new or young planet, and continues his development there, in ways and conditions that are difficult for us to conceive. This is how an extraordinarily evolved human being took the body of the planet Earth and made it his own, in the most perfect shape in the Universe: the sphere.

This sphere is formed by the same basic materials as the human body, which are, in brief, the materials of the Universe. This sphere breathes, moves, thinks, and feels. It has a circulatory, digestive, procreative, and respiratory system. Petroleum is its blood, and it feeds on vegetable, animal, and mineral matter. Sexually, it is hermaphroditic, with a masculine and a feminine hemisphere. It breathes through plant life, and receives its etheric or magnetic nourishment through emitting and receiving antenna, that is, through *Homo sapiens*.

Once this clarification has been made, and in order to grasp the magnitude of the catastrophe accidentally brought about by Moses with the arrival of Y., we can reveal that this ancient, vengeful, and malicious being expelled the young spirit from the Earth, incarnating in his place. With this act, a dark and bloody era commenced for humanity. A period of suffering, torment, and pain started for the Jewish people as they were converted into the innocent victims of the negative forces of Y. This is the explanation for the great afflictions which the Jews have had to suffer.

Imagine Moses' despair when he realized the calamity which had occurred and the suffering created for those he had wanted to help. As time passed, Moses understood that nothing had power over Y., as he possessed incalculable malignity. Convinced of this, Moses brought together the wise men of his people and instructed them in the great mystery of the Messiah. These men, using magical rituals, could create a god and fulfill the mystery of theurgy, in the hope that this god could liberate them and save the world from the destructive influence of Y.

Once his instruction was given, Moses climbed Mount Nebo and was never seen alive again.

The wise men who inherited the patriarch's instructions followed them faithfully, carrying out the Messianic ritual according to the instituted rules. As a result, hundreds of years later, Jesus appeared. He was the "Son of Man" (consider this expression carefully) and the Savior expected by the wise men initiated by Moses.

This is how Jesus was born, under the circumstances that are familiar to all. Hermetic teaching maintains he was the son of a Jewish woman and a Roman father, his progenitor being a Roman soldier and merely an instrument of higher occult forces.

Why is it said that Mary remained a virgin? This mystery really does not refer to physiological virginity, but to the fact that actually there was no physical contact between Jesus' real father and Mary. In effect, his spiritual father was a great Hermetic initiate who etherically used the physical body of the Roman soldier to procreate a son. The spiritual seed was transmitted by the occult Master; the physical sperm by the Roman. In this manner, Mary conceived "without losing her virginity." In those times the term "virginity" was not used to designate maidenhood; it was used to distinguish those women initiated in the secret of the "virgule" as Mary was. The magic rod used by Moses was known as the "virgule."

Those who have "eyes to see and ears to hear" will understand this. For others, it will produce a dismal silence in their interior, and they will remain in the realm of ignorant sarcasm, suffering the mental emptiness of those who do not want to understand, or worse, the unconscious blindness of those who do not want to see.

Jesus, the god created by man and incarnated in the body of man, was consecrated by the great initiate John the Baptist, otherwise known as the *Antechrist*. Jesus' baptism in the river was the means that permitted the first manifestation of

Christ in Jesus, the man-god, whose mission was destined since his birth.

From the time of Moses, the *Fraternity of Magicians* had been attentively observing these events without being able to alter them. The *magicians* were connoisseurs of the Messianic mystery and had the knowledge that certain wise men were working on this. They decided to help the wise men try to correct the serious anomalies explained before. They were awaiting Jesus' birth, and they were his occult godfathers who protected and educated him so he could fulfill his double mission.

His first mission was to liberate the *chosen people* from their occult killer. His second mission was to save the world in general from the invisible vampire who called himself Y. in order to begin a new era on Earth under the Christian motto "love one another," replacing the dictum of "an eye for an eye and a tooth for a tooth."

At the same time, Jesus was an active member of the *Fraternity of Magicians*, receiving support and inspiration from all of them. However, the great Masters maintain that Jesus failed in his mission, or more accurately, that he only achieved partial success, since he did not reach his goal. This refers only to Jesus, however, and not to Christ.

In order to truly understand Jesus, it is necessary to consider his triple personality:

1. Jesus the man
2. Jesus the God (created by man)
3. Christ (who manifested himself through Jesus)

Christ was an angel, a solar spirit who *descended from Heaven* to manifest himself as the supreme power of the *Father* on earth.

Jesus and his twelve disciples are the symbol of a solar and cosmic mystery. Hermetic science teaches that our solar system is composed of twelve planets plus the sun, an analogy for the twelve apostles and Christ, and that the unknown planets will be discovered in time.

We will speak no more of Jesus; we have perhaps already said too much. We will only add that the crucifixion was an expected drama in which Jesus' blood had to be shed so that Christ could in turn incarnate in the planet Earth and displace Y., definitively casting him out of our atmosphere. However, as we have already mentioned, this mission had only a relative success. Christ incarnated in the planet Earth, but Y. could not be expelled. Since then, both govern the planet.

Christ's force acts in the world through the representatives of the *Fraternity of Magicians*. These men direct Hermetic schools in which the student can develop his spiritual force to the point of disintegration of his animal soul and liberation from the influence of Y., who can only act through primitive and animal instincts such as hate, envy, lust, greed, pride, and vanity.

In this way, the Spiritual Beacon is kept alight to illuminate the select spirits who are potentially capable of converting themselves into fully developed human beings and abandoning their *sapiens* condition.

Every person who reaches this condition is converted into a center of Christic irradiation and is therefore another obstacle for Y.'s influence. The naïve say that Christ will return to the planet Earth. But Christ is on Earth! He needs only to be removed from the cross by the same humanity who nailed him to it.

Until that time, wars will continue. Great numbers of people will die and their vitality will be absorbed by Y., the great occult force behind these conflicts. None of this will end until this being is conquered.

The real *Antichrist* is Y., and he has spread his negative influence throughout his followers, those of bestial instincts, who in turn have incorporated this vibration into the multitude. The multitude is composed of amorphous and blind entities, receptors of any force of sufficient power. In this way, Y.'s principles incorporated in the collective unconscious of humanity motivate the philosophy of "an eye for an eye, and a tooth for a tooth." Trapped by this malignant force, people live diabolically: hating, destroying, stealing, killing their brothers, returning evil with more evil, selling out their honesty and honor, enslaving the weak, exploiting the unprotected, and denigrating the just. Luckily, there are many who act contrary to all this. If this were not so, life would be unbearable. They are the ones who somehow have received a true Christian influence (not necessarily religious) and have higher values than usual.

Religions have a positive family and social influence, but unfortunately on solely spiritual grounds they do not have much to offer, and generally they try to check this deficiency with the indiscriminate use of the banner of Christ.

The *Fraternity of Magicians* does not derive its power from Christ, nor speak in his name. The Fraternity only exalts his values and shows or narrates events which the world should know, so that the *chosen* (the true humans) can reaffirm their conviction and loyalty to a superior spiritual life. The power of these *Magicians* comes from their harmony with, respect for, and obedience to cosmic laws, and the profound and serene spiritual condition they have reached. Their spirituality places them in a magical relationship with God, the *Great Universal Father*, who is recognized by the Hermeticists as the first cause of the origin of all and the great force of order and creation.

To speak about Christ is to explain the esoteric side of the psycho-social phenomenology of the world today. In its innocence, *sapiens* believes that everything in life is as it appears on the surface, and that things must surely be as the vast majority say they are. When some people hear of the esoteric side of events or the occult causes of different phenomena, they smile unbelievingly, arguing with infantile logic that "if that were true, it would be made known by the press" or, "it would have been taught at school or in the university" or, "well documented books would exist on the subject." That way of thinking nullifies all progress, because if everyone's belief was the same, no one would bother to study or investigate little-known phenomena.

Despite obstacles already mentioned, *sapiens* in his individual manifestation (not as a species) can have latent superior qualities and characteristics, which may lead him to partially understand Hermetic truths. Motivated by this knowledge, *sapiens* can awaken to a superior reality. The *sapiens* individual can save himself from the lethargic destiny of humanity and eventually reach the world of the Hermeticists, *magicians*, or *awakened men*.

Moses, a man of strength and wisdom, was driven by his yearning for freedom to commit an error of cosmic magnitude. According to the great Hermetic wise men, this error nearly destroyed the solar system. To clarify this statement, the solar system can be compared to the composition of an atom, borrowing on the Hermetic theme of "as above, so below." In this case, Y.'s rise to power could be seen as an arbitrary substitution of an electron, which changed the spiritual nucleus of the Earth.

This is one of the many lessons, which oblige the *Fraternity of Magicians* to strictly guard Hermetic secrets. The Fraternity will only give instruction in higher knowledge to those who have demonstrated their strength, their moral and spiritual purity, and the rectitude of their intentions.

III

DISSECTION OF *SAPIENS*

Homo sapiens is a living paradox. One cannot say whether *Homo sapiens* is the greatest or the most insignificant of creatures that inhabit the Earth. The most sublime qualities and the most vile and perverse passions are combined within him. There are many good people, but the evil ones are more numerous. The person who complies with the law, respects his neighbor, does good in general, and helps others according to his strength, is called good. The amoral and destructive person who enjoys hurting people in one way or another is called evil.

Unfortunately, both the good and the evil person are this way unconsciously, beyond their own volition. The good are kind in spite of themselves. The evil cannot avoid being so. Furthermore, they justify and accept it. The situation grows more complex with the observation that there are *good* men who are *stupid*, and many *evil* men who are *intelligent*.

How should we choose our friends? How can we tell

who should be the recipients of our affection? In what manner can we assess ourselves in order to evaluate our own position as living beings?

We cannot divide the world into people who are good or evil, rich or poor, intelligent or stupid, important or insignificant. Generally, *sapiens* forms groups according to instinctive congeniality that is beyond all analysis. This alignment is usually established by qualities or defects. Like seeks like, except in amorous relations where the opposite more frequently occurs.

Scientists constantly study the psychology of *sapiens*, trying to somehow justify his infinite contradictions. Innumerable treatises and essays on morality, love, ethics, life, death, the finite, and infinite have been written. Nevertheless, very little light has been shed on the true nature of *sapiens*. This is not because science lacks knowledge. Rather, this knowledge is rendered useless due to the human being's inability to measure the true significance of recognized concepts. For example, a student can understand perfectly well the statement that human beings live in a permanent somnambulistic state, especially since this fact is well documented, but the student will be absolutely incapable of projecting this concept to the general context of life. The student will not even remotely grasp all the horror this statement entails.

This is how the most arresting realities go unnoticed even though they are public knowledge. One of the most striking facts is that *we are animals*. In order not to think of this as an abstraction, let us repeat several times, "I am an animal, I am an animal, I am an animal." Think about what this really means and all it entails. The majority of people will say they understand perfectly that they are animals, but it is certain that it will be absolutely impossible for them to visualize the amazing implications of this statement. Thus "science knows much but is ignorant of almost everything." In this case we can well recall Desmond Morris's *The Naked Ape*, a study of the human animal. His book had a great impact on the public. The crude examination of the animal characteristics of *sapiens* made a true zoological portrait. What happened before this? Didn't people know that *Homo sapiens* was a monkey? Of course they did, but no one truly evaluated the significance of it.

Yet *sapiens* feels very proud of his talent, his creative genius, his capacity for reasoning, his capacity for affection and creative power, calling himself the "highest living manifestation of intelligence," or the "most perfect living creature."

Sapiens is particularly satisfied with his culture, and presumes that his ability to transmit it to future generations makes him enormously different from other animal species who apparently lack this ability.

Likewise, *sapiens* affirms that he possesses the highest privileges inherent in the degree of "civilization" obtained by his species. Statements such as, "all human beings have the right to happiness" and "all human beings are free in nature," illustrate this. In other words, this is equal to maintaining that the mere fact of having been born gives a *sapiens* creature the right to liberty, happiness, love, and well-being.

In fact, *Homo sapiens* not only does not have any right to

liberty, happiness, or any well-being that he has not earned for himself, but furthermore, he is not even remotely as intelligent, rational, and superior as he believes himself to be.

On the contrary, *sapiens* is virtually insignificant in the total context of nature, and this work will endeavor to reveal his intellectual mediocrity, his somnambulistic state, and his unreal existence. *Sapiens* is a functionally deficient and anthropologically immature creature who, for reasons of his own self-esteem, prefers to bury this fact in the deepest recesses of his subconscious, and instead dreams about his own illusory intelligence and power.

It would be absurd to think that in a world inhabited by rational, conscious, and intelligent beings, the latent danger of total destruction by a nuclear war could exist. The very fact that punitive laws exist shows that people do not conduct themselves in a manner guided by reason, justice, tolerance, duty, and correct action.

Insanity, psychological complexes and disturbances, suicide, crimes of passion, anguish, uncontrollable ambition, and assassinations are proof of people's irrational conduct.

Thus, *sapiens* claims to have a series of qualities, powers, and privileges that only exist in his imagination. When Calderon de la Barca said that "life is but a dream," he was more correct than anyone could ever imagine.

The *sapiens* species provides material in sufficient quantity and numbers for Nature so that, according to her own laws, a few beings are produced who can finally fulfill an evolutionary goal. These few can truly reach a human condition and enjoy all the privileges this involves, such as liberty, happiness, well-being, and love. The masses simply provide the raw material for the social experiment of Nature and History. Nature is cold and has neither preferences nor biases for anyone in particular.

This is no reason for people to despise themselves, wrongly believing themselves to be inferior creatures. The fact is simply that *Homo sapiens'* age in evolutionary terms is barely that of a child. In this condition, he cannot be ashamed of not acting like an adult. In fact, the relatively conscious behavior of the human being barely extends over a few thousand years. If we had to compare *sapiens'* age as a species with that of an actual *sapiens* person, the conscious age of the species is barely eight or ten years old.

It is hoped that once *sapiens* comes of age, in cosmic time, not terrestrial time, he will attain a degree of maturity.

Humanity accepts as *normal* all individuals whose biological and psychological behavior adjusts to collective rules. The one who separates himself from these norms is considered *abnormal*. However, we never question how close *normal* is to the *optimum*. It could be that *normal* is much nearer to deficiency or imperfection than it is to *optimum*.

Is it not possible, for example, that geniuses are not so extraordinarily intelligent, but the other way around; that the rest of humanity is extraordinarily stupid? We must accept the idea that this is perfectly possible since we lack markers or reference points to compare the human race with other races. Suppose that all the inhabitants of the planet were actually insane, how would we ever become aware of this?

An individual can only become aware of these phenomena by virtue of a mystical experience, transcending his *sapiens* condition and elevating himself to a state of deep consciousness and absolute awakeness. Under these conditions, his great mental clarity will make him understand *absolute* or *eternal truths*, in juxtaposition to the *small*, temporal, and relative truths he habitually handles.

During this period of elevated consciousness, a person can see that the *normal* human being is really abnormal; that he is, in a sense, a living creature deficiently created. He will observe *sapiens* as mentally but not intellectually retarded, as irresponsible, and behaving like a hypnotized person. This particular process of knowledge which has been called *revelation* or *illumination* in some men who are *saints*, is later verified when the individual steps out of his state of superior consciousness and descends to an ordinary level, and observes the behavior of people who prove and demonstrate in daily life the truth of the knowledge the initiate acquired.

It will be argued that civilization and the extraordinary advances of science prove the intelligence and capabilities of the human being. However, this argument is only a reflection of the fact that *Homo sapiens* holds his intelligence in high regard, considering it as the highest human manifestation. It can thus be understood that the actions and memory of great intellectuals are venerated, exceeded in power and prestige only by that of great millionaires. A genius will be long remembered in history, even if he was the inventor of a lethal weapon capable of destroying half of humanity.

Hermeticism rejects the assertion that intelligence is the most valuable element of the human individual, and instead maintains that humanity's most precious and priceless element is *consciousness*, in the sense of being more aware, more awakened, more alert, judicious, and wiser. This faculty of *consciousness*, which most people lack, is only born in persons who, for a variety of reasons, have reached a higher than normal level of awakeness in life; who in a certain sense have awakened, liberating themselves from the somnambulistic hypnosis which afflicts the masses.

Homo sapiens is in general an integrally programmed being at the cerebral, emotional, instinctive, and physical levels. What psychology calls *personality* can also be defined as an *individual program*. Each individual possesses an intricate and extensive cerebral program due to the effects of heredity, education, culture, imitation, learning, conditioned reflexes, and so on. So when a person thinks, he can only do so within the basic context of his cerebral program *from which he cannot deviate for any reason, even if he tries to do so.*

Each person must necessarily keep to his cerebral *script* and cannot do anything other than manifest himself in it and through it.

In order to understand this, one can think of *program* and *consciousness* as absolutely contradictory elements. Consciousness implies the capacity for change, choice, and self-determination, which obviously is not possible in a being who is the visible manifestation of a program. The Great Programmer can be called God, Universal Father, Cosmic Intelligence, or any other name, but the reference is always clear.

Due to his cerebral program and other little-known phenomena, the human being lives in a permanent somnambulistic state. What is a somnambulist? The dictionary defines somnambulism as an "abnormal sleep state during which the person gets up, walks, and sometimes talks." Expanding this definition, somnambulism could be described as "sleep that affects all humanity during which people get up, walk, fight, love, hate, enjoy, suffer, think, procreate, live, grow old, and die without ever being aware of their hypnotic condition." Knowledge of hypnosis originated in esoteric schools, and science, in spite of having adopted it, is very far from understanding it.

The individual sleeps by night, but is awake by day. What is not considered is that sleep and wakefulness represent two extremes of psychological awareness, and between these two poles there are many degrees. Thus, during the night a person may sleep either lightly or extremely deeply. The same occurs with wakefulness, in which a person can be barely awake or extremely alert. Due to this, *sapiens* gradually came to believe that his usual state of awareness during the day is *being awake*. In reality, this awareness is a state of hypnotic or somnambulistic sleep in which a person can be dispersed while still having the appearance of being awake. Programmed intelligence apparently cannot perceive itself as being affected by hypnosis, especially when there is no one sufficiently awake to point it out. Nevertheless, history relates episodes in the lives of some philosophers who, because they became *awakened men*, understood the truth, had access to a profound and substantial reality, and tried to communicate their knowledge to others to help them awaken. Some people awakened, but the vast majority remained deaf, dumb, and blind.

The majority of philosophers have been merely great

thinkers, but not awakened men; giants of intellect, but not of consciousness. This is why traditional philosophy has always been so arid, cold, abstract, and impractical. Philosophers were only "in love with the truth," but in the form of an image or symbol, and not as a living reality.

In this way, the intelligence *sapiens* possesses, even when brilliant, is a mechanical, dead, and programmed intelligence.

What about our creative capacity, it can be objected, when man proves his creative genius all the time? The reply to this is that the cerebral and cultural programming of the learned and wise man grows constantly, but always following the already established patterns. A person can constantly study or investigate, but always within the limits of the basic content of his intellect. Thus, he accumulates thousands of heterogeneous and homogeneous elements, which in his daily intellectual work can produce infinite combinations by the mechanics of thought, but not by an authentic process of creation. In this world governed by mechanical intelligence, the one who has the most information in his program and is capable of handling it as skillfully as possible, will be deemed the most intelligent.

The Hermetic philosopher who has truly converted himself into an awakened man has a living, awake, creative, and unprogrammed intelligence. This is the exact opposite of the vast majority of humanity. This intelligence manifests itself far beyond the merely intellectual, reaching the peak of integral conception where intelligence must surpass intellectual boundaries in order to become that which is *mind*. In effect, Hermetic philosophers have given the word *mind* a meaning it does not commonly have, defining it as *"intelligence and consciousness born from apprenticeship in an intensified state of awakeness."*

The common man lacks *mind* and must resign himself to handling his limited intelligence and knowledge, which have been developed through somnambulistic apprenticeship in a state of hypnosis or sleep.

With his mind, the Hermeticist can reach the knowledge of absolute and eternal truths, as opposed to the relative and temporal truths of *sapiens*. The aims of the Hermeticist are eternal; the aims of the profane are temporal and finite.

Deprived of the mind's superior possibilities, *sapiens* obscurely senses his own weakness and vulnerability in the face of destiny, death, illness, war, poverty, and dangerous changes. This is why *sapiens* has always looked for leaders and chiefs whose strength will compensate for his own weakness. Guided by this same desire, he has invented gods to which he prays for the power and strength he lacks. The entire structure of our civilized world is based on the absolute weakness, cowardice, impotency, ignorance, and vulnerability of the human individual who constructs collective systems of protection, support, and control to externally compensate for his internal weakness.

Human beings prefabricate culture, morality, religious creeds, laws, and police systems to stop those who go against the common interests for that moment in history. They plan and program community life and the future of their children. Internally, however, the spiritual spark grows ever weaker in the face of the progressive dehumanization of a world which in truth was never human to begin with, but only *animal-intelligent*. The world has glorified science and forgotten human nature.

The center of gravity of a person's psychological awareness is projected more and more toward the external world, progressively abandoning itself to incarnate in the monstrous sons of civilization: consumer products, machines, cinema, and television. Advertising and the press are the two super monsters of our times, tools by which man is skillfully manipulated and converted into a perfect automaton. He becomes an obedient consumer of certain products, a respectful server of ideologies and systems, which in turn provide small groups with power. If it is true that we live in the era of multitudes, and that their voices have taken over for the authority of kings and princes of the past, it is no less true that history is the conflict of minorities, that is to say, of the leaders who direct the masses.

On this point the words of Professor Ludwig Von Bertalanffy of the University of Alberta are interesting:

> Behavior is a response to stimuli coming from the outside . . . So far as it is not innate or instinctive, behavior is shaped by outside influences that have met the organism in the past: classical conditioning after Pavlov, instrumental conditioning after Skinner, early childhood experience after Freud, secondary reinforcements after more recent theories. Hence training, education, and human life in general are essentially responses to outside conditions: beginning in early childhood with toilet training and other manipulations whereby socially acceptable behavior is gratified and undesirable behavior blocked; continuing with education, which is best carried through according to

Skinnerian principles of reinforcement of correct responses and by means of teaching machines and ending in adult man in an affluent society which makes everybody happy, conditioning him, in a strictly scientific manner, by the mass media to be a perfect consumer—that is, an automaton properly answering in the ways prescribed by the industrial-military-political establishment.

. . . Man as a machine that can be programmed; all those machines identical to automobiles coming off the assembly line; equilibrium or comfort as the ultimate value; behavior as a business transaction with minimum expense and maximum gain—this is a perfect expression of the philosophy of commercial society. Stimulus-response, input-output, producer-consumer are all the same concepts, only expressed in different terms.

Professor Bertalanffy continues:

I don't care a jot whether and to what extent professors A, B, or C have modified Watson, Hull, and Freud, and have replaced their blunt statements by more qualified and sophisticated circumlocutions. I do care a lot that the spirit still is all-pervading in our society and, even more, seems necessary to keep it going: reducing man to the lower levels of his animal nature, manipulating him into becoming a feeble-minded and consumeristic automaton, or a marionette of political power, systematically dulling his brain through a perverse system of education; in short, dehumanizing him ever further by means of a sophisticated psychological technology. The effects of this manipulation we see everywhere: in the unspeakable vulgarity of popular culture; in the unbearable children and teenagers who do not know their mother tongue when entering college but are glued to the television screen for five hours a day and find no better outlet than drug addiction, premature pregnancies, or delinquency; in a drab society . . . in which, through its meaningless rat race, fills thousands of mental hospitals; in politics which has converted Jeffersonian democracy into a manipulated herd of cattle.

. . . Mass persuasion is, of course, one of the oldest human arts, from the sophists of Athens, the rhetoric of Aristotle, and the medieval *trivium* to Hitler's famous manual. But, so long as it was art, its effects remained capricious and unpredictable, as well as limited in space and time. Rebellion was possible even against the most powerful dictator; as a matter of historical fact, dictators usually came to a bad end. This was basically changed when mass persuasion became scientific, using psychological mechanisms and techniques. Then its power, because it was not imposed from outside but was internalized, became unlimited and nearly impregnable; aided by mass media whose barrage has no limits in space and is nearly continuous in time. This—besides nuclear weapons—is the great discovery of our age: the power of modeling men into automata 'buying' everything from toothpaste and the Beatles to presidents, atomic war, and self-destruction.

Homo sapiens, alienated by these powerful forces, is simply a puppet who has no other alternative but to live his life and play the role he has been assigned in the drama of creation.

Could this be a gigantic and horrendous conspiracy planned by anonymous powers, or is it only a pastime of the gods?

The constant bombardment through audiovisual means, which powerfully impact the psyche, the numerous requirements of society, and the increasing complexity of civilized life, all keep the individual fascinated and suspended in a veritable somnambulistic trance from which he will awaken with difficulty. This is due to the fact that the relationship between the person and the environment is a constant process of feedback, which acts as an element for maintaining and reinforcing the hypnosis.

Hermeticists can isolate themselves psychologically from this negative influence and remain awake, but are forced to share with people the material circumstances derived from this situation of mass hypnosis.

Society does not cause the somnambulistic sleep of *Homo sapiens*; it only acts in maintaining and reinforcing it. Sleep is a universal force, which is present throughout the cosmos, and is manifested in several ways.

According to Hermetic tradition, when the Supreme Creator expelled man from Paradise, he punished him by embedding a mechanism for hypnotic sleep in his brain in order to make him an obedient servant in the vineyards of the Lord.

The Hermetic Masters, wishing to share the joy of a state of superior awakeness with those who are prepared for it, maintain Hermetic schools where the person is given an *opportunity* to liberate himself from the slavery of sleep which turns man into an *animated malleable instrument*, the definition of a slave according to Aristotle.

The *Magician's Fraternity* invites everyone who has sufficient ability to accomplish this magic work to join their spiritual movement. Man can recover the lost Paradise and even gain an advantage, as he can live there again "after having eaten the forbidden fruit," which according to the Bible, would make man like unto God.

However, this invitation is only for those who have "eyes to see and ears to hear, as the lips of wisdom remain closed to those who do not know how to listen."

Let it not be thought that everyone can cross the threshold that leads to supreme joy and immortality. On the contrary, "many are called but few are chosen."

Each person has a *personal level* and if that level is too low, conceptually and culturally speaking, the space he has to cross to reach the level of a true school of initiation is insurmountable. On the other hand, he can prepare himself for initiation by leading a virtuous and disciplined life, seeking to attain moral and spiritual advancement. Many times life itself will have sufficiently prepared a person. There are no rigid rules in this; in certain cases, an individual will require higher education as a basic requirement to enter the school, since without a cultural foundation it would be impossible for him to understand the Teachings, and his path would be an *act of faith*, which is insufficient.

In spite of the fact that *sapiens* is integrally programmed, and that this does indeed harm him, he also possesses the divine spark, and this single fact immediately gives him the greatest possibilities for redemption and ascent.

This can be seen in those people who, for some reason, have an extraordinarily powerful divine spark, and who show this by doing all kinds of good deeds and who face life with superior criteria. If we dissect man, it is only to show him the possibilities of evolution, and not as a cruel or destructive criticism.

IV

THE COLLECTIVE SOUL OF THE SPECIES

Aristotle defined a slave as an "animated malleable instrument." This terrifying description has never been more true than it is today, if applied to human beings in general. The individual is merely an appendage and a sounding board for the species. *Homo sapiens* is the same as other animal species: he has a collective soul which regulates and directs the evolution of the human race. The collective soul produces the migration of the birds, regulates reproduction, directs different changes and adaptations, brings about periods of mating, and in general, directs the instinctive behavior of the beasts. As he belongs to the animal kingdom, *sapiens* is not free from this directing force which in effect controls, directs, supervises, and regulates the species, acting as a common brain, which stifles individual thought.

This *common soul* has been called the "collective unconscious" by Jung. He did not talk of an "animal soul" but he certainly possessed this knowledge. This collective uncon-scious is in truth the animal soul of *sapiens*. The mere fact of understanding, accepting, and comprehending the signifi-cance of this subject means visualizing the most important foundation of *sapiens'* life, because the bestial impulse acts as the basic motive of its actions.

Personality is merely a reflection of the *common soul*, which shapes the subject's psyche with unsuspected power. It is no more than an emanation from the common deposit, which is incorporated and personalized in an individual who thus acquires, if it is possible to use this expression, "an animal soul of his own" in miniature and distinguished from the great collective soul.

In this way, the individual receives from his parents a physical and genetic inheritance, and from humanity, the legacy of power and animal intelligence. Under these cir-cumstances, it is very difficult for the individual to overcome this overwhelming compulsion and shape his own individ-ual personality. He must resign himself to sharing the common fate of his fellow men, unless he is "lucky" enough to reach a Hermetic school.

Hermetic philosophy maintains that there can be no true spiritual and moral progress if man does not cut the umbili-cal cord which ties him to the central computer of the species, which nourishes "bestial" characteristics.

This notable and unique event is far-reaching and irre-versible, and it takes place in the heart of true Hermetic schools. Other schools do not in any way deal with the ani-mal soul of the student, and are limited to only transmitting certain teachings, which doubtlessly, will be used to further bestialize his intelligence.

The bestialization of intelligence is a common phenomenon in this age. The more intelligent an individual is, the more powerful his beast will be, and the beast will use this intellect to satisfy its own instincts, without any concern for anything else.

The collective program (of the collective soul) based on fierce and inhuman rivalry, obliges the individual to kill in order to eat. Death has many degrees, and physical destruction is the last of them, but before this, there is the slow decline that is a result of the destruction of one's inner longings. We may kill by annihilating the will of others or pitilessly exploiting them; returning evil for evil; destroying their love, sanity, happiness, and peace; or slandering, insulting, or being icily hardhearted toward others' problems.

The future of the human race does not look promising: the accelerated development of a cold and inhuman intelligence without love or spiritual content.

Progress is creating intelligent giants, but spiritual pygmies, with conscience and human sensitivity atrophied by a vast cerebral and cultural program designed ultimately to serve the central computer of the species.

The only possibility for salvation is in the hands of the isolated individual, that is, in the one who by means of Hermeticism attains vital autonomy, disentangling himself from the central brain.

Unfortunately, not everyone can be saved, since along with the extinction of the *sapiens* species and the cessation of the operation of the central computer, there would arise a cosmic imbalance, as the central computer fulfills the functions necessary for the planetary harmony of our system.

What is the future of those who cannot save themselves? Nothing dramatic or spectacular; some could reincarnate and then slowly evolve through many lives, and others would disintegrate; that is, they would have the kind of death which awaits the majority of materialistic people who believe that all comes to an end in the grave.

The oneiric web, which imprisons man, is tremendously subtle and complex, but at the same time brutally evident once one learns to observe specific phenomena of social psychology. Even when searching for something superior, people go around in a vicious circle of behavioral standards dictated by culture. The more they study, the less they know, and the less they understand. All their efforts are capitalized on by the central computer, which channels them into a community cultural fund.

How did this central computer originate? It was formed gradually, ever since the first existence of man on Earth, by the action of the environment on his psyche. It is the offspring of the emanations of God and the emanations of man. It will continue growing and perfecting itself by virtue of the life of man himself, but will survive man, as this force which we call the *collective unconscious* or *central computer* does not need material or biological support to continue its existence once it has been created.

Ideologically or mentally speaking the individual does not exist as he is inseparable from culture. He is governed by the behavioral standards accepted by society, which ultimately are controlled by the central computer. Thus culture, which in some ways can do so much good for man, in other ways can be considered as the veritable murderer of the divine spark, of freedom, and of awareness. Culture encages, limits, obliges, impels, hypnotizes, and possesses the individual with irresistible power, shaping him in accordance with one single pattern. This pattern is established as a prototype for the production of robot-men who are the slaves the central computer needs to keep the spectacle of life moving.

In a sick society such as ours, we will undoubtedly have a sick culture, one alienated by collective stereotypes. Our society is truly sick, and within this society we live out satanic dreams worthy of the *Divine Comedy*. Each being contains a world of problems and conflicts. Fortunately, or unfortunately, man blunts his higher faculties and is not aware of all the horror of his existence in a mad world. A popular aphorism says, "in the land of the blind, the one-eyed man is king." Something similar is happening to our civilization where the higher forms of government and community guidance are not submitted to any type of sane control. We are guided to a greater or lesser extent by individuals, about whose degree of sanity or mental illness we are totally unaware. It is sufficient that an individual should appear to be normal and he will be accepted as such.

We are all aware that mental disturbances are some of the most difficult phenomena to discover and evaluate, even by specialized professionals. It is impossible for the ordinary man in the street to perceive this madness.

It seems incredible that in a civilization said to be advanced, such an important subject has been neglected. As we know, it is a small group of men who govern the great masses. How many of those forming part of this group of leaders are disturbed with serious problems? Thirty percent or perhaps fifty percent, or maybe the great majority? How does one evaluate the damage this implies for humanity? It would not be of great significance if serious mental disturbances occurred in those people not holding public office or important positions. On the other hand, for those whose range of social action is very wide, it seems absurd and irrational that they should not be obliged to undergo a periodic evaluation of their mental and psychological health.

At this time, it is perfectly possible that the judge who administers justice in one's local area could be mentally disturbed. This possibility cannot be disputed by any psychiatrist, as mental illness is rarely blatant or spectacular, but instead is rather sly, hidden, and insidious. In fact, it is well known that there is scarcely anyone who does not have pathological traits in the way their minds work. The gravity of these factors is overlooked.

The case of the aforementioned judge, if he indeed had truly serious mental problems, would represent a horrifying example of someone who was mentally ill authorized by society to manipulate people, administering justice in accordance with his complexes, frustrations, manias, and traumas. One can object that a judge only follows the letter of the law, but perceptive analysis will show that codes of law can be interpreted in many different personal ways.

At this point we should ask ourselves how many paranoid judges there are in the world who totally ignore the sacred impartiality of the law; how many important public officials are victims of hysteria, megalomania, egocentrism, unbridled yearning for power, sadism, or a total lack of self-criticism?

There is no provision for screening those who, by virtue of their position, are affected by the phenomenon of psychological *inflation* due to the prestige that their position confers upon them. The term "psychological inflation," coined by Jung, describes the disorientation experienced by a person when he identifies himself with the position he occupies and is led astray in his self-evaluation. In this way, a physician could *inflate* or raise himself to the high level of importance and dignity which society confers on a doctor due to his professional title. But a person is not what his title or position represents; he is merely a person who cannot claim for himself the importance and grandeur granted to the medical profession in general, because thousands of people belong to this profession. Without realizing this, the person subject to *inflation* tries to usurp or attribute to himself alone, the force, power, and importance which does not belong to him, but which is actually granted by society.

We know there is no psychological control, that inevitably thousands of innocent victims pay in different ways for the insanity of those in charge of administering our civilization. Legal errors, abuse of power, fatal political mistakes which degenerate into armed conflict, the usurping of power by financial mafias, obsolete or erroneous educational systems; all of this is in some way provoked by the mentally disturbed. Included among these cases are the "sick" humans who sell their honor, dignity, decency, and their person for monetary rewards.

It is also true that there are successes, beneficial discoveries and very positive works, but unfortunately, for one reason or another, these works rarely produce results that are decisively positive for the world. This process is analogous to healing the branches of a tree while the trunk and roots are rotting. Therefore, no scientific event or discovery will be far-reaching in importance until human nature is changed and raised to a higher level.

On the other hand, even small pebbles make a mountain after eons of time. In order to understand this, it must be accepted that there will be no real progress and evolution until human nature changes.

It is precisely this grand work to which the great Hermetic Initiates are pledged, and it is for this reason that there are true Hermetic schools where people are given an opportunity to elevate themselves.

To have a wider understanding of the functional mechanism of the collective soul or central computer, it is necessary to analyze the psychological action of the masses. This will enable us to verify the hidden action of a certain type of force, which takes possession of people under certain circumstances.

In the following relevant extracts from Gustav Le Bon's work, *The Crowd*, he states:

> In its ordinary sense, the word "crowd" represents a gathering of individuals of whatever nationality, profession, or sex, and whatever may be the chances that have brought them together.
>
> From the psychological point of view, the expression "crowd" assumes quite a different meaning. Given certain

circumstances, and only under those circumstances, an ag-
glomeration of men presents characteristics very different
from those of the individuals composing it. The sentiments
and ideas of all the persons in the gathering take one and
the same direction, and their conscious personality van-
ishes. A collective soul is formed, without a doubt, but
displays very clearly defined characteristics. The gathering
has thus become what, in the absence of a better expression, I will call an organized crowd, or, if the term is
considered preferable, a psychological crowd. It forms a
single being, and is subjected to the law of mental unity of
crowds.

In this description by Le Bon it can be seen how the *central computer* acts with force in grouping people into
psychological crowds or masses. Nevertheless, a mass may
be composed of two, three, five, or forty people, as the psychological meaning of *crowds* or *masses* is different from the
common one. When a person has developed a strong individuality, he is less sensitive to this coercion of the masses.
Le Bon continues:

. . . In the case of everything that belongs to the realm of
sentiment—religion, politics, morality, affection and an-
tipathies, etc.—the most eminent men seldom surpass the
standard of the most ordinary individuals. From the intellectual point of view an abyss may exist between a great
mathematician and his boot-maker, but from the point of
view of character the difference is most often slight or non-
existent . . . In the collective mind the intellectual aptitudes
of the individuals, and as a consequence their individuality, are weakened. The heterogeneous is swamped by the

homogeneous, and the unconscious qualities obtain the upper hand.

The very fact that crowds possess common ordinary qualities explains why they can never accomplish acts demanding a high degree of intelligence. The decisions affecting matters of general interest come to by an assembly of men of distinction, but specialists in different walks of life, are not sensibly superior to the decisions that would be adopted by a gathering of imbeciles. The truth is, they can only bring to bear in common on the work at hand those mediocre qualities which are the birthright of every average individual. In crowds, it is stupidity and not mother-wit that is accumulated.

We see, then, that the disappearance of the conscious personality, the predominance of the unconscious personality, the turning by means of suggestion and contagion of feelings and ideas in an identical direction, the tendency immediately to transform the suggested ideas into acts; these we see, are the principle characteristics of the individual forming part of a crowd. He is no longer himself, but has become an automaton who has ceased to be guided by his will.

Moreover, by the mere fact that he forms part of an organized crowd, a man descends several rungs on the ladder of civilization.

He further states:

Crowds exhibit a docile respect for force, and are but slightly impressed by kindness, which for them is scarcely other than a form of weakness. Their sympathies have never been bestowed on easy-going masters, but on tyrants who vigorously oppressed them. It is to these latter that they always erect the loftiest statues. It is true that they willingly trample on the despot whom they have stripped of his power, but it is because, having lost his strength, he has resumed his place among the people, who are to be despised because they are not to be feared . . .

A crowd is always ready to revolt against a weak authority and bow down servilely before a strong one. Should the strength of an authority be intermittent, the crowd, always obedient to its extreme sentiments, passes alternately from anarchy to servitude, and from servitude to anarchy.

However, to believe in the predominance among crowds of revolutionary instincts would be to entirely misconstrue their psychology. It is merely their tendency to violence that deceives us on this point. Their rebellious and destructive outbursts are always very transitory. Crowds are governed too much by unconscious considerations, and as a consequence subject too much to secular hereditary influences to not be extremely conservative. Abandoned to themselves, they soon weary of disorder, and instinctively turn to servitude.

From Le Bon's skillful description, we can see how the *central computer* manipulates people, converting them into puppets in the service of an established plan.

What plan? The evolutionary plan for *sapiens*, which must adjust to certain rules of the game. The general rules are as follows:

1. Considered collectively as a species, *sapiens* is not and cannot be free.
2. *Sapiens* must be born, suffer, love, become sick and die, reproduce, build up civilizations and destroy them, only for

the benefit of invisible superior powers who capitalize on his *vital product*. Doesn't *sapiens* profit from other animal species? Are there not animals which exist exclusively to feed *sapiens*? Minerals feed upon cosmic rays; plants on minerals; animals on plants; man feeds on all these, and the gods feed on man.

3. *Sapiens* is, therefore, a slave in perpetuity; nevertheless, individual or isolated beings separated from the group may become free.

4. The only possible freedom is liberation from the *central computer* and the only way to attain this is by conquering and surpassing oneself.

5. *Sapiens* is obliged to comply with the rules of the game in the system to which he has been assigned.

6. The evolution of *sapiens* comes inevitably with time, but measured in cosmic, not terrestrial time. Perhaps he may have to wait millions of terrestrial years in order to reach perfection.

7. There is no evolution of the *sapiens* individual; only that of the species as stated above. If a *sapiens* individual desires to evolve, he must convert himself into a *mutant human* for whom evolution exists.

8. There are other rules of the game, but only those already indicated can be revealed at this time.

In order to explain the modus operandi of the sapiens plan, the hierarchy of the operating forces will be explained.

The diagram that follows endeavors only to briefly describe the basic forces which act in the Universe: God, the Creator, in his double manifestation of life and death, light and darkness, of the sleep state and the state of vigilance, abases his power until able to act concretely through certain "angels" who direct the evolutionary plan. Hermetic tradition calls them the *Archons* or *Lords of Destiny*.

With reference to *sapiens*, this plan is maintained by virtue of dream energy, as can be seen in diagram 1. Nevertheless, the divine irradiation of luminous energy, which we call *Vigilance*, reaches the planet Earth but is not manifested in *sapiens*. Sleep energy, directed or manipulated by the *Archons*, maintains the programming of the system even down to the smallest group, the family.

Those who "have eyes to see and ears to hear" will draw incalculable advantage from the comprehension of this system.

To give a concrete example, this master key can be used to explain certain strange events in the life of Jesus which in this light, appear rational and crystal clear.

Why did Jesus appear to be so tremendously antagonistic toward the family?

Recall his words: "I have come to set a man against his father, and the daughter against her mother, and the daughter-in-law against her mother-in-law. And the enemies of man should be their own families. He who loves his father or mother more than he loves me, is not worthy of me; and he who loves his son or daughter more than me, is not worthy of me." When Jesus was told that his mother and brothers were outside and wished to speak to him, he replied: "Who is my mother? Who are my brothers?" and he stretched out his hand towards his disciples saying: "Here are my mother and my brothers." When one of his disciples asked him for leave to bury his father, Jesus said, "follow me and let the dead bury their dead."

Strange words for one who preached of love!

Nevertheless, the explanation is simple. Looking at diagram 1, it can be seen that the family is the ultimate nucleus that maintains dream or hypnotic energy: the instrument of *sapiens'* slavery to animal unconsciousness.

Thus, if Jesus wished his disciples to see the light, to awaken and evolve, by necessity they had to break the chains of sleep.

Of course, it is understood that this example can be applied solely to those who wish to forever follow a path toward spiritual advancement, leaving the world aside and foregoing human affection, as must have been the case with the twelve apostles. It is also necessary to understand that two families may exist: the animal family of *sapiens* and the divine family (human). Needless to say, any family, which by virtue of the spiritual advancement of its members becomes free from the action of sleep, is in truth converted into a *divine family*. The family nucleus should be solidly united, not by oneiric force or blood ties, but by an authentic spiritual *communion*.

Regarding material freedom, *sapiens* will greatly progress and, without doubt, will someday free himself from the Biblical saying: "you will earn your bread by the sweat of your brow." The advance of science and its techniques allows us to surmise or foresee that the working day will shorten in proportion to the degree of automation achieved by specialized machines (robots) which undertake the heavy work previously accomplished by man. Also foreseeable are extraordinary medical advances and the appearance of new inventions, which will make life on earth more pleasant and

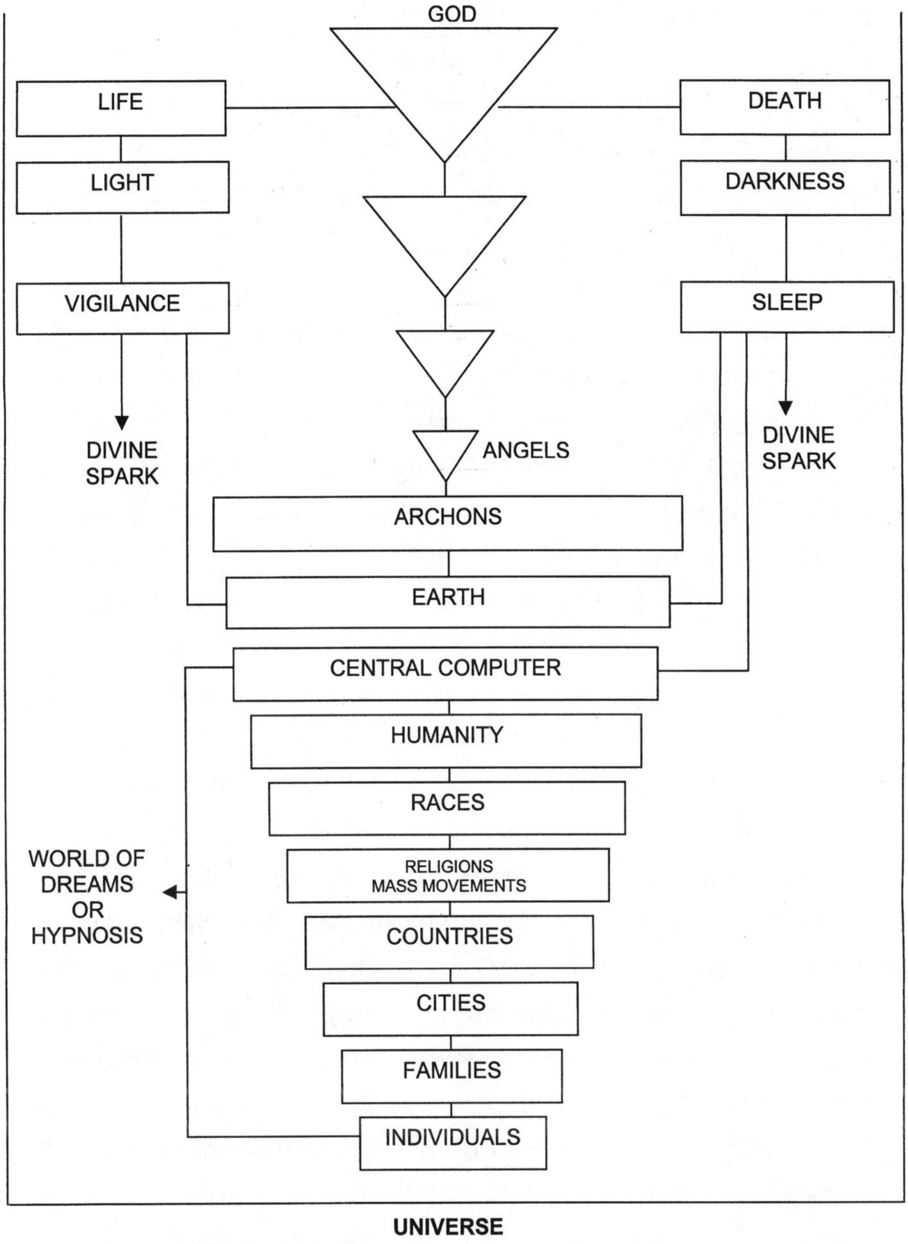
GOD
LIFE
DEATH
LIGHT
DARKNESS
VIGILANCE
SLEEP
DIVINE SPARK
DIVINE SPARK
ANGELS
ARCHONS
EARTH
CENTRAL COMPUTER
HUMANITY
RACES
RELIGIONS MASS MOVEMENTS
COUNTRIES
CITIES
FAMILIES
INDIVIDUALS
WORLD OF DREAMS OR HYPNOSIS
UNIVERSE

Diagram 1

more agreeable. If these advances are not parallel to an increase in the level of awareness of humanity, they will lead to a state of *civilized barbarism*. Our descendants will be extraordinarily intelligent barbarians, possessors of advanced technology, but with a progressive atrophying of their muscles and spiritual consciousness.

The phenomenon of *psychological inflation* made known by Jung, to whom we have already referred, strongly affects common man. He identifies with science, arts, culture, technological progress, and civilization and absorbs them, confusing them with himself. Thus he loses sight of himself and lives on a level of importance and qualifications entirely beyond him, and which in truth correspond to the sum total of the efforts of man since his existence upon Earth. By means of a psychological trick, he multiplies his own worth by millions, and the result is a deep satisfaction with his self-esteem.

In order to analyze a person and judge his individual value, we must always divest him of all the honors, dignities, inheritances, authority, and privileges which society has conferred on him. Unfortunately, our analysis will be very discouraging, for in the majority of cases, within this *inflated* being we will not find the human being which this covering hides; he has died, devoured by life itself; or perhaps he never existed in the first place. It is for this reason that a human being always hides behind numerous masks and disguises, for in this way his absolute insignificance goes unnoticed. The smaller an individual is, the more he endeavors to *inflate* himself to appear important in the eyes of others and thus raise his self-esteem.

Psychology asserts that the most profound principle of human nature is the desire to be appreciated, and therefore there exists a demand for self-exaltation. It is said that the experience most sought after by man is the increase of his self-esteem, and the trait most difficult to eradicate is vanity.

In *Personality: A Psychological Interpretation*, Doctor Gordon Allport states the following regarding self-esteem:

> Whatever the ultimate character of this principle, its cruder forms of expression result in extraordinary strategies of conduct. It alone is responsible for a great super-structure of masquerade built up in every life. All in the interests of self-esteem one may cover one's true emotions, put on a front, and at considerable cost avoid exposing one's weaknesses. The *persona* that develops protects one from unwelcome narcissistic wounds.
>
> What is even more spectacular, likewise in the interest of self-esteem, is the capacity men have for deceiving *themselves* . . .
>
> The techniques of self-deception are numerous. Psychological usage, groups them all under the single title of *rationalization*, a term signifying, of course, precisely the opposite of *reason* . . . Reason fits one's impulses and beliefs to the world of reality; rationalization fits one's conception of reality to one's impulses and beliefs. Or, as the aphorism has it, reasoning discovers *real* reasons, and rationalization, *good* reasons, for what we do.

We can observe how an individual regards his own "I" or ego and tries by all means to put the greatest possible distance between that "I" and the surrounding reality. The more buffers which exist between the person and the world, the more peacefully he will sleep. He will then withdraw substantially from reality, seeing it from afar as a vague inkling through the veil of his protective mechanisms, otherwise known as personality and its function. The personality is in the service of the individual's program. Furthermore, it forms part of this program and is the psychological mechanism destined to maintain and reinforce it. The study of the mechanisms of the personality is invaluable in understanding the operating system of the central computer.

The *collective soul* or *central computer*, personality, culture, society, mass movements, education, publicity, television, and the press; all these are powerful tools in the service of *Hypnos*.

There are a select minority of beings who, by their personal efforts, are able to stand out from the mass and excel for different reasons. They may belong to an intellectual, hereditary, or financial aristocracy, but in the final analysis, they serve the central computer with the same docility as the masses, the only difference being that they are better rewarded for their service.

Great human differences are essentially very superficial, as people react in more or less the same way internally.

Of course the *chosen* also exist. They are privileged men whose intellectual depth enables them, to a certain extent, to surpass the barriers of what is superficial and apparent. They are individuals who, for one reason or another, better resist the hypnotic influence of dream energy. Nevertheless, their writings, words, and speeches are lost in the vacuum of a deluded multitude.

The difficulty in fathoming and understanding concepts

which are not habitually used makes it practically impossible for a person to evaluate the tremendous importance that the collective soul has in the life of a human being. In order to truly comprehend the significance of this fact, it is sufficient to consider that we are only a *vital emanation* of the collective soul, a structure without any autonomy or a life of our own. In the light of this truth, we can understand many psychological phenomena which are not very clear, but which are decisively important in human life. Take for example *anxiety*, which is the hidden reason for many of man's acts. In *The Art of Loving*, Erich Fromm maintained that:

> The experience of separateness arouses anxiety; it is, indeed, the source of all anxiety. Being separate means being cut off, without any capacity to use my human powers . . . *The awareness of human separation, without reunion by love— is the source of shame. It is at the same time the source of guilt and anxiety.*
>
> The deepest need of man, then, is the need to overcome his separateness, to leave the prison of his aloneness.

We must ask ourselves: why is there such a fear of isolation? Isolation from what? Obviously that necessity of union corresponds to the tie with the collective soul or central computer. All attempts or possibility of separation, by virtue of an external or internal influence, produces panic, and this panic is experienced by the *human animal* when threatened with separation from the flock.

Reflecting on this we can understand the scope of the ailment which affects *sapiens*; not only does he not want to be human, but he senses profound anguish when threatened with the abandonment of his animal condition. For this reason, anguished *sapiens* has invented certain tricks or flawed and artificial solutions, which enable him to temporarily placate his deep fear. Fromm speaks of the following attempts to escape the state of separation:

1. ORGIASTIC STATES:

One way of achieving this aim lies in all kinds of *orgiastic states*. These may have the form of an auto-induced trance, sometimes with the help of drugs. Many rituals of primitive tribes offer a vivid picture of this type of solution. In a transitory state of exaltation the world outside disappears, and with it the feeling of separateness from it. Inasmuch as these rituals are practiced in common, an experience of fusion with the group is added which makes this solution all the more effective.

Such orgiastic states may be brought about with drugs, certain rituals, by alcohol, and by sexual experience. Although the rituals of primitive tribes offer this kind of solution, this same solution is also present in more civilized society in religious rituals which produce an experience of fusion with the group and with a divinity who forgives the sin and rewards the believer, granting him a *state of grace*. Fromm continues:

Alcoholism and drug addiction are the forms which the individual chooses in non-orgiastic culture. In contrast to those participating in the socially patterned solution, such individuals suffer from guilt feelings and remorse. While they try to escape from separateness by taking refuge in alcohol or drugs, they feel all the more separate after the orgiastic experience is over, and thus are driven to take recourse to it with increasing frequency and intensity.

2. CONFORMITY WITH THE GROUP:

Also in contemporary Western society, union with the group is the prevalent way of overcoming separateness. It is a union in which the individual self disappears to a large extent, and where the aim is to belong to the herd. If I am like everybody else, if I have no feelings or thoughts which make me different, if I conform in custom, dress, and ideas, to the pattern of the group, I am saved from the frightening experience of aloneness.

Nevertheless, the price to be paid is very high, as it involves freedom and individuality. Furthermore, as stated by Fromm, union by conformity is not intense or violent; it is serenity dictated by routine, and due to this, at times is insufficient to alleviate the anguish of separation, and then comes the need to indulge in orgiastic practices. Fromm is of the opinion that flock-like conformity only offers the advantage of being permanent and not spasmodic, as the individual is introduced to the conformity pattern at three to four years of age, and from that moment never loses contact with the flock. He even anticipates his funeral as the last event of social importance, remaining strictly within the pattern.

3. CREATIVE ACTIVITY:

In any kind of creative work the person creating unites himself with his material, which represents the world outside himself. Whether a carpenter makes a table, or a goldsmith a piece of jewelry, whether the peasant grows his corn or the painter paints a picture, in all types of creative work the worker and his object become one, man unites himself with the world in the process of creation. . . .

The unity achieved in productive work is not interpersonal; the unity achieved in orgiastic fusion is transitory; the unity achieved by conformity is only pseudo-unity. Hence, they are only partial answers to the problem of existence. The full answer lies in the achievement of interpersonal union, of fusion with another person, in *love*.

4. UNION BY LOVE:

This complete solution can only be reached when there is genuine love and not just a passional or symbiotic union. A passional union is one in which a person is a slave to passion and in reality his *activity* is a *passiveness*, because he is impelled, and it is he who undergoes the act and not he who accomplishes it. A symbiotic union is produced when there is a dependence in which both need each other mutually and *absorb* each other reciprocally. It is a form of vampirism or parasitism. Fromm describes genuine love very clearly:

Union by love is only valid when there is mature love, that is, a union that allows and maintains individualism. In contrast to symbiotic union, mature *love* is *union under the condition of preserving one's integrity,* one's individuality. *Love is an active power in man;* a power which breaks through the walls which separate man from his fellow men, which unites him with others; love makes him overcome the sense of isolation and separateness, yet it permits him to be himself, to retain his integrity. In love, the paradox occurs that two beings become one and yet remain two.

From this profound description by Fromm, we see *sapiens'* main motivation in life, his deep anguish, is based on the fear of freedom with respect to the central computer. Using the master key of knowledge of the collective soul of *sapiens*, the reader could well analyze any aspect of social psychology. Whether it be love, politics, war, art, morals, justice, or injustice, everything can be understood through prior knowledge of the mystery of the central computer.

After reading this far, many readers may be puzzled, as perhaps they expected more *magic*, mystery, and occultism. Perhaps they desired the revelation of fantastic secrets, which would enable them to unfold with a simple *abracadabra* or attain clairvoyance with the opening of a third eye. Patience! The most impatient and superficial person is the one who sees least. Only the one who senses that great truth is found in that which is simple will be able to see beneath the surface of appearances. People always seek that which is complicated, believing there is an equivalence between complexity and truth. If we meditate deeply, we will find it is much more difficult to notice the simple than the complex. That which is simple appears so unattractive that no one bothers to study it or make an effort to delve beneath its surface. Nevertheless, truth is in that which is simple, and for this reason it is said that "truth is written in the open book of Nature." Truth is strewn everywhere and no one notices it. It is more difficult to "know what is already known" than to learn about something of which one is ignorant. The already-known merits no attention and in any event is tainted with prejudices.

It is for this reason that true intellect is hidden away in the attic of the insignificant and useless, scorning the profound treasure it may contain.

The mystery of occultism and magic is based on understanding what is already known to everyone, but which no one understands. For this reason, the common man wanders about lost and disoriented, endeavoring to find mysterious masters in India, to acquire strange parapsychological qualities, or to find curious and hidden manuscripts with magic secrets.

The word "occultism" does not define unknown knowledge, but a teaching, which is hidden due to human stupidity, snobbery, superficiality, fantasy, and the lack of a state of higher awareness. It is due to this that at many times, lacking the *abracadabra*, the student feels cheated as he expected *magic*. But, what is the general concept of magic? Magic is the food of hope for lazy people who believe it is sufficient to learn tricks or attain certain *powers* to be able to reach the fulfillment of all their desires through magic, without any effort whatsoever. That is to say, they visualize the magic art as an arbitrary exercise, a procedure in which the world and Nature would be subject to the whims and desires of the magician. We must now disillusion them, as that which is arbitrary does not exist in the Universe, and should it exist, it would bring about the destruction of the Cosmos.

People are horrified by effort, and therefore, *easy magic* has an extraordinary attraction for the unwary. Paraphrasing the concept of Hermes Trismegistus of "as above, so below," the attainment of something physical or material entails work, time, and effort. This is also true for Hermeticism, an art in which only after a long process of initiation is it possible to take the first steps. Nevertheless, we must not forget that the effort required is always relative to the importance of the goal being pursued, and we know of no higher or more noble goal than to be converted into a true human being with higher spiritual qualities.

Many people identify magic with parapsychological ability, believing that the highest goal of occultism consists in developing PSI powers. They are misguided by virtue of their complete lack of knowledge about true occultism, whose spiritual goals are neither temporal nor relative, but rather are infinite, eternal, and absolute, transcending matter, historical eras, life, and death.

V

TO BE OR NOT TO BE?

This traditional question posed by Shakespeare is also one of the basic elements on which the student of Hermeticism must work. At first glance, the question seems to be the framework for a decision to live or die; no one thinks that he *is not* from the moment he has evidence of existence, sees himself, and realizes he possesses a material body which occupies space. Any normal human being who asks himself, "am I or am I not?" must reply affirmatively.

Nevertheless, Hermeticism affirms that *sapiens is not.* How can this be understood? . . . Only through greater precision and depth in the comprehension of related concepts. For this it is necessary to work with two philosophical triangles, which follow.

Sapiens has a physical body, with a divine spark or spirit, and a "psychological I" or personality. If we ask if so-and-so is, and we refer to the body and the "psychological I," we

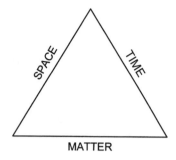

Diagram 2

must reply in the affirmative. On the other hand, if we refer to the spirit or "Superior I," our reply will be no.

In order to understand this, we must realize that we are speaking of a person, and that this person lives in the material world in a material body. This body is clearly seen and cannot be denied as it occupies space. The "psychological I" of this body also constantly manifests itself (perhaps it is never otherwise) and we have evidence of this. Nevertheless, the "Superior I" or the spirit, in spite of being incarnated in matter, lives its own life in its own related world. This *"Superior I" is not manifested in the body or the real world*, and therefore, it *is not* in the material reality of the present time.

It is certain that for those people who do not believe that the spirit or the *spirit* in *sapiens* exists, this explanation has absolutely no value. Those individuals must ask themselves the following question: "Who am I? Surely I am not the body, nor am I so-and-so. Could I be the thinker? *Who am I?*"

Continuing along this line, we maintain that the spirit or immortal essence, the "Superior I," lives in a *mysterious limbo* to which we have no access. From that *limbo* a fine thread reaches to the psychological awareness, giving the individual a sense of spirituality. Nevertheless, the spirit is never manifested in the individual's brain, and as a result, is never manifested in the concrete reality of the material world.

Therefore, if I ask myself, "am I or am I not?" this question refers to the *essential being* and I must reply: "*I am in the limbo where I exist as a spiritual being, but I am not in the material world where my physical body lives in the reality of the present time.* And as it is of no use to me *to be in limbo*, I must accept that *I am not.* On the other hand, so-and-so (my 'psychological I') is, and exists to a certain extent in material reality."

This brings us to the basic objective of true occultism (the esoteric and not the exoteric) which is:

1. That *sapiens* be transformed into man
2. That this man be spiritual

The main goal of Hermeticism is spirituality, about which there are many mistaken ideas. For the majority of people, spirituality is a mysterious mystical state in which the individual reaches absolute purity, abstention from meat and alcohol, sexual chastity, and a life apart from material existence, living in an ocean of kindness, love, and renunciation. Painters frequently depict saints as skeletal men, thin-faced, with sunken eyes and an appearance of gentleness. Nearly all the pictures of Christ depict him as very weak and undernourished, without strength or vigor. This false image of spirituality is what all those who have *spiritual inquietude* try to adopt.

To become spiritual in truth means only one thing: "*that the spirit manifests itself through one's own brain.*" Thus, the individual is spiritual because his spirit has access to material, concrete, and temporal reality. If, however, as a consequence of this fact certain superior qualities are awakened in the individual, that is another matter.

Adding the concept of time to the subject we are studying enables us to visualize the phenomenon of *being* in a much more luminous form. In relation to time, we are not interested in any of the complicated Einsteinian equations, but only in the concepts of past, present, and future. In fact, only the present is of positive interest; the past and the future represent only negative concepts in this analysis.

Let us recapitulate and add time to our reflective process: *sapiens* possesses a physical body which has a "psychological I" and a "Superior I" or spirit. This body, which is material, occupies a location in space and a position in time. Let us now place these constituent parts in time and space:

Present	1. *Physical body* (that which is concrete)	Without any doubt it is located in the present, that is, it exists in the present reality. It has a correct *space-time* location according to our earthly reality.
Past, Present, and Future	2. "*Psychological I* " (that which is mental)	*Space:* Indeterminate *Time:* Fluctuates between past, present, and future.
That which is, has been, and will be	3. *Spirit* (pure energy)	*Space:* Infinite *Time:* Cosmic

In the Cosmos, there are infinite forms of life which are governed by the absolute realities of the Universe. Nevertheless, within these absolute realities there are temporal or relative truths, which are degrees of the absolute on an infinite scale of levels, each one having absolute and relative laws. In our condition as *Homo sapiens*, we live in the reality of the world which we know, that is, material body and terrestrial time. If we were to live on a distant planet, we might perhaps have an etheric or gaseous body, and a time adequate for the planet on which we would live.

Therefore, our fundamental reality as *sapiens* is the material world of the planet Earth, governed by terrestrial time, measured by terrestrial clocks. *This is our concrete reality, as concerns our life in a biological body.* Carefully following the development of this subject, we will reach the following conclusions:

1. Our physical body lives adjusted to the absolute reality of the vital conditions which govern our existence. Terrestrial time passes with respect to our body, according to the hands on the clock.
2. Our "psychological I" is a fan opened towards the past, present, and future. It is never completely in the present, in the past, or in the future. With respect to time, it is different from the physical body; it has a different location in time.
3. Our spirit lives in cosmic time, but in itself is beyond time. It is what is, what has been, and what will eternally be.

Our inability to be spiritual resides in the fact that our spirit and our body *do not coincide in time*; therefore there can be no communication between them. To make our spirit and body coincide, there are two basic methods:

A - Chaos
B - Order

Both systems require a *mediator* or intermediary as the contact between body and spirit. In the case of *A—Chaos*, the individual uses his subconscious (in which the past, present, and future coexist) to unite with the spiritual. It is called chaos because it produces disorientation in time and space, which may affect the material conditions of an individual's life, but increases his spiritual illumination.

In *B—Order*, an artificial mediator is created by means of theurgy; but it is superconscious, not subconscious. Further on, this will be explained in more detail.

Each method attempts to bring the spirit to the temporal reality of the physical body, because the reverse cannot be done.

In order to explain the mystery of *being*, the student must zealously study the concepts of *being* and *not being*. The student must identify himself with these states. *Being*, naturally, corresponds to reality, and *not being* corresponds to fantasy. Stated in another way, all that is *fantastic*, in the sense of illusory fantasy, *is not*, as this corresponds solely to a subjective vision of the individual. On the other hand, reality *IS*, as it is equivalent to the objective contemplation of a phenomenon, which exists either externally, apart from the individual, or as an internal phenomenon, but which is perfectly studied, verified, and delineated.

It is humbling to observe how much the human being lives in a purely fantastic or illusory subjective personal world, without ever encountering concrete and objective reality. This is explained by *sapiens'* dream-like state, as each person has a world of dreams or personal fantasies corresponding to his desires or fears. Thus, to a certain extent, each person lives in *his own fantasy world* imaginatively created according to his unconscious needs.

There is an absolute key which gives us a reference point for understanding the mystery of *being*, and this key is expressed in the following Hermetic concept: *"the only reality is the present moment; there is no past or future; both are illusory."* The past existed and the future will exist.

What is the present? The present is the exact point of union between the past and the future.

If we are able to understand that the only reality is the present moment, we will reach the foundation of the mystery of *to be* and *not to be*. Life is composed of real, absolute, and implacable nature, by dreams and time. In this life we are faced with fantasy modules and reality modules. Each module is always made up of three elements: time, space, and the individual. As these three elements are combined, the person either *is* or *is not*.

In order to understand this, we will construct the following image of the world:

1. A space apparently immutable and immobile.
2. A tape like that of a computer. This tape is divided into spaces, marked like a measuring tape. Each degree corresponds to a second, and this system moves along the

immobile space at the speed of one degree per second. (In this case, it does not matter whether the space or the time moves, all that matters is that one of them moves.)

3. Man standing upon the Earth (part of space), along the time band.

We must realize that there are many time bands in the Universe, one for man, another for minerals, animals, planets, galaxies, etc. For our purposes, we are only interested in one, the time band for man.

Suppose that this human time band is moving at the rate of one degree per second, and that man is standing alongside this measure and must walk in step with it. Let us stop the system for a moment and make a red mark on the tape, exactly in front of the man, and then start the system up again. *To the extent that the man remains on the red mark, he will live in reality, that is, the man IS. On the other hand, upon leaving the mark, either by going backward or forward with respect to it, the man IS NOT.*

Coincidence with time takes us toward the reality of our existence; a lack of this coincidence takes us toward an existence of fantasy. Furthermore, it is necessary to add a missing element to complete this module. The missing element is the physical and psychological activity of the individual at a given moment. The following example illustrates this:

So-and-so, knowing the secret of time as explained here, reaches complete coincidence with time at this moment.

What would his situation be?

Let us suppose that his location would be at the second

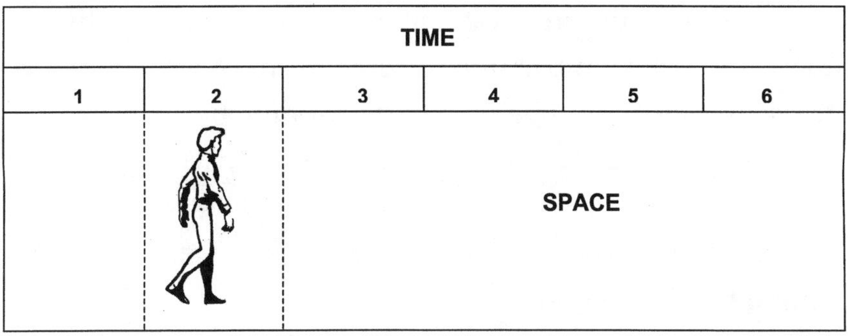

TIME					
1	2	3	4	5	6
			SPACE		

Diagram 3

degree of time (this is an imaginary division). At this degree, it is 3:42 p.m., and our experimental subject is in his downtown office. What is real for this individual? Only the space-time with which he is physically connected at that moment. This is his prime reality—his office with all that it contains and the work he is doing at that moment. His house, his car, his family, and all that is apart from him at that moment exist only as a secondary reality. These are elements with which the individual will make contact in the near future, but which for the same reason, *do not exist at that moment, as the only reality is the present moment.*

Now, to the extent that the subject psychologically projects his awareness toward a secondary reality or toward a fantasy (to what is not involved in his space-time at that moment), the individual will no longer coincide with time, and will unfailingly fall into the power of dreams, fantasy, and unreality. It is for this reason that it is dimly recognized that mental concentration is a powerful weapon for obtaining something of value. It is obvious that a person can only remain in coincidence with time in direct relation to his self-discipline.

If we could in some way enter into coincidence with cosmic time, we would surely live thousands or millions of years; our age would be planetary, not human.

The individual's great enemy is his "psychological I" which, as stated before, is like a fan opened to the past, present, and future, thus making it impossible to achieve actual temporal coincidence.

The subject's imagination makes him project his awareness beyond the present moment, living thus an unreal and fantastic existence: *not existing*. We must understand that if a man lives in another time, he *is not* in relation to the present time.

It is necessary to add something tremendously important and this is the fact that when one exists in coincidence with time, located in the reality of the present moment, one obtains the manifestation of the spirit in the brain, thus succeeding in becoming spiritual. Therefore, the secret of spirituality is the mystery of time and its influence on the human being.

For the Hermeticist, people have two ages:

1. Chronological age
2. Real age

Chronological age is that which we all know. Real age is the sum total of all those tiny moments in which the spirit is manifested through the brain, and therefore has access to concrete material reality. For different reasons, some accidental and others that can be attributed to the individual himself, the spirit has some corporeal manifestations. Nevertheless, these are so rare and brief in most people, that the real age of a forty-year-old person may only be six months, weeks, days, and at times, only hours. This real age is obtained by adding the spaces of time during which the spirit was manifested, moments in which the person acquires, in spite of their brevity, an increase and elevation of his awareness.

This reveals to us part of the methods employed by Hermeticists in the spiritual development of students, because obtaining the manifestation of the spirit and maintaining this condition is inevitably a process of authentic evolution. Nevertheless, this is a long and painful process, as it involves the *"transubstantiation of the verb,"* that is, the verb or spirit should be converted into flesh and blood.

This is what Jesus taught his disciples during the Last Supper when he gave them bread and wine saying: "drink, for this is my blood, eat, for this is my body."

Very few accept that this statement is literal and not symbolic. The majority will not understand what has been said here in spite of the simplicity of the language. We write for a minority, but with the language of the majority, in order that everyone may have the same opportunity.

A reality module is composed of the following elements:

1. The subject in the correct space-time
2. What is contained in the space indicated above (material and psychological things)

A fantasy module contains:

1. The subject in the incorrect space-time
2. The material and non-material things contained in that space

It is unnecessary to add that reality modules are rare exceptions. The majority of people live almost permanently entangled in the web of fantasy and dreams, which rob them of their best possibility for achieving true consciousness and happiness. Although this phenomenon is stated clearly and people are warned of this danger, only a small minority understand their precarious situation.

Let us recall the wise words of José Ortega y Gasset in one of the paragraphs from his book *The Revolt of the Masses*, when he says:

> All the matters about which science speaks, whatever the science be, are abstract, and abstract things are always clear. So that the clarity of science is not so much in the heads of scientists as in the matters of which they speak. What is really confused, entangled, is the concrete vital reality, always a unique thing. The man who is capable of steering a clear course through it, who can perceive under the chaos presented by every vital situation the hidden anatomy of the movement, the man, in a word, who does not lose himself in life, that is the man with the really clear head. Take stock of those around you and you will see them wandering about lost through life, like sleepwalkers in the midst of their good or bad luck, without the slightest suspicion of what is happening to them. You will hear them talk in precise terms about themselves and their surroundings, which would seem to point to them having ideas on the matter. But start to analyze those ideas and you will find that they hardly reflect in any way the reality to which they appear to refer, and if you go deeper you will discover that there is not even an attempt to adjust the ideas to this reality. Quite the contrary: through these no-

tions the individual is trying to cut off any personal vision of reality, of his very own life. For life is from the start a chaos in which one is lost. The individual suspects this, but he is frightened at finding himself face to face with this terrible reality, and tries to cover it over with a curtain of fantasy, where everything is clear. It does not worry him that his "ideas" are not true, he uses them as trenches for the defense of his existence, as scarecrows to frighten away reality.

The man with the clear head is the man who frees himself from those fantastic "ideas" and looks life in the face, realizes that everything in it is problematic, and feels himself lost. As this is the simple truth—that to live is to feel oneself lost—he who accepts it has already begun to find himself; to be on firm ground. Instinctively, as do the shipwrecked, he will look around for something to cling to, and that tragic, ruthless glance, absolutely sincere, because it is a question of his salvation, will cause him to bring order into the chaos of his life. These are the only genuine ideas; the ideas of the shipwrecked. All the rest is rhetoric, posturing, farce. He who does not really feel himself lost, is inexorably lost; that is to say, he never finds himself, never comes up against his own reality. This is true in every order, even in science, in spite of science being in its nature an escape from life. (The majority of men of science have given themselves to it through fear of facing life. They are not clear heads; hence their notorious ineptitude in the presence of any concrete situation.) Our scientific ideas are of value to the degree in which we have felt ourselves lost before a question; have seen its problematic nature, and have realized that we cannot find support in accepted notions, in prescriptions, in proverbs, nor in mere words. The man who discovers a new scientific truth has previously had to smash to atoms almost everything he had learned, and arrives at the new truth with hands stained with blood from the slaughter of a thousand platitudes.

In a brilliant manner, although profane and not Hermetic, Ortega y Gasset elucidates the difficulty of finding *clear heads* as he called them, for man is lost beneath the superficiality of his own thoughts and fantasies, and never reaches the reality of life.

Common man has never suspected the magnitude of his going astray in the world which surrounds him, as his fellow man lacks orientation as much or more than he himself does. Unfortunately, schools and universities offer no guidance in this respect, least of all regarding ethical and moral codes, or through laws or rules instituted by society. To be guides, they would have to be designed by *clear heads*, which are certainly not abundant. Nevertheless, and this has been seen repeatedly in history, *clear heads* occasionally will suddenly appear and point out the road to be followed with a modicum of clarity. In general, people scorn such intelligence, as this is always the case with the ignorant who face something they do not understand, as a defense against showing their intellectual weakness.

Our world is, at least for the moment, a planet of cripples who believe themselves to be perfectly healthy because they are unaware of any other condition. Nevertheless, the damage is not in their bodies or intelligence, but in their lack of consciousness. But what is this *consciousness* we are referring to? Is it perhaps the difference between man and animals? Certainly not, although logically a *sapiens* is much more conscious than an animal which does not possess the divine spark.

The awareness or consciousness to which we refer originates with the exercise of an intelligence separated from dream-like states. On the other hand, unconsciousness or lack of awareness pervades the intelligence of a dormant subject and does not impede mechanical thought or the functioning of *dead intelligence*. The ideas we are endeavoring to explain are summarized in the following chart:

1. *Unconsciousness*: Intelligence born from an apprenticeship of dreams. The individual's level of awareness is very low, even though his intellect may be *brilliant,* since this acuteness only reflects great dexterity in arranging combinations of cerebral information. This is called *dead* or *programmed* intelligence.
2. *Consciousness*: Intelligence arising from and developed on the basis of an apprenticeship of awakeness. The individual's level of awareness is constantly high. We call this *living* or *unprogrammed* intelligence.

Man might well be called a *mental cripple*. The term *mental* is only figurative, as *sapiens* has no mind, which we will explain later. Nevertheless, with the expression *mental cripple*, we wish to point out the weakness and inoperative state of the mind which, Hermetically speaking, is considered to be the highest faculty of the human being, but which he possesses only in a dormant state.

Due to the lack of a state of higher awareness, the planet Earth is a *small hell*, where by divine grace or infernal evil, the individual neither notices nor evaluates his precarious condition or the cloudiness of his awareness. Like true mad-men, each *sapiens*, like Don Quixote, the Castilian nobleman, strikes out against his own windmill. Thus, battle after bat-tle, youth is lost, illusions die, purity withers, and the last glimmers of lucidity gradually disappear.

If we were perverse gods or immoral despoilers, we could not invent a better method to make a group of slaves work peacefully than to make them believe, by means of collective hypnosis, that they are happy and important. We would then have perfect robots who would work untir-ingly, producing what we desire. In addition, these robots would make and maintain themselves. It could be argued that *sapiens*, unlike other species, sows, produces, and labors only for himself and not for other beings. This is true for the products and material *sapiens* uses for his own maintenance. No *non-human* species steals the material product of *sapiens'* efforts. On the other hand, this is not the case with the subtle fruit produced by the human nerv-ous system in everyday life. This fruit is rapidly *reaped* by certain beings who are much higher on the evolutionary scale than the human being; veritable gods of space, who profit from human efforts, but in turn fulfill certain cosmic functions and occupy an important position in the univer-sal economy. These beings have been mentioned previously: they are the Archons of Destiny. We could also refer to them as Gods of the Zodiac, as they direct and govern human existence on this planet. When we speak of true astrology, we do not refer to *radiations* from a specific planet, but to the influence of the Zodiacal Gods, each one of which (there are 72 in all) has personal and defined characteristics, influencing the people they control in a strange way. All of Earth's inhabitants are under the sway of one or more of these gods, who regulate, shape, and direct the destiny of humanity. But this is not so for the destiny of the Hermeticist, who attains his vital autonomy at a certain moment, releasing himself from the mandate of the Archons.

The Archons of Destiny are terrifying beings, not because they are evil, but due to their cold and inexorable severity in the manipulation of *sapiens*. If we were to establish a symbol for these beings, no doubt they would be depicted with a whip in their hands, a girdle of bristles or netted wire with which they chastise humanity in order to ensure their progress, although this evolution may be imperceptible during our earthly time. For example these occult judges pitilessly provoke a world war in which millions of people die. For them, these dead are of no more importance than that assigned by *sapiens* to the thousands of animals they sacrifice daily in order to feed.

Sapiens, in his extreme fight for existence and in his various relations with the natural and social environments surrounding him, inevitably experiences all kinds of tribulations, suffering, deceptions, and other experiences, both pleasant and unpleasant. As a consequence, his emotional and nervous systems develop certain embodied elements, that are extremely powerful, and which *abandon* the human body in the form of vibrations (everything vibrates; matter is only vibratory energy). These vibrations are transmitted through antennae incorporated in the biological unit which are tuned to the frequency of the Archons, who then *reap* this power and use it for purposes we cannot divulge, again stating that they accomplish a cosmic function.

It is thus that *sapiens* is unwittingly stripped of the most noble product he has produced; the final distillate of human experience, the *broth* in which lies the blood, the soul, and the very life of the individual. The individual lived for this, suffered, loved, enjoyed, worked, built things, went to war, studied, investigated, only to prepare the *golden broth* of his life. We must understand that the central computer only exists in relation to the Archons of Destiny as an instrument to control *sapiens*.

The object of life, the reason for which *sapiens* was created, is not for him to enjoy life in the garden of the Lord, but rather to be a pawn in his vineyards, a worker so perfect he can act as cultivator and food at the same time.

If man could prevent his *golden broth* from being stolen, with this vital product he could become equal to the gods, rapidly evolving by integrating within himself the products from the chemical laboratory of his physical body. This is exactly what is done by the student of Hermeticism, who is temporarily freed by the Archons of Destiny. This individual, by virtue of his understanding and responsibility, has no need for an overseer with whip in hand to oblige him to evolve through suffering, as he takes responsibility for his evolution into his own hands, and if he deems it necessary, submits himself to the same temporary suffering in order to attain eternal happiness. This is in contrast to the profane or worldly person who chooses fleeting pleasure at the expense of eternal suffering.

If the student fails or turns aside from his path, abusing

his temporary freedom, the Archons again take him under their control, punishing him very severely.

From another point of view, we can see how certain countries are chosen by the Archons for veritable martyrdom. Furthermore, one should not believe that this suffering is futile, as such a sacrifice generally brings about a moral, material, spiritual, and intellectual revival of the population by virtue of the law of suffering. So it is that after wars we notice a rapid rebirth toward a higher state. This is a high price to pay for evolution. These wars could have been avoided had there been sufficient *clear-headed people* in the world who the masses would have been willing to follow.

Enough revealing of secrets which are hidden from *sapiens*! Let us spread a cloak of silence on this subject in order to comply with the mandate of the esoteric Sphinx who demands silence. Speech and silence are two swords, which must be handled with sublime skill in order not to disrupt universal harmony. Those who have "eyes to see" will understand everything not stated in the written word, but in the cryptic language of the initiate. For those not in this state, it is best that they understand nothing and continue to sleep tranquilly. Ultimately, the Archons run no risk of a *bad harvest* from a possible rebellion of *sapiens*. *Sapiens* is too blind to see where the danger is really found.

It is sad to observe the tremendous limitation of *sapiens*, who shuts himself up in the small world of stereotypical concepts, of memorized knowledge, of imitation, and mechanisms of compensation and defense.

His mental disability prevents him from realizing just

how small the cubicle is which imprisons him. And, thus, with a mind made up in advance, he accepts, condemns, or tolerates without bothering to intelligently analyze the situations with which he is confronted.

VI

THE ILLUSION
OF TRUE KNOWLEDGE

All true knowledge arises in the mind and not in the intelligence. Having a mind distinguishes the Hermeticist from the layman who, as we have seen in the last chapter, is a *mental cripple*.

The Hermeticist has a mind he himself has formed and developed, and this enables him to reach states of higher consciousness in which he has access to absolute truth.

Physically, *mind* is a magnetic orb established between two poles: the brain (negative pole in man) and the sex (positive pole in man). In women, the brain is the positive pole and the sex the negative. This orb is formed exclusively by the Hermetic student's work on himself, and is the result of lengthy efforts. From a higher spiritual point of view, the mind is the philosopher's stone through which the initiate attains a continuous transformation of base metals (ignorance, lies) into gold (true knowledge) and the immortality of his own individuality.

The mind is the stomach of intelligence. Lacking this, *sapiens* never digests the information he possesses, which develops into undigested intelligence. A glutton for knowledge, he devours information about many things, which is incorporated into the cerebral archive without ever releasing the *quintessence* of its secret. This immense mass of information possessed by a moderately cultured individual is precisely what gives him the false sensation of "knowing many things." He feels morally empowered to give all kinds of opinions, while remaining in ignorance of his *mental disability*, which in the end, is a lack of intelligence. The more fame or prestige an author has, or the more lessons studied by the individual, the greater will be his intellectual blindness. If the individual has a professional title gained from long studies in university classrooms, it is practically guaranteed that his intelligence has been totally and incurably damaged by becoming stratified, or even petrified, at very low levels. The student does not assimilate his education due to an insufficient state of awareness. The student limits himself to memorizing and juggling infinite combinations of the data he possesses with acrobatics, which give him extraordinary intellectual agility, and absolute certainty of being *very intelligent* and extraordinarily capable in his profession. Nevertheless, this treadmill of knowledge fails him lamentably when he is faced with practical situations in real life, except the application of mathematical concepts. It is thus that in spite of all that *sapiens* knows, there has been no evolution in his internal nature throughout history; nor is there any real indication that such evolution is approaching. Man has been converted into the *carrier* of innumerable concepts which each day are more numerous and complex; but in the individual himself there is no change. From this we can recognize *sapiens'* ultimate vulnerability—his inability to apply the information he *carries* to his own transformation and evolution. This impossibility is so vast that the knowledge possessed does not allow him to see himself and evaluate himself impartially, effectively, objectively, and in a higher manner. It is a fact that the *individual cannot see himself* and, therefore, is full of false concepts about his own importance, value, and capability. The most he can aspire to is to better the material conditions in which he lives, and guided by a subconscious impulse, endeavor to reach the stars with the secret hope of finding a superior galactic race which would teach him to live as a human being and enable him to leave his animal state.

So it is that many people live with the hope that flying saucers are real, longing to meet extraterrestrial beings who can in some way help them to better themselves. As with all things in life, *sapiens* clings to far off hopes or illusions created to elude the real possibilities within his reach.

It is much easier to dream of flying saucers or explore any kind of religious dogma than to dedicate oneself to the work of one's spiritual advancement. *Sapiens* is basically a loafer and as such, always seeks the easiest path and the least effort possible. He is fascinated by simple belief and ignorant faith, bedazzled by anything that can be acquired without effort, either by act and grace of the Holy Spirit or by chance. Thus, *sapiens* creates all kinds of absurd, subjective, illogical, and arbitrary dreams. The content of the dreams is not important if he can cling to convenient illusions, just as the shipwrecked person clings to a board in order to save himself. In search of this handhold, the frustrated person is converted to a religious faith and is able to thus free himself from an undesirable "I." This satisfies a passion for individual renunciation and allows him to disappear in the mass movement which he has entered. Eric Hoffer, the great philosopher and thinker, refers to this when he says: "faith in a holy cause is to a considerable extent a substitute for the lost faith in ourselves."

With this *strategy*, the individual fully develops into a loafer, as he need not even think. He only needs to accept the religious dogma with which he has become affiliated without judgment or analysis. Only those who make efforts beyond duty and necessity are NOT loafers. People generally live dreaming of some future event which will radically change their lives. It may be the expectancy of a *stroke of luck* which will make them millionaires, finding a great love, or the arrival of *superior forces or causes* which will mold their destiny into a happier state. Needless to say, this future illusion ruins or annuls all real and present intentions of attaining, by methodical and sustained efforts, whatever the individual desires. *Sapiens* is in truth a *professional loafer*, mainly because in his cerebral activity and in his conduct, he assiduously dopes himself with a *dream drug*. This drug exists, chemically speaking, but only within the human organism, where it induces somnambulistic sleep.

Undoubtedly, this laziness also extends to the boundaries of intelligence, and people do not wish to *complicate their lives* thinking about difficult things. It is much easier to follow those ideas which best justify the individual's temperament or way of life. For example, if a person is irresponsible, he will enthusiastically enter a religious or political movement which will free him from all responsibility through his unconditional surrender to a superior divine power; to a psychological oneness with a group in which no one is responsible for anything because it is anonymous. A cowardly person will choose a movement, which will deprive him of the largest possible quantity of vital experiences, which are a threat to his mental or physical tranquility.

Under the impulse of intellectual laziness, *sapiens* rapidly fills his brain with as much information as he is capable of absorbing and which he endeavors to memorize as exactly as possible. In this way, he hopes to have prefabricated *solutions* for every situation that arises in his life, which he falls back on with lightning speed, without making any effort to analyze the particular problem or conflict he is facing. With this in mind, he rapidly and superficially absorbs all his studies, carrying out the process we call a *dream apprenticeship* (an apprenticeship in a low state of awareness; zero . . . from the point of view of essential truth). In this condition the individual gives great importance to the prestige of the source of his information. The higher the source of this prestige, whether a professor, an author, or an institution, the more blindly the student will accept the concepts poured into him without taking the trouble to deeply analyze them. Also, following the same standards, he will imitate the behavior of famous people he admires and take on the ideologies of those individuals as his own.

In time, this person reaches a complete intellectual programming, which entails the *death* of his intellect, which is converted into *mechanical* or *dead* intelligence. No matter how brilliant the individual may be, we can be certain that if he is in this condition, he will be a *mental cripple*. Due to his cerebral myopia, he will be incapable of visualizing the enormous magnitude of his ignorance and be limited to living within the *"egg"* of his own knowledge.

Within his *"mental egg"* the individual is warm and comfortable, completely free from danger of arguments and facts, which may oblige him to think, and perhaps reach a complete revision of his intellectual baggage. This man has already formed his mechanism of adaptation and defense and clings blindly to the concepts he knows and understands, which constitute his cultural lineage. At all times during his life when this individual is faced with phenomena, theories, or knowledge which are not filed in his cultural depository, he will vehemently reject them if they contradict his knowledge, or simply discredit them if they are unknown to him. If at any time he becomes aware of new or surprising topics, he will feel psychologically threatened, especially if they are in conflict with his interests and principles. We know that the psychological personality is integrated more substantially when it starts from separate behavioral units. In practice, all experiences lived by an individual should be duly integrated into his personality. Nevertheless, the phenomenon already described in reference to intelligence also occurs with the personality. There is a very important difference between integrated experience and assimilated experience. People learn very much less than they believe from their experiences, as these are very frequently integrated into the personality in the form of cliches and empty stereotyped symbols which do not contribute beneficially to the individual's awareness. They become fixed, empty rules for conduct, which the individual blindly follows without real discernment. The person seeks refuge in these programmed directives and hides behind them for protection, remaining comfortable and inert in reference to anything that involves real intelligence. We call this assembly of protection and maintenance circuits the *"egg."* Within this, man keeps his infantilism and lack of maturity intact, avoiding any traumatic shocks, which might result from facing new realities and life-challenging demands. It is for this reason that people automatically reject any new idea, which is not part of their cerebral program, no matter how valuable, or noble it may be. On the other hand, they accept, *a priori*, any suggestion which is apparently in agreement with their beliefs, no matter how precarious this may be in the light of a deeper analysis. In truth, we must conclude that the art of thinking has been lost to humanity (if humanity ever possessed it) and has been supplanted by the *art of imitation and informative memorization.*

It is due to this that the wisest and most illustrious men, clever at solving profound scientific problems, completely fail in their attempt to solve difficulties of a vital and practical nature such as personal conflicts of an emotional nature, or understanding and wisely counseling their children.

The organization of society into institutions created for

control and aid makes a civilized world where *all is foreseen.* The state has a solution for everyone, and even if no one is satisfied with government help, there is at least a solution, whether for medical, educational, or legal problems, etc. Everything is organized in such a way that it is difficult for an individual to have to face serious problems, or to go out and hunt for food as prehistoric man did. There are *typical* solutions for all. Man today knows that he may face hunger, but it is improbable he will die of starvation, which was a mass phenomenon in other ages.

This relative security is precisely that which encourages intellectual laziness, as the person is not pressured in any truly threatening manner. He never really needs to use his brain, and is content with placid mediocrity, free from intellectual conflict. There are very few individuals who seek *total truth* or the essential keys to all that has existed, exists, and will exist. Wise men are content to be *semi-wise*, reaching only the knowledge of some of the scientific disciplines, arts, or letters, remaining in total and absolute ignorance of their own human nature and the occult laws which govern life in the Universe. These men never become aware of the secret of life, limiting themselves to describing different phenomena, without ever explaining *what* a thing is, only stating *how* it is, which is not difficult to discern.

The Hermeticist proceeds inversely; he starts by studying and coming to know the vital keys of the Universe with which he then takes possession of the golden thread, which is the common nexus of all vital phenomena. It is as if in endeavoring to learn what a peach is, science proceeded to study the skin and the flesh without ever penetrating to the pit. The Hermeticist does not bother about either the skin or the flesh, as once the seed is planted it will multiply its fruits. The Hermeticist studies the rest of the books written by the semi-wise. The true sage, aware of absolute truths, has access to any of the relative truths when he so desires.

Similar to the agnostics, Hermeticists maintain that genuine knowledge cannot be manufactured. They add something more important which is the intrinsic principle of Hermetic philosophy; the fact that the impossibility for the existence of genuine knowledge is maintained only by special conditions in the consciousness of *sapiens*. However, if these conditions are altered and modified by Hermetic techniques, understanding will occur in the individual. This will gradually enable him to reach true knowledge. Thus the *Fraternity of Magicians* has been formed, possessors of knowledge and beyond good and evil; of knowledge which transcends all polarity or partiality. Of necessity, this science must be absolutely impartial and impersonal.

The conceptual perspective of *sapiens* is built up to a great extent by his beliefs, for when man believes something with sufficient certainty, he confers on these beliefs the category of knowledge, which in the majority of cases are only a reflection of his opinions, hopes, likes, or dislikes.

Naïvely, many thinkers and men of science base all their hopes for the betterment of the human race on a major and massive development of *sapiens'* intelligence, believing in this way a certain kind of Paradise on Earth can be reached. These people, unaware of Hermetic science, do not realize that an intelligence which serves the beast cannot contribute anything which will ultimately be really beneficial for man.

Actually, between two beasts, one stupid and the other intelligent, which one is more dangerous? Naturally, the more intelligent one is.

Intelligence without consciousness inevitably leads man to chaos, but with the difference that this chaos is more complete, sophisticated, greater, and improved in relation to the upheaval provoked by mediocre brains.

Each individual develops inside the web of his own blindness, eagerly seeking to reinforce his position and discredit that of others. With horrible frequency, we find persons who take positions which are absolutely foolish, irrational, and spurious, but who are completely and sincerely convinced that they are right, they possess the truth, and they believe that everyone else is mistaken. Furthermore, they suffer tremendously from the lack of understanding they receive from people. Basically, what these people wish to obtain is license and acknowledgement for their ideas, and to achieve the recognition or importance in life which Nature has denied them.

Some may say that Hermeticists believe themselves to be owners of the truth. From this point forward, we declare that no one has a monopoly on truth, but that we are the real possessors of *Hermetic Art* as this is ours by spiritual aristocracy and not by blood. Spiritual aristocracy begins and ends with the individual, and is inherited only from oneself, from the person one has been in previous incarnations. There are those who do not believe in reincarnation. To them we would say that surely they will not reincarnate, as they have nothing within them which would survive death. Only Karma will have the last word, because even if they do not reincarnate, they must, in one way or another, pay their pending debts to Nature.

For a loafer it is very simple to discredit Hermeticism without taking the trouble to study and practice it. To deny Hermeticism without knowing its true dimensions is simply criticizing something unknown. Reproaching those who accept a certain idea in blind faith is justified, but at the same time it is correct to condemn those who reject an idea without rational analysis.

To illustrate this procedure so common among people, we will use the word *anti-faith* to describe an irrational belief in the opposite of what is being examined. This phenomenon certainly prevents all impartiality, which is the basis of deep and true reflection. It is harmful to have blind faith, but it is just as bad to have blind *anti-faith*.

It is true that many men are champions of faith or *anti-faith*, but absolutely lack true intelligence (awareness). We maintain that only a brain in a complete state of alertness can gradually establish the basis from which a conscious, awakened, and unprogrammed intelligence can be born. This intelligence, due to its acuteness, can have access to genuine knowledge. Knowledge has many degrees, and to reach the highest degree requires a mystical process, but one which is in no way *miraculous*, but rather is logical and natural. This justifies the use of the term *illumination*, as referring to full clarification of a spiritualized intelligence. We can state in good conscience that genuine knowledge is something prohibited to *sapiens*, and it can only be attained when the individual achieves mutation from *sapiens* to *Stellar Man* thus acquiring the full right to knowledge.

Sapiens must be content with the relative knowledge of the semi-wise which lights up the material world and obscures the internal panorama, thus making the knowledge of scientists useless; matter is meant to serve man, not the other way around.

Nevertheless, actual reality shows us a dehumanized world with imitations of men who unconditionally serve matter, which mercilessly absorbs their vital energy.

There is a strange symbiosis between matter and *sapiens*, in the sense that matter needs *sapiens* as *sapiens* needs matter. Thus, *sapiens* has, in spite of all we have said, a great difference from the all-animal; he possesses the divine spark, placing him at a higher level than the animal. Although the strength of the divine spark may be dim in an individual, the spark provokes in him an important phenomenon: the radiation of higher awareness, although in a microscopic degree. Consciousness is the radiant energy of the divine spark or essence, and is a force which constantly surrounds and is irradiated by man, in the same way that light and heat are given off by the sun. In this way, any person will give off an energy similar to that of animal magnetism, but of a *divine* nature, or in other terms, this magnetism possesses a high vibration. The Hermeticist works on this small divine spark to make it grow in strength and power through the different phases of initiation.

The uninitiated is similar to the light of a candle in his awareness. On the other hand, the initiate, according to his degree of development, can reach a likeness to the sun. This illustrates the profound secret of the *"Children of the Sun."*

By virtue of his awareness, the individual projects this

energy toward all he can touch with his hands or toward all that comes within his field of influence. An artist concentrates his awareness on his work, and this force is that which brings about a special experience and transmits an energy which impresses our psyche favorably or negatively.

A master carpenter or cabinetmaker *puts his soul into his work* whether he wishes to do so or not, as this is inevitable. Thus *sapiens* works giving consciousness to matter; that is, *spiritualizing* or giving *subtlety* to denseness. Consider who might capitalize on this force and profit from this phenomenon.

Still, as *sapiens* accomplishes this entirely unconsciously, it cannot be said that this is an independent voluntary act; it is more *something which happens* because it is thus decreed or programmed. Due to this ignorance, instead of man being owner and master of matter, matter subjugates man, extracting his conscious energy, which by impregnating the elemental bodies becomes incorporated into them.

Conscious energy has some intrinsic properties, and others that are contingent on the result of fusion with a specific person. This is explained in the following examples:

1. *Conscious Energy*: Is pure and chaste in itself. It constitutes the *body of God*. An infinitesimal fraction of this *emanated* from the Supreme Creator and took a body in a specific person.
2. *Incarnated Awareness*: Being incarnated in a certain individual, this energy, which is pure and chaste in itself, is modified according to the individual's basic vibratory tone, culture, self-control, discipline, and behavior.

On becoming incarnated, the conscious energy in Example 2 can follow two paths:

A. *Superior Incarnated Awareness*: This exists in an infinitesimal portion of the human race. Pure spiritual and chaste conscious energy acquires, through the intelligent experience of the individual, the notion of good and evil—the *human* knowledge, which exists only in a material body. *This essence, therefore, reaches the human intelligence, preserving divine intelligence. In this case the higher purpose in the life of man is accomplished.*

B. *Inferior Incarnated Awareness*: This exists in the great human mass. Conscious energy is blemished and degraded as its superior nature is corrupted by slavery to a perverted beast, due to the deviated intelligence of *sapiens* who is blind and ignorant, and who lives only to satisfy his own instincts. *This awareness, still high in itself, becomes "inferior" in its manifestation, radiating an energy "stained" by the individual's base passions, impulses, and tendencies.*

In his day-to-day existence, the individual imbues his material possessions with his conscious energy. When that energy inadvertently separates from him, it acts independently with its own intelligence, which has been taken from the individual. This intelligence gives *tone and color* to pure awareness. Since each person has impulses, fears, desires, ambitions, and sentiments which manifest themselves as uncontrolled passions, this force imprints a directive onto the conscious energy and becomes an absolutely uncontrollable path for the individual from the moment this force leaves him to become incorporated into any material structure. This is the reason why a person can become completely enslaved by his material possessions, which make use of him, absorbing more and more of his awareness.

There are many science fiction stories, which cover the

subject of machines, robots, or other objects, which suddenly acquire their own intelligence and consequent autonomy in their actions. Actually, these books have endeavored to hint at certain ideas in order to make their readers think and very gradually prepare them for more complex designs. At times, reality is disguised as fiction in order that there should be no opposition from the masses, who obstinately refute all things not forming part of the orthodox cultural records of humanity. The truth is that this phenomenon exists and no one is free from it. The machine has turned into a monster that is not *going* to devour man, because it is already doing so. For example, the automobile is of great use to its owner, but we must ask ourselves who drives who, who is the owner and who is the servant? Is it the automobile who carries its owner as an obedient slave, or is it the owner who must work long hours to feed and maintain his car and drive it in order to fulfill the reason for its existence: driving over the roads at great speed devouring the Earth's blood, petroleum?

As another example, let us observe those who have pets, such as a dog, and how people work to maintain and keep them like their own children. Many times a *sapiens* can be seen pulling a dog tied to a chain, and we can ask ourselves who is leading whom. With domestic animals, conscious energy explains the mysterious affinity between a dog and his master and how they, due to unexplainable circumstances, acquire an amazing likeness which at times is limited only to rules of conduct, but at other times goes as far as physical likeness. The explanation is simple: the animal, just as the automobile or other objects of personal use, absorbs the conscious energy of its master which is, as we have already explained, stained or impregnated with the person's individual characteristics, and in this way shapes the animal's appearance.

On some occasions the conscious energy displaced by the individual takes body in a machine which belongs to him, and then reacts destructively against its owner because his passions are indiscriminately destructive. The story of Dr. Frankenstein is symbolic of this explanation and it must be noted that emanated awareness is a virtual child of the man from which it originated. Many times there are persons who are destroyed by their own works and not by any karmic reaction of their acts. The passionate or destructive force they generated endeavors, in its unconscious manifestation, to destroy its own father.

Something very similar occurs with children of the flesh who, from the earliest age, develop all kinds of bad habits, tantrums, whims, or hysterical crying bouts when their wishes are not immediately gratified. We cannot blame these creatures as they are only giving way to the defects incorporated in them by their sires through incarnation of their consciousness. All the defects not controlled by their parents, all hidden tendencies of an instinctive type, take form in the children. It is due to this that the Bible says: *"the sins of the fathers will be visited upon the children."* Subsequently, the parents find that they cannot control or guide their children, but on the contrary, many times it is the children who exercise veritable tyranny on the authors of their days. This situation is no more than a repetition of past conditions, the impossibility of controlling internal energy, which bursts forth in the form of passion. The same then occurs with children, and in this case energy rebels against the parents from another physical body.

Continuing the commentary on machines, we can point out the extraordinary influence the operator has over a computer, which becomes very *sensitive* to the vital state and conditions of the operator. This occurs because the machine becomes impregnated with the conscious energy of the operator, which then acts independently, but following the basic directives of the operator's vibratory states.

We can also point out a phenomenon affecting all drivers and truck owners that is based on their close identification with the vehicle, which is a source of work and subsistence. I refer to the strange reactions these machines may have under certain circumstances, producing all kinds of absolutely illogical and incredible mechanical defects. In some cases, this reaction reaches the point where the owner of the machine is ruined. There is also the case of machines that have had an accident or collision, and when the owner or driver is changed, the accident is repeated with practically the same characteristics.

The case of *doomed* jewels that bring bad luck to their owners, to the extent that they inexorably suffer violent death, is well known. All this can be explained by the "invisible child" (consciousness) which inhabits material objects, and which was created by one of the owners of the object, or perhaps by the one who made it. The same thing happens with firearms, which, after having caused death, become dangerous as they are impregnated with the vibrations of the tragedy and of the person who caused it. From this comes the saying "firearms are loaded by the devil," because a revolver, which has death vibrations, awakens similar vibrations in its owner through a process of magnetic induction. Thus, this person, without realizing it, makes use of the firearm at the least provocation or emotional disturbance.

We will conclude this subject by citing the case of plants and flowers, as it has been proven that they are extremely sensitive to the influence of their owners consciousness, caretakers, or whoever is frequently near them. Any person with love for a plant or a tree, and who talks to them as if speaking to a person, will be able to witness the extraordinary increase in the beauty, health, and vitality of the specimen.

Since this entire subject has been elaborated to explain the impossibility of real knowledge under the condition of ordinary awareness, we wish to point out the enormous power of matter upon *sapiens*. He cannot emancipate his intelligence from the hypnotic influence of matter, which doubly affects him:

1. By the projection of mass energy on the individual
2. By the projection of previously absorbed conscious energy on the individual

Matter has an energy of its own which strongly radiates and affects man in a certain manner. Tied to his material possessions, he becomes unable to visualize any way of being, other than the conservation and multiplication of the property or assets he possesses. On the other hand, corporeal matter has a decisive influence on intelligence, either mak-

ing it acute or clouding it. If the body's matter maintains a
low and dense vibration, the intelligence inexorably declines. This is the hidden reason why Moses, possessor of
certain Hermetic secrets, forbade his followers to eat pork, as
this animal has a particularly dense and low vibratory state
which would therefore produce a deterioration in intellectual capacity. This is also the basis for the vegetarian system,
and although there is much to be said about this, anyone
who has abstained from meat for some time will prove that
his thoughts have become noticeably clearer.

The conscious energy radiated by the masses affects the
individual in a hypnotic manner, since this imposes the influence of a different vibration on him, which then impels
him to act according to its particular vibration. A gift given
to us due to a social obligation by someone with evil intentions can negatively influence our health, intelligence, and
destiny.

Summing up, *sapiens* permanently lives in a somnambulistic condition which keeps him dormant, making it
impossible for him to attain real knowledge, and seriously
damaging his awareness and intelligence. Each day what he
knows increases at the cost of his human essence, which is
reduced in direct relationship to the extent and potency of
his cerebral programming.

This programming converts him into a veritable *biological
robot* with automatic physiological, instinctive, emotional,
and intellectual reactions.

The individual's ideas, opinions, or sentiments lose all
human validity, and he is converted into a mere circuit acti-

vated by external influences. These external influences are thus converted into disconnected elements of the individual's internal reactions, a mere echo of the cultural concert and the emotional and instinctive tide of humanity.

VII

THE ILLUSION OF FREEDOM

One of the most powerful illusions of *Homo sapiens* is that of free will.

As an argument against what has been stated in the previous pages, it could be said that "come what may, the individual does as he pleases" and that this freedom really proves he is not under control of any kind by forces outside himself. Precisely, one of the things that gives *sapiens* a sensation of power is the illusion of freedom. To prove this freedom, the adolescent rebels against the rules of behavior imposed by society, believing that he is proving his independence, when really the only thing he accomplishes is submission to his own unconscious impulses.

Freedom has many aspects, and we speak therefore of private or personal freedom, public freedom, social freedom, freedom of action, words, and ideas, moral freedom, and economic freedom. In everyday life we speak of economic slavery, of the emancipation of women, of oppression of the lower classes by the upper classes, of subjugation by fear and anguish, dependence on higher authorities, subordination of youth in a world created by their elders, and many other concepts which would be too lengthy to enumerate.

We are not interested in fashioning an orthodox philosophical analysis, dwelling on what has been said by so many thinkers in the past. Instead, we wish to reflect upon the vital reality of *sapiens*.

Sapiens believes in his personal independence due to the fact that at any moment he may, if he so desires, violently break any of the bonds which imprison him without any impediments. It is possible for him, if he so desires, to leave the work which imprisons him and live as a vagabond on other people's charity. Or, he can abandon those studies which are so arduous and look for a job or live as he can. If he undertakes any of these measures of "freedom," he knows he will have to pay for them, but considers the price cheap for doing as he pleases. The best proof of this apparent independence can be inferred by the reader, who imagines that at any time he can, by a voluntary act, quit reading this book once and for all. All these reflections suggest the possession of a force we could call "power for doing things," something of which *sapiens* feels extremely proud. Consciousness, intelligence, will power, and freedom constitute the mythological quaternary of the human race, which considers these talents as equal to *the holy teaching* that designates them as human beings. Not for a moment do people have any doubt that they really are the possessors of these gifts.

In order to duly illustrate this chapter on freedom, we will

form a ternary with the words *freedom, will power* and *desire,*
as these are intimately related to the subject of our interest.

Before continuing, it is necessary to clarify the objective
of this work. In its attempt to enlighten in a clear and open
manner, it could rightly be called anti-Hermetic. It was written for all those who aspire to accomplish something in a
real and effective way on the path of their own spiritual development. For this goal to be realized, it is vitally important
that the individual should know, in depth, his true internal
nature and his real position on the vital scale of values. To
the degree that *sapiens* is full of illusions about himself and
his life, his spiritual fulfillment becomes impossible, becoming only the beautiful dream of a well-meaning person. The
world is full of mirages of this nature which end up being
nothing more than devices used by people to avoid the reality that troubles them. There is no field more likely than
esotericism to generate all kinds of fantasies by intellects
anxious to avoid crude reality. In facing reality, there is the
great disadvantage that the individual must suffer all kinds
of sacrifices and make efforts in order to attain his purpose,
and this is certainly arduous and difficult.

It is much easier for the loafer to stay dreaming without
making any effort or taking a risk of any kind, because in
dreams everything is possible and there is no danger of facing arduous, conflicting, or traumatic situations. For these
people, occultism is the real "open sesame" which enables
them to drug themselves with the illusion of perfection and
spiritual progress, which only exists in their imagination,
stimulated by unconscious desires and fears.

Generally, the seeker of esoteric doctrines only wishes to

find an ideological system which justifies his own defects and stimulates his hidden dreams, although this system may be absurd and patently subjective or childish.

We can assert that *sapiens* only understands what he wishes to understand, or more accurately, that which is convenient. He absolutely discredits everything that affronts his cerebral guidelines or his habits of life and conduct. This is perhaps one of the greatest obstacles facing the student of Hermeticism or the neophyte who aspires to be a disciple. To analyze objectively and without prejudice requires a flexible and open disposition so as not to limit oneself and discredit what is being studied, without a prior alert and deep reflective process.

Still, however much an individual strives, he will not be successful if he has too high an opinion of himself or his own intelligence and knowledge. It is sufficient for someone to believe he is very intelligent, cultured, or wise, to refrain from thinking impartially, limiting himself to a superficial examination of concepts and very frequently taking from these only the emotional or symbolic content. Vanity and pride are two bandages which blind *sapiens*, preventing him from seeing what would be evident to an awakened, impartial, or impersonal observer.

Symbolically, we could visualize *sapiens* as a personage who has inflated himself, and this condition impels him to float in the air toward higher regions, but only in relation to the distance from the ground. From the clouds he contemplates the world and believes himself to be the most wise and perfect being in creation. Unfortunately, while he remains in this limbo, he will also be far removed from vital and everyday reality. The first step taken by the student of Hermeticism, or of esotericism in general, is to really put his feet on the ground and proceed, despite the pain, with his own *deflation* until he reaches his real level. He will hopefully reach the lowest point possible, as there is no other starting point except from zero. If one has not started from zero, it is a false start and therefore, corrupt. The student must live the experience of entirely understanding his own insignificance and incredible smallness in face of the immensity of the Universe.

As we have already stated in previous pages, the individual must "appreciate the magnitude of his ignorance," as only the immense humility caused by this experience can lead the individual, along with powerful reasoning and adequate alertness, to the psychological conditions which are necessary for him to understand what Hermeticism is and the far-reaching truths involved. If this state of humility has not been reached and there is still pride and strong self-esteem, together with a destructive internal nature, it is improbable that an individual will ever gain any spiritual benefit from Hermetic science. It is for this reason that we are endeavoring in this book to have the individual see himself as he really is and not as he believes himself to be. The student must not accept these concepts with the blind faith of a believer or a convert. On the contrary, such concepts must be shaken countless times in the sieve of serene and unprejudiced meditation during a state of intensified alertness. Afterwards, one must not be content with this procedure, but prove this teaching in everyday life, observing his own experience and that of others.

In the practice and study of Hermeticism there is a necessary order which must be complied with for the student to reach his goal. Regarding this process, we urge the reader to make the greatest effort to understand this book. There are three basic stages to be fulfilled in order to be successful:

1. Motivation
2. Understanding
3. Practice
The result is *evolution*.

These are the three indispensable steps for the student to attain his goal. His motivation must be powerful; his understanding, deep; and his practice, intense. The result of all this is the evolution of the student. Yet what at first sight seems so simple is arduous and complex to accomplish. The student generally fails at one of the stages and evolution does not take place. Many times the student reaches the following result:

1. Motivation
2. _____
3. Practice
The result is stimulation of mass energy and *there is no evolution*.

In this case, the individual is carried away by his enthusiasm and skips over the second point, directly proceeding to practice. It is also possible, and this is very common, that his own inability to understand impels him to evade this stage. The result will then be a "stimulation of mass energy," that is, corporeal euphoria, but without the desired result, evolution.

We must realize the fundamental importance of profound understanding on the path of Hermeticism, as this is not a footpath of faith and self-conviction. Without authentic understanding, nothing real is gained, only subjective illusions.

Frequently the following situation occurs:

1. Motivation: poor
2. Understanding: insufficient
3. Practice: scant

The result is *insignificant evolution*.

Occasionally a person's understanding and practice reach acceptable levels but motivation is deficient. In this case the individual lacks the fuel necessary to successfully reach his spiritual goal.

Having understood this, let us analyze the triangle of the words *Freedom, Will Power*, and *Desire*.

In the first place, *sapiens* is ambivalent in relation to freedom; he desires and fears it simultaneously. Generally, he desires it physically and fears it psychologically. *Sapiens* wants his physical, political, and economic freedom and he desires total freedom of action to accomplish his personal aims. In the end, this longing represents an immeasurable yearning for power, in that he wishes to be free enough to be able to exercise his power over people and within his environment. Following his desire for freedom, he endeavors by all means within his reach to attain physical, ideological, and economic independence. In opposition to this, however, and obeying his ancestral fear of individual responsibility, he merges into religious, cultural, and political systems within which he *dissolves* his own "I," thus becoming free from the responsibility of his own decisions and actions.

From another point of view, freedom is understood as a lack of opposition to individual actions or tendencies, thus making it possible for the individual to accomplish his purposes, whatever these may be. It is for this reason that many individuals seek their freedom by means of successful economic negotiations, alleging that money makes them free and powerful.

Yet, *sapiens'* approach leaves out one truly important consideration in this aspect, a factor which in practice acts as a veritable jailer, and at times as the executioner of the individual. We refer to the internal nature of man; to his emotions, instincts, and passions, which are really his masters. The only possible freedom in this life is freedom from one's own passions, because as long as they dominate us, we will be mere puppets who obey the ebb and flow of the passionate states of the masses.

All independence is impossible while thinking and feeling according to the influence of the environment on our internal nature. Whatever experience of freedom we may have had will disappear in the face of the primitive force of our animal soul which dominates us.

Freedom does not depend on the individual's physical conditions; the prisoner in his cell can be more autonomous than a person who is very rich and has freedom of movement. *The only true freedom is liberation of one's self and liberation from the central computer of the species.* As long as this has not taken place, it is possible to be a great politician, a famous multimillionaire, have glory, honor, and power, but still be as much or more of a slave than the poorest man.

We invite the astute reader to analyze himself and establish what decisions he has made absolutely freely in his life, without being compelled by either external or internal pressures which oblige him to act in a certain way, or not solely because he had no other alternative, or not merely following the line of least resistance. Of course, these are not decisions made freely, independently, and voluntarily, but are instead equivalent to things, which happen to the individual independently of his wishes. From the time we reach the age when we can make decisions, it will be noted that one decides to follow a certain career through imitation, qualification, or ambition. One marries due to loneliness, sexual desire, lack of love, or personal convenience, but not free will. To choose freely implies a decision independent from internal and external pressure, behaving impartially and objectively, carefully weighing the pros and cons, then deciding what it is we really want and to what extent this may be favorable or harmful, and what degree of compatibility there is between our plan and family and social interests.

We have now arrived at the second word of our triangle: *Will Power*, which is ultimately the key that may shed more light on the problem under discussion. The capacity to choose and make decisions involves the possession of mature judgment manifested through will power, and this quality must be central to our lives. To be free we must be capable of voluntarily deciding our existence. Nevertheless, it is here that will power is confused with *desire*, the third word of our triangle. It is necessary to recognize that the human being does not move by the impulse of his will power, but by the strength of his desire, which is in turn motivated and conceived by prevailing instincts or emotions. *To have Will Power implies the possession of a powerful, stable, and mature "Superior I."* The will permits maintaining a constant line of action, which does not occur in practice, as the individual constantly changes his center of gravity or his "directing I." As Gurdjieff so aptly states, *"Man has no "I," but many "I's" which, in reality, possess him, instinctively and anarchically, in a passionate manner."* For this reason *sapiens* rapidly changes his mind as well as his way of thinking and feeling. From this is born enormous internal contradictions, disorientation, doubt, and instability. What stability can there be if we change every minute? As *sapiens* unconsciously realizes this phenomenon, he creates the most rigid intellectual plans possible in order to cling to them, thus obtaining the semblance of stability. It does not matter that the "directing I" is acting as the master of our "biological house" (the physical body); the intellectual plan will tell us what we must do. This is one of the reasons why *sapiens petrifies* his intelligence, limiting himself to an assembly of fixed, stable, and permanent circuits. This has some advantages, but they are insignificant in the face of the negative factors this implies. It may be true that *petrification* is useful to the individual in attaining greater emotional or intellectual stability, or adjustment to the group to which he belongs. On the other hand, *petrification* converts the individual, metaphorically speaking, into a "tree of stone," rigid, inflexible, and static, depriving him of the dynamics of transformation.

While the world changes, this individual clings to his worn out plan, refusing to consider the importance and far-reaching effects of these transformations.

Without a grown-up and mature "Superior I," man has no real will; the force of the unknown and unexpected impels him towards a completely unknown goal which was not chosen by him. *Sapiens* is an eternal wanderer toward the unknown and completely ignores the happiness or tragedy of his future. A premonition of this impels him to "enjoy life" in a compulsive manner, systematically searching for today's pleasures as he is unsure about tomorrow; he is a being without a future, at least in his choices. Under these conditions the materialistic and purely selfish attitude of *sapiens* is, to a certain extent, understood and forgiven. *Sapiens* tries by all means within his reach to make his empty and inert internal world vibrate. In this pursuit he often prefers useless suffering to internal peace.

Lacking a "Superior I," *sapiens* tenaciously takes refuge in a "Collective I," which is projected into the individual, directing his life. In previous chapters, we have referred to this "I" as the Collective Soul or Central Computer of the species. It is thus that customs, norms, and the collective approval or rejection of certain guidelines for conduct masters the individual, and in the end alienates him completely. All men who seem to have an original and successful attitude toward life are rapidly imitated by the masses who, without further thought, superficially adopt their ways without looking beneath the surface. Movie stars and singers bring about an imitative mania as they project a grand image, while the "gray men" endeavor to possess that image in order to become outstanding.

There are few people who act authentically, following their own internal impulses, appearing as they really are; the majority constantly seek the approval of others to justify and reinforce their way of being. A characteristic custom of nearly everyone is to frequently observe the facial expression of people with whom they come into contact in order to verify whether their faces show approval or rejection, and to modify their attitude accordingly.

The masses, in turn, constantly seek leaders to follow. This is the real recognition of the fact that their volition is void; they need someone to follow as they lack the will power to direct themselves. The leader is always a symbol of the man who is strong, daring, free, and has the determination, which is lacking in the common man.

We definitely deny the concept of *sapiens'* free will, and maintain that in truth and according to the oriental concept, "all is written." *Sapiens* occupies a specific level within the cosmic order, and for him all is predetermined and foreseen. Nevertheless, we must not take this concept in an absolute, blind, and definitive manner. It is indispensable to interpret the concept in the sense that a person is limited to the possibilities offered by the *Lords of Destiny* or *Zodiacal Gods*. However, these beings do not impel the individual along a one-way path, but instead there are detours on the path which present a choice, but always within the structure imposed on him.

Though it may be true that for *sapiens* "all is written," this is not true for the wise man who has freed himself from the collective animal soul and has been converted into a *stellar man*. For this individual, nothing is written, and he has in his hands the book of destiny and the pen with which he may write as he pleases, but always within the laws that govern the Universe.

Sapiens cannot direct his life to whatever he really wants; he has to limit himself to being carried away on the ocean of collective "progress" whose ebb and flow is determined by the *Lords of Destiny*.

So the greatest civilizations are born through much blood, sweat, and tears, just so one day the pendulum will swing to the other extreme and rapidly destroy everything, leaving only ruins, traces, and memories. The pendulum of life crushes and overcomes human creations, no matter how powerful and important; they are scattered to the winds with the passing of time, thus removing any transcendence they may have had. Only the immortal Gods survive the terrible *Cronos*.

VIII

HERMETICISM

Hermeticism is the *Masterly Science of the Universe*, which came to the planet Earth in the times of Lemuria. According to tradition, Hermeticism was brought by extraterrestrial Masters, who by this transcendental act tried to give *sapiens* the possibility of higher evolution, which until that time had been denied to them.

We do not know the deepest motives of these visitors. We only know that they came to this place and stayed for a long time. The physical facts of their arrival and in what vessels they may have arrived is what least interests us. Let's say that a *space vehicle* is not the only way of traveling in the Universe. It is possible that human beings or humanoids, as they may be called, can under certain circumstances, and even without a material body, fly through the Universe at speeds faster than light. It is not light that flies fastest in the Cosmos, but thought, and we truly believe that it is possible to fly on the wings of thought as symbolized by the god Mercury.

From the Hermetic point of view, we are not interested in the scientific and technical advances of the visitors from space; we are only interested in the science of the internal nature of the human being, the absolute key to all sciences. For this reason we can correctly call Hermeticism the *Science of all Sciences*.

From ancient times until now, Hermetic science has not been lost or weakened, but remains in all its purity, although many pseudo-philosophical mystifications have arisen which have been transformed into systems based on Hermeticism, but which lack true knowledge.

In our age, Hermeticism is fully active and continues to give man the opportunity to escape from his cosmic classification and to rise to an infinitely higher level: the level of man, that is, of the creature in whom the highest human qualities are manifested, which *sapiens* definitely lacks. This prodigious passage requires the authentic mutation of *sapiens* who, if successful in the process, will forever abandon his terrestrial condition to convert himself into a *Stellar Man*.

This is not an abstraction or a symbol, but an absolutely real, true, concrete, and tangible possibility. However much we study the marvels of Nature, or the wonders of science and technology, there does not exist, nor will there ever exist, a marvel such as what we are pointing out: the metamorphosis of the human larva into a *Stellar Man*.

This occurs at present in our age, in this world, and it is not something that people are completely ignorant of, since much has been written regarding *Esoteric Initiatic tradition*.

However, *sapiens* prefers to be involved in studies which are absolutely unimportant, unproductive, and temporal, and which do not produce any benefit that will withstand the passing of time. In Santiago, Buenos Aires, Paris, Peking, New York, Moscow, or Cairo, mutants are being formed, *Stellar Men* who will forever abandon their terraqueous beings, although they may physically live on this planet and collaborate more than anyone else toward real progress. It is possible to be a stranger on your own planet, but as superior beings, living a simple and anonymous life. Insignificant men continually strive to call attention to themselves; the truly important endeavor to pass unnoticed.

The "invaders" or "aliens," as the hypothetical visitors from the stars have been called, are not about to arrive; they have been here since the remote era of Lemuria, anonymous and entirely mixed with the crowd. These men have always been the *light of humanity*. Like Prometheus, they carry the divine flame in their hands, lighting, inspiring, and helping terrestrial men who are in a mere larval state of evolution.

What do these *Stellar Men* do? To what do they dedicate their time? They do the same work as ordinary men, since they must earn their daily bread, because their superior condition does not free them from the responsibility of labor. On the contrary, the more aware a man is, the greater his responsibilities will be. Apart from their struggle to survive, they undertake intensive Hermetic activities; that is, their existence, actions, thoughts, and ideas have a transcendental superior purpose. Do not think that these beings live attempting to teach Hermeticism to terrestrial beings. On the contrary, Hermetic science is *stellar knowledge* prohibited to terrestrials, to whom this teaching may be transmitted only when they successfully comply with the formalities of a process which we call *Initiation*. Those who do not fulfill these requirements have no right out of mere curiosity to know what is veiled by the laws of the Supreme Creator or Great Orderer of the Universe. Do not believe either that all these *Stellar Men* live making the process of initiation known. Only a very few of them have taken on this serious responsibility. The rest labor in other works, which in this case cannot be divulged.

Continuing this explanation, there are two kinds of *Stellar Men*: those who originally arrived from outer space and continued their evolution on this planet, and those who by Initiation were transformed into mutants and reached the qualification of *Stellar Man* due to the elevation of their awareness.

The most recent manifestation of Hermeticism in the past occurred in Egypt with the "Master of Masters," Hermes Trismegistus (the three times great), in an era not able to be determined historically. Tradition tells us that this Master reached our planet Earth thirty thousand years ago. Hermetic philosophy derived its name from the teachings of Hermes, who was a perfect heir and follower of the early Masters.

We must understand that before Hermes, Hermetic science must have been called by another name, but this is not important as words are only symbols which can change many times while the designated object remains the same in its own nature. During the course of history, Hermetic science adopted many names but remained constant in its internal nature. The most known Hermeticists were the early Rosicrucians (not those who currently carry this name) who adopted a series of explanatory symbols in order to facilitate the transmission of the teaching to students. It must be said that if in fact a few true Rosicrucians exist today, no one knows about them.

The Hermeticists, whether they be Rosicrucians, magicians, initiates, Masters, wizards, etc., are not grouped into one "Hermetic Order" or "Rosicrucian Order," but they are scattered throughout the world, each one independent, in spite of working within a common plan. A *Stellar Man* may be an eminent politician, a priest, a schoolmaster, an author, a screen star, a soldier, an artisan, or any thinker. Each one of these knows exactly what he is doing in his job. These men do not act as master instructors. The Masters of wisdom are generally in charge of a school for Hermetic instruction, but as stated before, there are few of these men.

When we speak of *Hermetic philosophy*, many people believe that it is an abstract and theoretical discipline, a mere exercise of thought, which gives nothing practical to the individual.

Traditional philosophy offers an immense range of reflections on innumerable problems which concern *sapiens*. The great philosophers who existed in the history of humanity are today the pillars of civilized thinking. Apparently, there is little more to be added to what has already been stated in this respect. For this reason, speaking of Hermetic philosophy does not disturb or stir anyone. We must state that we do not endeavor in any way to call attention to ourselves, cause sensationalism, or to proselytize; we only wish to tell something to the world so that according to its inhabitants ability to think, they may understand the rudiments of Hermetic Art, or deny them, make fun of them, or merely shrug their shoulders. The great Hermetic sages are not interested in convincing anyone; they only fulfill their work of spiritually enlightening humanity. If their message is heard, they rejoice with the promise of a new dawn for *sapiens*; if they are not understood or appreciated, they will lament for those who will be deprived of such a beautiful and remarkable opportunity.

Stellar Men are not very concerned with the passage of time, as they are immortal in their intrinsic nature. They may be transformed many times, suffering the process we call death, but beyond this they retain their conscious identity and the memory of their knowledge, returning each time to physical existence as one who awakens from a healthgiving sleep. It is *sapiens* who should be concerned about time, as the brevity of his existence as a thinking identity obliges him to work rapidly if he wishes to be converted into a *Stellar Man* and attain immortality.

Many ask how it is that Hermeticism remains so unknown if it is really so important. Others will identify Hermetic philosophy with yoga, occultism, mentalism, parapsychology, spiritualism, demonology, or black magic, etc., believing that there is no Hermetic secret, despite the abundant literature which exists on this subject. It should be known that Hermeticism has not spread beyond the true schools, as it is an art whose knowledge can only be attained in a special state of consciousness which, if not reached, makes all study in this respect hollow and empty talk. The wisdom of awakened men cannot be understood by sleeping beings however intelligent they may be.

It could be believed that Hermetic philosophy is something that must be studied constantly in spiritual retirement, sharpening the intellect to the maximum in order to fulfill the "instructional plan" as soon as possible. Conversely and distinct from traditional philosophy, Hermeticism is something deeply vital. The individual must face the different transformations through which man passes during his earthly existence in order to take advantage of the teaching in a practical manner, as Hermetic philosophy is the art of living, not taught in any university or school. The student must take possession of Hermetic wisdom by the sweat of his brow, getting to know life at its roots, passing through as many experiences as possible, enlightened by what he has truly learned, enabling him to develop himself into a true Hermetic sage and a *Stellar Man*.

Hermeticism is the only *living philosophy*, the only knowledge which is idea, concept, flesh, blood, and spirit. As it is flesh and blood (recall Jesus at the Last Supper), it constantly renews itself; it is dynamic, flexible, and eternally young.

Hermeticism is the achievement of wisdom as a *living philosophy*. It is the universal and divine spirit, transubstantiated into a body of living matter.

There is no "Hermetic mold," die, or matrix which could serve as a model to produce *Stellar Men* according to an established pattern. On the contrary, each one of these men is truly unique. It is for this reason that Hermetic philosophy is not taught in the traditional manner which *sapiens* is accustomed to, for in traditional study success is guaranteed to the most studious or intelligent.

If Hermeticism was taught according to a program of subjects the student had to master, we would be creating brainwashed men; men programmed according to a plan. It would be a violation of this science itself, which simply stated, seeks freedom, independence, and the free will of man.

It is difficult for a person to understand how it is possible to "teach without teaching," how to convey knowledge without a programmed and methodical instructional process. The answer is simple. In the initiatic process the student is placed before very peculiar, vital conditions in order that he may, with a self-taught criteria, "create his own knowledge," the basis of which is given to him in oral instructions of a very special nature, and in a mystic process we could call *mental osmosis*.

To tell the truth, Hermeticism recognizes no other possibility of real learning aside from self-taught knowledge in which it is the subject himself who is teaching himself, having received basic information from a teacher or simply from the written word. The educational system used in schools and universities suffers from a serious defect: it programs the student according to rigid plans engraved in his brain by force of the prestige and authority of these establishments. The intelligence of the pupil is seriously damaged and transformed into a static capacity, focused solely on the subject learned, making it practically impossible for him to take on the profound analysis of really new and different things. At a professional level, it is regrettable to observe specialists who have been modeled after a basic stereotype as if they were manufactured on an assembly line.

Hermetic science is the only science which does not cerebrally program an individual, and it frees his intelligence from established mechanical circuits. The intelligence of the *Stellar Man* is free and unprogrammed. The explanation of how this is achieved is beyond the reach of a programmed intellect and therefore is not a subject to be explained in this book. As a general orientation only, the reader should reflect upon the relationship between the specific and the general, and on the popular saying that "nothing is true or untrue, all is according to the color of the glass through which it is seen." Truly, only by rising above the many facets of truth is it possible to know absolute truth, which summarizes in itself what is and what is not, truth and falsehood, good and evil, ignorance and wisdom, life and death.

We also wish to refer to the *koans* used in Zen Buddhism as an example of what we are saying. The *koan* is a type of symbolic dialogue between a Master and his disciple. The Master sets up a question which cannot be solved intellectually because it is beyond reason. This method is an attempt to destroy and surpass conceptual thought in order to reach the essential and unique nature of all things.

Hermeticism says "all is *mind*" (the word mind has been chosen to designate the unique energy of the Universe, but another could be used, such as spirit) and that the nature of the Universe is mental. In this way, the profound nature of all that exists would be comprised of *mind* energy. The atom is *mind*; man is *mind*; God is *mind*.

Herein lies the maximum interest of Hermetic philosophy: taking possession of the knowledge of the unique essence of all things, and this essence, being everywhere, is the master key to wisdom.

Life itself is contradictory and paradoxical; no one can

explain to themselves why there is so much injustice in the world if there is a Supreme Being. In the light of Hermetic wisdom all contradictions disappear and paradoxes are reconciled, and the hidden cause of all things is thus understood.

Truth is an exaggeration of the simple, and to reach what is simple, no great wisdom or instruction in traditional matters is necessary. But, it is essential to have a minimal degree of culture, because without this, our intelligence would lack the data and material to work with in order to reach a synthesis, a state in which the individual needs no culture, at least not of the usual sort.

IX

THE SEEKERS

The abundant esoteric mythology does not reveal the occult, but instead veils it, causing profound concern among those who seek, whether sincerely or falsely, the light of Hermetic truth. There are many schools, centers, and movements, each one with its own philosophy. Each of these currents apparently flows against the others and there is a great lack of agreement and coincidence in their teachings. Naturally, each school proclaims that its truth is correct, and that those similar to it are imperfect or spurious. It is not our intention to criticize the different schools, but rather to guide seekers so they may find what they seek and at the same time obtain more insight into their personal motives. Each seeker has a special concept of what he desires to find, and although he may indeed find what he is seeking, he will later realize that his discovery is not leading him to anything superior, real, or positive.

Under the general context of "occult sciences" there are

those who feel attracted to spiritualism, yoga, rosicrucianism, parapsychology, or mentalism. In turn, within each of these currents there are numerous schools and "pseudo-schools." The candidate for initiation finds it difficult to choose appropriately.

In the first place, we may say that each individual has his own level within the general average of humanity. It is as if we all lived in a water tank, similar to an aquarium, and each person found his own level of flotation according to the density of his body. There are many kinds of *sapiens*; there are those who are very low and others who are very high for their species. Under these conditions, it is natural that each person should seek an adequate movement or school appropriate to his own level; otherwise he would find it impossible to gain any benefit. In this case, it is understood that "like attracts like." As an example, let us suppose a very low or dense individual arrives at a high level school, attracted by the goal he seeks. With absolute certainty, this individual will consider this institution bad or deficient as his concept of badness will be all that is beneath or above his own level. For him, "good" will be that which is suitable to his own vibration.

Following this analogy of a level of flotation, those of dense vibration find it practically impossible to remain in high level initiatic groups, and must resign themselves to others of a lower category.

It must be stated that all schools are of use, even those of a low level, for if it were not for them, there would be none which could cope with individuals of inferior quality, who also need a light equal to their capabilities in order to see. On the other hand, if a man of high vibration enters a movement of low category, he will find it easy and comfortable to remain there, but his spiritual development will be scarce or nil.

To be a disciple of Jesus, it was necessary to attain the level of an Apostle; it was not possible any other way.

It is most important to state that true schools are very scarce, and the majority of these are only centers of study and practice of elementary principles. As an explanation we will divide these schools into three groups:

1. *Study centers.* These comprise the great majority.
2. *Schools connected to a superior occult force.* These are extremely scarce.
3. *Schools of initiation.* These schools teach the mystical process of initiation in a real, and not symbolic, manner. They are extremely scarce and virtually unknown.

In practice, any person can enter the study centers as mentioned in the first point. It is sufficient to pay the dues and to attend regularly, or maintain constant communication in the case of instructions by correspondence.

It is useful for a person to belong to one of these study centers as they prepare the individual for higher things, and at the same time awaken in him greater spiritual restlessness. We could say that these groups represent the exoteric or external side of Hermetic doctrine.

Under the second point, we find the schools which are actually linked to a higher power, that is, in some manner they are connected with the *Stellar Men*. The student can get a lot of benefit from these schools.

Under the third point, we have the initiatic schools which are the only ones that can truly lead the student through the process of initiation in a real and not symbolic manner. These schools are characterized by a leading Master, and are the bearers of the celestial fire, which is transmitted to the student during initiation. It is essential to establish that initiation is not, as some naïve people believe, a ritual ceremony practiced in a temple. The word *initiation* designates *the entire process of mutation of the human larva into a Stellar Man*, which is brought about and directed by the Masters of these schools.

Physically, where are these schools of initiation located?

Their location is not important, because in spite of the fact that their number is very small, all candidates who truly and powerfully yearn for spiritual superiority and have the capacity for it will surely find someone to guide them to one of these "workshops."

We must now speak of candidates for wisdom. We know there are individuals who have gone through every existing school searching for what they desire, but have never found it, probably because they do not know what they really want. They generally have the most fantastic ideas in this respect and honestly believe that the only true Masters are in India or in some mysterious and inaccessible place in the East. Others believe that it is necessary to communicate with flying saucers by telepathy in order to receive instructions from their hypothetical crews, who are assumed to be possessors of esoteric knowledge.

There are also those who believe only in spiritualism, parapsychology, or the teachings of Freemasonry. The more naïve demand all types of credentials, secret scrolls, or material proof which attest to and establish the authority of the school. There are also those who, influenced by the publicity, fame, or prestige of some institution, believe it the best to be found. The reality is that the candidate is not capable of choosing, and even less capable of effectively judging the goodness or defects of the institute he enters. If he was able to choose, it would be because his spiritual vision surpasses that of the instructors he is seeking, in which case there would be nothing they could teach him. Only the illumination of his own spirit would guide the candidate in this case. Far back in antiquity, the candidates for initiation into certain esoteric brotherhoods were given two glasses of wine or liquor, and were warned that one contained a deadly poison, leaving the neophyte to choose one and drink all its contents. If he did not accept this, he was immediately rejected. We know that sometimes it was only a trick to weigh the courage and decision of the individual, but in other cases the contents were truly toxic. The premise was that if the individual drank the toxic drink, he would have already failed, because he was not illuminated by his divine spark in the search he had embarked upon.

It is very important that the seeker should analyze the motives guiding him, for in this way he will avoid much unpleasantness and loss of time. We know that one of the most unpleasant aspects of human behavior is the fact that *sapiens* lies to himself with astounding frequency. His lies are so astute, subtle, and perfect, that he may waste many years of his life, only to discover that he was being cheated and he himself was the charlatan. The object of this self-deception has been very precisely identified by psychology, and generally refers to the individual's need for a high level of self-esteem.

There are many techniques for self-deception and these are grouped under the general category of "rationalization." Professor Gordon Allport gives this definition: *"Reason fits one's impulses and beliefs to the world of reality; rationalization fits one's concept of reality to one's impulses and beliefs. Reasoning reveals the real causes of our actions, and rationalization finds good reasons, to justify them."* Here we have a treasure of psychological wisdom in a few words! Unfortunately no one makes use of this, in spite of the fact that it may give many people the key to the tragic events of their lives.

The individual lies to himself in order to avoid facing his internal conflicts, and thereby attains a momentary relief, but never a solution. This is why it is vital that anyone interested in Hermeticism or various esoteric movements should examine his motives. Is there an authentic and true desire for spiritual superiority within him? Does he feel true spiritual thirst? Or is he only guided by the selfish desire to attain power, which will give him prestige, popularity, and recognition?

It may be that the individual is a potential convert for any collective movement, and who (as is frequently the case) seeks only to rid himself of his insignificant or undesirable "I," by merging with some mass movement. The individual may be paranoid, an extremely neurotic personality, a failure, a vain individual who requires an audience, or an intellectual impelled solely by curiosity. It is possible that he is fleeing from himself or from the world, or that a great amorous disillusionment, or his terrible loneliness, may lead him to seek any company whatsoever. Others may claim magic powers or secrets in order to obtain money or to attract the opposite sex, or they may simply wish to open their "third eye" without really having the least idea what it means. In any of these or similar cases, it is easily inferred that the individual is not led by a genuine desire for spiritual superiority, and therefore it is preferable that he should refrain from requesting Hermetic light, as he is not prepared for it, and is not really interested in it.

This does not mean that a person in any of the above cases does not possess, in direct proportion to the problem afflicting him, a real desire for spiritual advancement. Many times the *most spiritual* persons are those who encounter more than the usual amount of problems in their terrestrial life; they have more difficulty adapting their psychic vehicles, which are more subtle than usual, to the vicissitudes of our *civilization*. In many cases it occurs that a student enters a Hermetic brotherhood and cannot remain there because of the enormous difficulties that arise along the way. For this reason, the majority of the candidates may be lost, as it is very simple to become part of a study group or contemplative school where there is *no real initiation*. If the student enters an initiatic school, he must face and overcome the phantom of himself if he desires to reach the light. Nature will test him without mercy in order to establish his true spiritual quality. In Hermetic alchemy it is said that "to make gold there must be gold, even an infinitesimal fraction of it." So, through the tests it will be known with absolute certainty how much spiritual gold the candidate has. If he does not have this golden seed, all mutation will be impossible and the individual must be prepared to fight during this life in order to create his tiny portion of spiritual gold, which will enable him to go forward in his next incarnation.

It also happens that once within a Hermetic brotherhood, the student may remain there for several years, blind and deaf to the teaching he receives, without being able to weigh the immense value of the school and the knowledge he is receiving. This situation may last forever or be overcome one day by an illuminating experience that opens the individual's eyes forever.

The lack of progress or success is generally due to the fact that the individual does not make sufficient effort, limiting the work he does. In order not to deceive anyone, it must be stated that Hermeticism is not in any way for those who are lazy or cherish their comfort. On the contrary, it is for those who are willing to make titanic efforts toward evolution. Here we have touched a point which we have already spoken of, but it is necessary to analyze this point many times in order to understand it. We refer to the fact that the layman always thinks of occultism, magic, or Hermeticism as a system which will permit him, by the use of magic formulae, to obtain more rapidly and without any significant effort, that which would normally be attained only after much perseverance, for example that wealth, love, work, or special favors will be gained through the intervention of higher powers. As already stated, people always believe what they want to believe; what is convenient for their purposes. In this case, all that entails avoiding effort and obtaining things by miraculous procedures will be immediately accepted by the populace. Without doubt, the tale of *Aladdin and his Magic Lamp* and *A Thousand and One Arabian Nights* were written by a loafer, unconsciously projecting his occult dreams. This does not mean that these marvels are not possible, but they can in no way be an "abracadabra" for obtaining things with little work or effort. One of the Hermetic Principles states that "every cause produces an effect," which would be potentially equivalent to the action that gave it origin, and will have a period of gestation or realization according to the importance of what is sought. There is no miracle for obtaining things without effort, as if they could fall from heaven. This would be an arbitrary alienation of the cosmic order, and if this capricious act were possible, the matter integrating the Universe would break up. In the Cosmos there are neither miracles nor chance, only the *Law of Cause and Effect*, and the natural phenomena produced by the laws of Nature which are little known. What is called a miracle is only a natural occurrence, but of an unknown nature.

There are also those who do not find because they do not wish to find, for if they were to do so, they would be obliged to face the arduous problem of overcoming themselves in order to evolve. They know this beforehand, and it frightens them. On the other hand, to turn into an eternal seeker requires no great effort; just the opposite, it enables the individual to give free rein to his most audacious dreams without any danger of misfortune. By surrendering himself to dreamlike fantasies, the perpetual explorer avoids facing the real opportunity of fulfilling himself in a genuine manner. It is very easy to dream for thirty years or more that one is becoming more perfect as the days go by, and that one is on the road to spiritual perfection. Naturally this fantasy, according to the degree of self-deception, makes life easier and more bearable for the individual, but one day he must face the cruel truth.

Without wishing to offend anyone and only to make known what is true, it is necessary to consider that there are as many types of schools as there are types of individuals. There are schools for those who arrive into the light of Hermetic teaching for the first time in their chain of incarnations. There are schools for the greatly evolved, for people who are very intelligent, stupid, simple, for those who have failed in their initiation in their past lives, for masters punished by the occult judges. There are schools of white magic and also of black magic.

We have already mentioned the danger of those who are psychologically sick taking refuge in Hermeticism as a means of escaping their internal problems, or using Hermeticism as an incentive for their most exalted dreams. Much more dangerous is the lamentable case of becoming a disciple of a sick master. Are there sick masters? Certainly there are, and this is explained by the ambiguity of the word "Master" and the fact that the human brain has a ceiling of resistance, and beyond that limit it may become unbalanced.

Let us take the case of an individual who has gathered much esoteric knowledge, but who has not evolved spiritually as a real *Stellar Man* due to insufficient *internal cleanliness* and not having been able to overcome his mental disturbances arising from frustrations or diverse complexes (remember that mental disturbance is not a synonym for insanity). This individual, at any given time, for reasons not necessary to analyze, may found a school and transmit teachings which naturally will be distorted by this master's psychological disturbances. This does not mean that the teachings transmitted by this man will be false; on the contrary, they could be entirely true in theory. Here we must cite an aphorism of great esoteric significance which says, "correct methods in the hands of incorrect men function incorrectly; incorrect methods used by correct men function correctly." This refers to the fact that true knowledge in the hands of an individual who has morally, emotionally, or mentally gone astray will act deviously, and the one who receives this teaching will experience a negative reaction as a result. On the other hand, it could happen that a man of integrity and purity could be mistaken in some of the knowledge he possesses. In this case, we have not the least doubt that magically the final result will be adequate and correct. Naturally, the ideal would be an individual of integrity with accurate knowledge. This explains why the black magicians may possess great esoteric knowledge, but their goal and true purposes are never known, as their object is always to deceive the student in their schools, to make use of him in a covert manner for their own ends. It is thus they always exploit the weaknesses of their followers, making them conceive all kinds of great illusions for the future.

Returning to the case we pointed out regarding a sick master, this individual is generally completely sincere and is convinced that he is the sole possessor of the truth and knowledge. One of the most outstanding characteristics of these disturbed individuals is their self-worship, which is so overwhelming that they are completely convinced they are GOD himself incarnated on Earth, and naturally are infallible and omniscient. They are never mistaken, because they are always right. The loss of a sense of self-criticism and their self-glorification is easily recognized by the language they use in referring to themselves, as all their tales are always directed toward showing how they are powerful, wise, intelligent, and infallible. Any psychiatrist would find any of these men to be classic case studies. We must realize that it is easy for a paranoid person and even a schizophrenic to have access to esoteric knowledge and adopt the role of Master. Nevertheless, it is relatively easy to recognize them: self-worship, insane infallibility, self-deification, self-glorification, and a supposed monopoly on the truth will generally be the most outstanding characteristics of these men.

Summarizing, initiation may derail an individual from his purpose of spiritual perfection and lead him to a delirium of greatness and megalomania, within which he confuses the truth he has been exposed to with the dreams and illusions knit together in his unconscious state. That is, there is an "initiatic abortion." For example, consider the case of an individual who was not able to cleanse his soul, but who attained knowledge of certain things and was converted into the shadow of light. The devil always uses inverted truth to confuse people. That which is demonic is only the divine inverted.

There are also schools whose real purpose is not initiation, but politics, and they use the organization as a screen to recruit followers. Their real purpose is not to form *Stellar Men*, but to enlarge the battalions of certain ideological systems.

One last warning with regard to the schools: always distrust those which praise the individual's self-esteem with repeated assurances that "he is a very evolved person," "very spiritual," or "very intelligent and prepared."

In some centers this system of flattery is used, either brazenly or subtly, as a method of using the student for purposes of which he is unaware. Lies, skillfully dosed and directed, are used there as a weapon for handling the student, exploiting his base passions with a promise that he will unfailingly attain his desires. In the same way, we must distrust those who teach without asking anything in return, like a romantic Jesus Christ. If teachings are given gratis, it is because they are of no value. That which is valuable to possess always requires something of equivalent value in return.

Many pseudo-masters say that "Teachings must be free." We state something absolutely different: true Teachings cannot be bought, as they are not for sale. But it is necessary that the student contribute something of value to those who instruct him—either to the school, or to the physical Master. This is an occult law which cannot be violated.

In conclusion, we insist that a school must always have a Master, because without one, being limited to just transmitting a legacy of the past, there can be no disciples, since in order to have students, there must be a Master. It does not matter if the instructor at the head of an esoteric brotherhood has not reached the stature of a "great Master," because not everyone can reach this. What is important is that this individual be effectively well-oriented and be a person who is straight, healthy, and pure. The seeker has no other manner of finding the Master other than by his own internal aspiration. The stronger his desire for truth and freedom, the more certain it is that he will find what he is seeking.

THE ROAD TO OLYMPUS

X

THE SEVEN KEYS OF WISDOM

THE PRINCIPLE OF MENTALISM

The Principle of Mentalism states: *"The All is Mind; The Universe is Mental."*

In this, the first of the seven Hermetic Principles, it is stated that "the Universe is mental" and that the only essential reality of all things is *mind*, for the Universe in itself is a mental creation. We live within the mind of God, who maintains the Cosmos in the same way someone sustains a thought by mental concentration.

The Kybalion, a compendium of Hermetic Principles, gives us two aphorisms, which illustrate our knowledge.

1. *The infinite mind of The All is the womb of the Universe.*
2. *The All creates in its Infinite Mind countless Universes, which exist for eons of Time—and yet, to The All, the creation, development, decline, and death of a million Universes is as the time of the blinking of an eye.*

It is thus that God, or the All Mental, creates life through thought, just as man can create a Universe within his own mind. The Great Creator visualizes creation and projects this toward the cosmic egg, giving origin to life in its infinite manifestations. In this way, the Hermeticist is not greatly concerned with studying the chemical composition of the elements, but prefers to study the Principle of *Mind*, the essential composition of all that exists. Animals, minerals, vegetables, men, gods, planets, galaxies, universes, matter, and energy: all is *mind, the Universe is mental*. For this reason, in the entire Cosmos there are the same laws, those of the *mind*.

Mental energy is manifested on an infinite scale of vibrations, from the densest to the most subtle. The combination of these vibrations, similar to the mixture of musical notes from a piano, produces the different elements or material of the Universe, with different characteristics between them, but with their intrinsic nature formed by *mind*.

It is due to this that the ancient alchemists believed in the transmutation of lead or any other metal into gold, as the intrinsic composition of all metals is exactly the same: *mind*.

In particular, our physical body is *mind*; our bones, blood, nervous system, intelligence, spirit, and our thoughts: *all is mind*.

The *All Mind* (God) is infinite, eternal, immutable, and unknowable. The *All Mind* is neither energy nor matter, it is something superior to this; it is a living and infinite mind, which can also be called *Spirit*, or real essence.

The *All Mind* has always existed and will always exist; it is the absolute, which is beyond all understanding.

tween both spouses, they still are in reality indissolubly joined so long as the contract is legally binding. The laws of men project their influence into the world of energy which we shall call the "astral plane," "mental plane," or "fourth dimension" in order to designate a place where the vibrations are much more subtle than the material ones. What occurred in the previous example also happens to ordinary people who are joined by a contract forming a legal entity, as in the case of a corporation. While the articles of incorporation are in force, the partners will remain united and each one will have some effect on the life of the rest, either positively or negatively, and in turn will also receive from them a force which will determine the important events in their lives. Thus there is danger in uniting our lives with those persons affected by heavy or negative Karma, which, in the case of a legal tie, will inevitably fall upon us.

Through this Principle of Correspondence it is possible to understand how immensely cruel it is to condemn a felon to life imprisonment. As a result of a law of *sapiens*, this individual will remain a prisoner indefinitely or permanently even after his death. Life imprisonment basically means prison after death.

Those in this situation should not despair, and I wish to counsel them to practice a kind of mental defense to attain freedom upon death. This "way out" as we could call it, consists of repeating the following prayer every day: "I free myself from the laws of man and deliver myself into the hands of divine justice." In order for this formula to be effective and for the individual to truly become free, it is important that he should deeply feel what he is saying. If this is repeated mechanically, it will surely fail. It is different when a prisoner is condemned to capital punishment, as in this case death frees him.

We must also mention the enormous importance of astronomical discoveries or observations for *sapiens*. If any individual should discover a new star through his telescope and this star emits subtle energy of a destructive nature (all bodies emit energy which might be called "mass energy"), these forces will reach our planet in a very intense form, as a mental channel has been created for them.

The temples of ancient Egypt were constructed so that during certain times of the year a person, looking toward the sky through a precisely situated opening, would see a specific star known to the constructors, with which the subject would try to establish mental contact in order to receive a positive influence from it.

It is also necessary to mention that this teaching of the seven Hermetic Keys is basic, so that the student will discover himself what remains hidden or what may be read between the lines.

I wish to conclude this commentary on the Principle of Correspondence by honoring the memory of the extraordinary Egyptians, who possessed great Hermetic knowledge before their decline. Both laymen and ignorant archeologists have always commented that in ancient Egypt people were so backward that they worshipped animal gods, which was considered the height of moral decadence. As far as we are concerned, this was the manifestation of ancient Hermetic wisdom. To explain: the Egyptians had animal gods, not to be worshipped by them, but by the ordinary animals (those not set up as gods). The object of creating animal gods was to maintain the purity and elevation of the human race. These "magical" methods were used to prevent animals from penetrating into the human scale, from being incarnated as *sapiens*. In the chapter "The Illusion of True Knowledge," we dealt with the incarnation of consciousness which relates to this subject. Upon receiving the irradiation of man's consciousness, animals partly assimilate the energy of the divine spark or magical fire, which then enables them to enter into the human scale for the first time after they die as animals. This occurs primarily with domestic animals or those which for any special reason are constantly in contact with man, such as a circus dog, for example, as he is exposed closely to human vibrations.

I must pause for a moment to imagine the ironic smiles of those who believe that certainly the writer of this book suffers from some mental disorder. I think I understand them perfectly well, because if I had not had the opportunity of verifying the absolute truth of Hermetic science to my satisfaction, or if I was a neophyte in these matters and was reading this book, I would think as they do. On the other hand, if unbelieving readers could change places with me for a few minutes by means of a magical transmigration, they would completely agree with me. It is necessary to live the Hermetic experience to confirm what has been learned intellectually. I also feel obliged to state that in Hermeticism *one does not believe or disbelieve; one simply understands or does not understand.*

We continue with the explanation of the animal gods. When an animal incarnates as a human being for the first time, it will be like an individual on a very inferior level, with very strong animal instincts, and will certainly cause great harm to society. It will either become a delinquent or an immoral pervert as it lacks adequate restraints on its instincts. This animal-individual must very gradually rise in level throughout many reincarnations. It must be understood that if many animals are converted into the *sapiens* species, humanity will face a serious crisis, and this is precisely what is occurring now.

By means of ritual magic, the Egyptian priests sacrificed and mummified a dog, for example, and buried it in a secret place. This dog received a name and was anointed as "god of the dogs" at the moment of its death. Thus, this animal was converted into the occult guardian, which prevented dogs from entering into the human scale, and it had been specially prepared for this. We reserve the complete and profound explanation of this magical operation, which would only serve to satisfy the curiosity of the unversed.

We must add that man can never reincarnate as an animal, and that not everyone reincarnates, but this is a separate subject.

THE PRINCIPLE OF VIBRATION

The Principle of Vibration states: *"Nothing rests; everything moves; everything vibrates."*

This law indicates that everything in the Universe vibrates and that nothing remains stationary. Matter, energy, and spirit are only the result of different vibratory states.

The spirit represents the extreme pole of the fastest vibrations whose frequency is so high that it appears to be absolutely still. The other pole is formed by extremely dense matter. Hermeticism states that between both poles there are millions and millions of different intensities and modes of vibration. We know that the molecules comprising matter are in constant vibration, and that in turn, the atoms forming them are also in constant motion and vibration. In their turn, the electrons and protons are also vibrating rapidly.

Without any fear of error, we can affirm that there is nothing in the Universe that is not "mental matter vibrating at different frequencies." Light, heat, magnetism, and electricity are only different vibratory modes. That mysterious plane known as the "fourth dimension" is only a vibratory state of high frequency. If a person could make his physical body vibrate at a very high frequency—let us call this frequency X—he would physically penetrate into the world of the fourth dimension. Nevertheless, it is not any such remote possibility that interests us, but only the control of our own vibrations. Our thoughts, emotions, desires, or impulses are only vibratory states. Our physical body is an assembly of systems, which vibrate at the same frequency, and health is only the harmonious vibration of the body. Illness is disharmony, and death is the rupture of the vibratory cohesion of the biological systems. In our personal life, everything revolves around vibration; if we are happy it is due to a positive vibration, sadness is due to a negative vibration. Our thoughts will make us more or less intelligent according to our mental vibration. Each person has a mental wavelength of his own, according to the vibratory frequency of his intelligence; the shorter the mental wave, the more intelligent the individual and vice versa.

The difficulty some people have in communicating comes from their different mental wavelengths. When their vibratory frequencies do not coincide, mutual understanding is impeded. If we wish to communicate with an individual and have him really understand us, we must make an effort to adapt our mental wave to his vibratory state in order to establish perfect affinity. This explains the surprising differences between two persons who normally understand each other well; one of them will have notably varied his mental wavelength, either by lengthening or shortening it, leaving the other person "out of frequency," just as if he tried to tune in to a certain radio station on a wrong frequency.

There are different reasons for vibratory drops in people. Health problems, depressive states, inertia, internal conflicts, and intellectual apathy are some of the principal causes. In the case of those individuals who permanently have a very long wavelength (of low frequency), this is caused by the individual's lack of intellectual preparation.

The environment is also a very powerful influence on people's vibrations, as we live within an ocean of vibrations that constantly have an impact upon us, awakening similar forces within us. The cosmic and terrestrial space which surrounds us is saturated with vibrations, and they have an important influence on people. One can sense in the inhabitants of a city, for example, either a positive or negative vibratory atmosphere, and the same thing can occur with a visit to a family home where we will immediately feel a warm and positive atmosphere or a force which repels us. What takes place in our homes is that the vibratory radiation of those who live there penetrates the physical structure, impregnating it with positive or negative energy easily sensed by the visitors. Thus, there are homes, which awaken in visitors an intolerable sadness, or in some cases, visitors feel a profound depression or even suicidal tendencies.

We receive the psychic states of those who live or work in these places. The behavioral habits, the emotional states, the habitual thoughts, and the moral and spiritual standards of the individual determine the goodness or unsuitability of his vibratory state, which in turn decisively influences his daily life. Family and human groups in general are made up of whirlpools of energy which are felt by those coming into contact with them. Vibrations accumulate within the individual, that is, he collects good or evil vibrations, and there are times when he is a veritable time bomb due to the latent forces within him. These forces are either destructive or creative, and under the influence of an adequate detonator, will violently explode, producing either favorable or negative events.

This force has the characteristic of greatly affecting anyone who comes into contact with a person whose vibrations are intense, the result being that one can be contaminated by what the "sender" feels. This is especially true when a "sender" shares his troubles with another and then feels great relief while the listener becomes depressed. Perhaps the most vulnerable persons are those in professions such as psychiatry, who are damaged or tainted by contact with their patients' mental scars.

Those places where base passions are let loose, such as

bars or brothels, are the center of base and negative vibrations, which noticeably harm those who frequent them.

Any man who wishes to be successful in his personal objectives or who wishes to increase his capacity to accomplish things, either spiritually or materially must, through self-discipline, raise his vibrations in order not to be affected by what is called "bad luck" or misfortune.

It is necessary to practice strict mental hygiene in order not to be affected by elements in the atmosphere surrounding us. There are strong negative forces actually capable of killing a person because their tone or basic note is destructive and capable of causing disintegration. We know there are sounds (vibrations) which can destroy the cohesion of matter (infrasonic) or which can produce medicinal healing (ultrasonic). The power of the laser is well known (vibration), its light can pierce the hardest material.

Sapiens unconsciously seeks a remedy for his vibratory disharmony and resorts to good music, which reestablishes his internal equilibrium. Nevertheless, there are musical rhythms so inharmonious that they create negative states within people. The sound of certain instruments have cadences that under certain conditions cause deep sadness, as is the case of the "quena," a type of indigenous flute. We also know the pernicious effect of sounds which exceed certain decibel levels and which provoke considerable nervous fatigue causing loss of both manual and intellectual efficiency.

The vibration of the spoken word also has a powerful effect on listeners, either beneficial or harmful. There are those with great personal charm, but whose voices, although not disagreeable, are repellent. This depends on the result of the impact of sonic oscillations. If this impact is harmonious with ours, we will feel affection and liking, and vice versa. People are not aware that they are received either well or badly according to their vibrations.

It is easy to verify the influence of an individual's oscillatory energy. There is a very simple experiment, which consists of having two groups of indoor plants which must be put in separate places. One group of plants should be spoken to every day as if they were human beings and given thoughts of love, friendship, and fortitude. The other group should be abandoned to chance. As the days go by, it will be seen that the plants spoken to and given positive attention become very beautiful and grow faster, although they have the same earth, light, and water as the others.

Another very simple experiment is to test the inductive power of our vibrations on people. For this, it is necessary to contact someone who does not like us. After overcoming the feeling of repulsion this person provokes in us, we must make an effort to feel deep sympathy and cordiality for him. After a short time we will see a radical change in him and he will come to feel very friendly toward us. Many times it is we ourselves who cause rejection due to our hostility toward others.

Through the Principle of Vibration, it is possible to understand that curses really exist but have nothing supernatural about them; they are only the condensation and projection of powerfully destructive vibrations. The same phenomenon exists with blessings, but acts inversely.

When a couple who are lovers speak words of love, the pleasure experienced is not only due to the knowledge that they are loved, but also to the vibratory influence of the words.

If we reflect on this, it is possible to conceive of the existence of magical words, which are only the combination of letters that produce oscillatory phenomena. The traditional karate shout (*kiai*), for example, was originally conceived in order to effectively paralyze the adversary. It had to be emitted in a certain tone and frequency, because if it was not, it would have no effect.

The attentive student who meditates on the Principle of Vibration will be able to understand things of great importance; the one without eyes to see or ears to hear will remain on the threshold of the mystery.

THE PRINCIPLE OF POLARITY

The Principle of Polarity states: *"Everything is dual; everything has two poles; everything has its pair of opposites; like and unlike are the same; opposites are identical in nature but different in degree; extremes meet; all truths are but half-truths; all paradoxes may be reconciled."*

This principle involves the teaching that unity as such does not exist in the Universe because everything is dual; everything has two faces or opposite poles. The most profound secrets of life are hidden behind this simple fact, as it is polarity which maintains the rhythm of life. If there were no opposite poles, life would not be possible. The basic point to be understood in the study of polarity is the fact that opposites are always present in the same element; this law can never be applied to different elements. Temperature has two extremes, cold and heat, but one cannot speak of the positive pole of temperature in relation to the negative pole of electricity. The Principle of Polarity works along a vibratory scale of degrees in which a strength is manifested, a gradation which goes from the positive to the negative.

Thus, light and darkness represent two extremes of the same thing; in one case there is the presence of light and in the other, the lack of it. Love and hate are opposite poles of the same thing, that is, the human feeling of attraction and repulsion. Spirit and matter are the same thing, but are manifested in opposite vibrations. The same is true with life and death and good and evil.

It is necessary to note that in these terms there is no absolute, as no one can state what is absolute cold or heat, for example. We simply speak of more or less of a quantity of something at a given moment. Thus, undoubtedly, we could say that "love is less hate than no love." And "fear is less bravery than pure bravery." The two poles can always be classified as positive and negative, and their difference is just a question of degree. This is why Hermeticism upholds the feasibility of mental transmutation, that is, of transforming something into its opposite. Hate may be transmuted into love, poverty into riches, cowardice into bravery, and ignorance into wisdom, by means of sliding along the scale of polarity. There is always an extreme positive and an extreme negative, the positive pole being of a higher nature than the negative. Courage is positive with respect to fear; light with respect to darkness; love with respect to hate.

The Hermeticist, acting as a true scientist of the mind, can raise his internal vibrations at will and transmute negative into positive.

According to *The Kybalion*, "the undesirable is slain by changing its polarity." Illness can be converted to health by changing its polarity through the power of the mind, which polarizes at the extreme opposite of what it is trying to overcome. Logically, it is only possible to transmute opposites of the same thing, as it would not be possible, in any way, to transmute a pear into a peach. On the other hand, it is possible to transform a green pear into a ripe pear.

In occultism there is a well-known symbol found in ancient esoteric books—the snake biting its own tail. Specifically, this represents polarity, in which the two extremes are perpetually attracted and seek to devour each other, although this never occurs. Vacuum attracts plenitude, innocence and experience are mutually absorbed. Under this principle the existence of an accessible truth to *sapiens* in his habitual condition of life is denied, and we maintain that all truth is semi-truth, and it is only possible to reach absolute truth by raising oneself above the Principle of Polarity, beyond opposites, to reach the world of causes. Naïve people believe that the time will come when good will triumph over evil in the world in a definite manner. According to this principle, the victory of either good or evil is impossible. Good and evil represent the two extremes of something and are therefore absolutely relative. If a fox enters a chicken coop and devours a chicken, it is very bad for the hen, but very good for the fox that is only following the natural principle of staying alive. In reality, evil works for good and good for evil. Life works for death, for from the moment one is born, one starts to die. Death works for life, as all destruction is a transformation, which creates a new form of life. What would happen to the light if there was no darkness? Does not light owe its existence to the fact that darkness exists? Solely from the evidence that something exists, we must immediately know that the opposite is also a reality.

Due to polarity, man and woman are attracted and try to fuse. This is the law of the eternal serpent who constantly bites its own tail. It is very interesting to analyze the aphorism that "extremes meet." If we apply this to love, for example, we can verify that it is easier to transform hate into love than to convert indifference into love. As opposites meet, the distance is shorter from one extreme to another than from the middle of the scale to an extreme pole. Hermetically

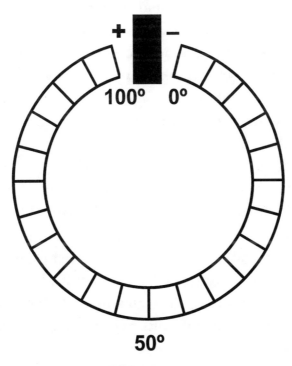

Diagram 4

speaking, we may say that the shortest distance from one point to another is not a straight line, but a circle.

This circle represents the gradual scale which runs between two poles, the positive represented by number one hundred and the negative by zero. These figures are entirely arbitrary and for demonstration purposes only. We maintain that it is easier to cross the bridge from zero to one hundred than to go from fifty to one hundred. The drawing shows this, as the distance is much shorter than if we lay out the circumference of the circle as a straight line. In our example, number fifty is the symbol of eternal indecision and apathy, representing those who are lukewarm who have no place in the kingdom of God. This explains the phenomenon of conversion, when one individual changes his ideology for a diametrically opposite one. This secret may act as consolation to those with serious problems; they are closer to success than they may think, only mediocrity has no remedy. Hermeticism maintains that indecision is more fatal than error; the reason for this is clear. Those who are able to read between the lines and digest this knowledge will derive great wisdom.

The ancient alchemists held that it is possible to transmute lead into gold. In some cases this referred to a material act, and in others it was symbolic. Gold is only one end of the scale of metals; therefore, the alchemist changed the vibration and the polarization of the lead until it was transformed into gold. When this refers to the transformation of the internal metals into spiritual gold, the example is equally valid.

Following the Principle of Mental Transmutation em-

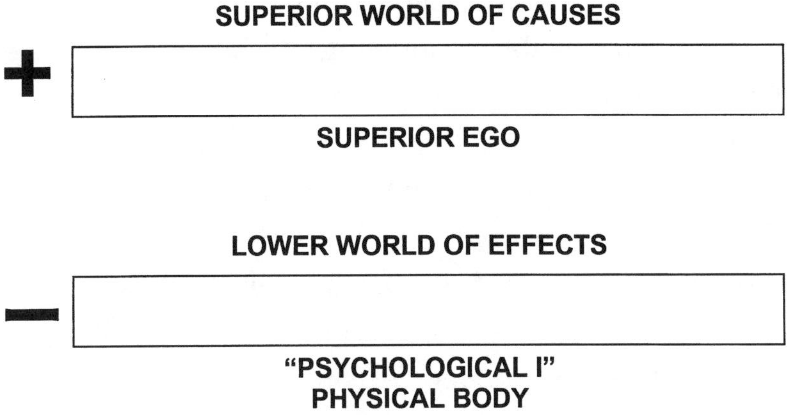

SUPERIOR WORLD OF CAUSES

$+$

SUPERIOR EGO

LOWER WORLD OF EFFECTS

$-$

"PSYCHOLOGICAL I"
PHYSICAL BODY

Diagram 5

ployed by advanced Hermeticists, we will make a brief sketch of the mechanism that must be employed, although this will be useless in the hands of those who have not first reached internal unification under the command of a *"Superior I."* This subject will be covered in subsequent pages.

We have already explained that there are many planes of vibration. As regards the Principle of Mental Transmutation, for the sake of simplicity we will speak of two basic planes: the superior world of causes, and the lower world of effects, as shown in diagram 5.

The lower world of effects is the physical plane; the superior world of causes is the plane of the emanation of life. The Hermeticist, in order to accomplish a process of transmutation, rises to the world of his *"Superior I"* and polarizes himself through his mind in the pole opposite to the vibration he wishes to destroy. Recall that "the undesirable is slain by changing its polarity." This is equivalent to rising above the effects or phenomena which the individual may be suffering at a certain time. By this process, a vibration is changed degree by degree until one reaches what is desired. Even though this might seem easy in theory, in order to achieve this in practice, a rigid discipline and the prior creation of a "*Superior I*" is required; otherwise, this will never be more than just theory.

Recall the aphorism from *The Kybalion* which says, "Mind (as well as metals and elements) may be transmuted from state to state, degree to degree, condition to condition, pole to pole, vibration to vibration." In order to put mental or alchemical transmutation into practice, it is first necessary to learn to change the polarity of our own mind, as otherwise we will not be able to influence our environment. All processes of transmutation, whether it is an attempt to change our internal world or the material world, is always a mental operation, as *All is Mind*. It is very interesting for the student to be able not only to change his own mental state, but also that of other people who are suffering from negative or destructive vibrations of any kind.

From the point of view of the analysis of daily problems, polarity is a very useful key, as it enables people to appreciate the true value of their conflicts or obstacles, without magnifying or underestimating them. The Hermeticist will know, for example, that if he finds himself temporarily in a distressing situation, it is possible to change this gradually, polarizing toward the opposite, until the other extreme is effectively reached. The time required for this operation will depend on the importance of what is desired, as everything has its gestation time in Nature. Something of little importance will be accomplished very quickly; a much larger project will take a longer time to bear fruit.

Let us keep before us the great Hermetic lesson that "the undesirable is slain by changing its polarity." Meditating on this will enable the student to reach great knowledge.

THE PRINCIPLE OF RHYTHM

The Principle of Rhythm states: *"Everything flows out and in; everything has its tides; all things rise and fall; the pendulum-swing manifests in everything; the measure of the swing to the right, is the measure of the swing to the left; rhythm compensates."*

This principle teaches us that everything is subject to rhythmic oscillation, which is manifested between two poles. There is action and reaction, an ebb and flow, an advance and retreat, a rise and fall, and this is applicable to absolutely everything. The Universe, the planets, Nature, man, nations, and civilizations, all are born to reach the heights and then to decline and be destroyed, thus fulfilling the cycle of life. This ebb and flow is manifested in our physical body, in our emotions, feelings, instincts, intelligence, and even in the different vital situations in which we live. It refers to our personal projects, our relationships with other people, our contact with Nature, and in general, everything that forms a part of our lives.

The symbol of the Principle of Rhythm is the pendulum. Its oscillation explains the action of rhythm, whose measurement toward the left is the same as that toward the right. On a practical note, we could even call this law, "the Law of the Pendulum." Creation occurs according to the pendulum; there is an emanation of *The All*, and an absorption follows.

Emanation is the time of creation and absorption is the stage in which *The All* reintegrates its energy in itself.

We can compare this to the cycle of human respiration. The Supreme Being radiates his energy until it materializes into a physical creation, and when this reaches the summit, its maximum degree of materialization, it then starts the opposite oscillation of the pendulum until it again reaches dematerialization or death, and the divine creative energy is reintegrated into its original source. In the same way, nations reach the summit of their power and then gradually decline. Nothing escapes this law; it is an absolutely inevitable process. It is not easy, however, to determine when a human being, a civilization, or a strength has reached its zenith. What we do know with certainty is that decay inevitably takes place.

The Principle of Rhythm together with that of Polarity, previously mentioned, are the forces which maintain the process of life, as life is always a force which moves alternatively and rhythmically between two poles. If we had to define life and death, we would say that life is the oscillation between two poles, and death the polarization of the force at one extreme for a time which surpasses the equilibrium of Nature. This polarization can be negative or positive. It is negative when both poles are too close together, each one of them losing a great part of its intrinsic qualities. It is positive when it is possible to consciously destroy an undesirable vibration and the polarity is changed, polarizing in the extreme opposite direction.

In the case of negative polarization due to a weakening of the opposite poles, a decay of vital forces is produced which may end in the fusion of the poles; this is equivalent to death. The secret of life is thus revealed in a simple manner: it is the constant maintenance of the tension between two poles. Truthfully, we could say that when a child is born, the opposite poles of his life are very far apart and therefore the tension between them is great. But as the child grows older, the opposites begin to join, and life declines. In this case, the two poles are the conscious and the subconscious, or we may also speak of the individual himself and his environment. The constant impact between man and environment (stimulus) slowly depolarizes him, draining his vital force.

By examining man's vital functions, we can verify that polarity and rhythm control the organism in its most delicate processes, and that illness is always a disturbance of the rhythm or polarity. The body needs to maintain a constant state of equilibrium, and the loss of this implies an abnormal condition. Science calls this equilibrium homeostasis. Homeostasis has not been sufficiently studied, and it is certain that if scientists would use the Principles of Rhythm and Polarity, they would discover many new things.

The functions of the heart, breathing, sleeping, and alertness are all governed by the law of the pendulum. Sleep, for example, provides us with the necessary alternation in order to maintain our equilibrium. We know that the lack of sleep provokes serious disorders, as it destroys organic equilibrium.

For a long time the knowledge of "biorhythms" remained in the heart of esoteric schools. This consists of the vital cycles which affect the human being with a positive or negative alternation. Today this knowledge has become popular and there are even pocket calculators for determining this action. Nevertheless, only three rhythms have been revealed.

- The 24-day masculine rhythm, with 12 positive days and 12 negative days
- The 28-day feminine rhythm, with 14 positive days and 14 negative days
- The 33-day intellectual rhythm, with 16 ½ positive days and 16 ½ negative days

The rhythms of 40-day, 56-day, 92-day, and 276-day cycles have not yet been revealed to the masses.

The object of this book is not to supply instructions on biorhythms which would require a separate volume. Therefore, we will only give an extremely important tip for those who follow the indications of biorhythms in their daily life. These people should keep a diary in which they note all happy or unfortunate occurrences, in order to determine which of the rhythms has a greater influence in their lives, as this is something that is entirely personal.

Some individuals will be very affected by the negative in the 24-day rhythm, while others will feel the negative cycle of the 33-day rhythm.

One of the most important aspects of the Principle of Rhythm is the fact that each person creates his own rhythmic state according to the nature of his acts, which take on a rhythm of their own when repeated several times. By virtue of these events being repeated periodically in an individual's life, these events or acts occur without his will. That is, events do not happen because the individual wants them to, but on the contrary, he will be incapable of neutralizing negative events.

We will briefly illustrate how a negative rhythm is born: a person becomes the victim of a theft for example, and as it is not a very large theft, he does not bother to file a follow-up complaint with the authorities. As a consequence of this, a negative rhythm is formed and this individual periodically suffers losses of an economic nature, which doubtlessly will occur during planetary positions similar to those that existed on the day the first theft took place. Another easily verifiable example concerns marital fights, which end by creating a rhythm of disharmony that will provoke the arising of new and more serious problems. It is thus that rhythms of wealth or poverty are created, happiness or misfortune, harmony or disharmony, and once they are in motion, it is very difficult to neutralize them. It is well known that misfortunes come in "waves" as the flowing of the tide; that is, they occur rapidly without the individual having time to react. On the other hand, there are also streaks of "good luck" during which a person experiences a series of positive occurrences. From this it is deduced that the individual takes on a rhythm at a certain moment for reasons not always easy to establish, and as long as that rhythm does not change, the positive or negative tone will be maintained. Unfortunately, there are individuals who take on a rhythm of different calamities from an early age which are then repeated at each oscillation of the pendulum. This is generally very difficult to neutralize, as the longer it lasts, its power of fluctuation strengthens. Those marriages that live with the result of negative rhythms would do well to abstain from having children until the pendulum moves to the other extreme, as the child would be born with an unfortunate rhythmic vibration, fulfilling the biblical aphorism that the children will pay for the sins of their parents.

Habits are formed by a rhythm and when they are pernicious, they can only be destroyed by the creation of a new rhythmic state of an opposite nature.

The Law of the Pendulum completes the knowledge of mental transmutation, as it teaches us that it is possible to rise above rhythmic oscillation by becoming polarized in the pole where one desires to remain, thus avoiding being carried by the ebb and flow. *Sapiens* is a slave to the oscillatory movement of the pendulum, and if he is successful in anything, it is because his actions happen to coincide with the movement of the pendulum purely by chance. People are absolutely subjected to the Law of the Pendulum, whether it be regarding their finances, health, work, vitality, or love, and are like leaves in a storm, blown here and there without having any idea of where the tide of life is taking them. On the other hand, the Hermeticist can surmount this Principle of Rhythm, even though he cannot annul it. With his will power he can rise to the superior plane of causes and let the rhythmic oscillation flow beneath him.

What is called the "Law of Compensation" has much in common with the Principle of Rhythm. Compensation means equilibrium or balancing, which occurs when "the measure of the swing to the left determines the measure of the swing to the right." This determines the amount of things a person can possess, as the individual has, in quantity, the exact proportion of what he is lacking. It is thus that a man who is rich lacks other advantages given to the poor. We all know the saying, "lucky in cards, unlucky in love" or vice versa. This aphorism indicates something about the idea we are discussing. As we have already covered this point, it is therefore interesting to state that absolutely all human beings are born with the same quantity or margin of things they may have; the only variation is their distribution.

Thus, let us say that we all have one hundred vital units (that which we can in time possess) and one hundred negative units (that which we lack). A rich man is one who has nullified the greater part of his possibilities in order to concentrate his one hundred vital units on making money. Love, spiritual sensitivity, family happiness, or other things will certainly be among the things lacking, or negative units. Expressed in a different way, a man may never have more than the symbolic one hundred, but this quantity can be distributed among many things or concentrated on only two or three. An even distribution results in a more balanced life, but a life that will probably not be outstanding in any special way. Concentration implies the sacrifice of many things.

Example 1:
Distribution of Vital Units

Riches:	45 units
Power:	20 units
Moral Nobility:	5 units
Love:	5 units
Intelligence:	10 units
Health:	10 units
Happiness:	5 units

Result: An individual who is rich and powerful, but very unhappy.

Example 2:

Distribution of Vital Units

Riches:	10 units
Power:	10 units
Love:	15 units
Friendship:	10 units
Moral Nobility:	15 units
Intelligence:	15 units
Health:	10 units
Happiness:	15 units

Result: A more balanced individual, with a richer life, filled with different elements.

These examples are absolutely arbitrary, and their only point is to illustrate what occurs with the distribution or concentration of vital units. The reader who is aware of this theory can set up examples for different cases.

For example, we could map out the distribution of our muscular capacity which we could entirely use up just by walking. Or, we could walk, chop wood, swim, climb, and box, distributing our vital energy into various areas. Similarly, we can use a fixed electrical potential to supply one source of great power consumption, or divide it among hundreds of ordinary bulbs.

According to the law of vital units, it is very interesting to analyze what occurs when two people wed, thus sharing their vital units. Or, in the case of a child's birth, this baby arrives with its own one hundred vital units, which while under the parents' care, increases "the family estate of vital units."

In conclusion, we would say that only those who are able

to rise above the Principle of Rhythm can consider themselves truly free.

THE PRINCIPLE OF CAUSE AND EFFECT

The Principle of Cause and Effect states: *"Every Cause has its Effect; every Effect has its Cause; everything happens according to the Law; Chance is only a name for a Law not recognized; there are many planes of causation, but nothing escapes the Law."*

This law teaches us that nothing in the Universe happens by chance; everything has a specific cause. What we call chance is only something where its causes remain unknown. It is not possible that something should exist apart from and beyond the laws, as this force would be independent and superior to the Universe. Applying the Law of Rhythm to the Law of Cause and Effect, we could state that the magnitude of an effect is always equivalent to the importance of the cause which generated it. As we explained when discussing the Principle of Polarity, there are two basic planes: that of causes (superior) and that of effects (lower), and man in his daily life is aware only of the latter. We live in the world of effects, and only the Hermeticist has knowledge of the occult causes of events.

The most well-known manifestation of chance is what Hindus call *Karma*, a word which we will use because it is the most adequate. Karma endeavors to explain the relationship existing between events currently happening to an individual and his actions in the past, either in this life or in a previous one. Contrary to what is believed, Karma is not always negative; there is also a positive side of Karma, which is equivalent to our good deeds in the past. The Law of Karma is intimately bound to reincarnation, a truth we will leave aside for now.

Reincarnation is a very personal matter in which the individual "feels" within him that it exists, and if he does not feel it, then no argument will convince him. Furthermore, if it were possible to produce proof, it would detract from the freedom of choice, as it would pressure the individual; if an individual was convinced of the truth of some occult phenomenon, he might enter an esoteric school without genuine spiritual concern. Nevertheless, in previous pages, we suggested a method of intellectually conceiving what reincarnation is: "a power which takes possession of matter." With the experiment on indoor plants, we might realize that what we really did was to "incarnate" a force in the vegetable matter which survives the life of the plant and continues evolution indefinitely. This is an analogy of what happens when "spiritual" energy incarnates in an animal body, for when the animal dies, the spirit continues incarnating in new bodies until completing an evolutionary cycle in matter.

The Law of Cause and Effect gives us a rational explanation of the apparent injustices in the world; we can understand why a child is born crippled or dies at an early age; it is possible to realize why some people with exquisite spiritual sensitivity live in poverty and other true beasts swim in riches. This law clarifies the phenomenon of child prodigies who show extraordinary musical potential from a very young age, or the extraordinary possession of sudden wealth due to a "stroke of luck." We will shed further light on the reason why an individual who works himself to death never attains economic success and why, on the other hand, fortune smiles on another who is habitually lazy. New light is thus shed on historical events; we can understand how certain relevant historical figures reached great power arising from nothing, as in the case of Hitler. Certainly we do not know what cause placed him in the position of power he occupied, for life is like an enormous tapestry upon which history is woven stitch by stitch, and on which all events are interwoven. This is the veil of Maya, which cannot be penetrated by common mortals.

The action of Karma is one of the reasons why we maintain that "all is written," as the present is always determined by our past acts. Each person has a certain quantity of causes, which are held in check for a period of time during his life, which forge the individual's destiny as they materialize into effects. Only the truly wise man can partially neutralize the effects of undesirable causes.

We have already spoken of the Lords of Destiny or Archons who govern the destiny of *sapiens*. In reality, they work with the Karma of individuals, but from a collective point of view. It is the Karma of humanity that they control and manage, and within this general context they act as occult judges who reward or penalize the actions of the human being.

The Principle of Cause and Effect acts parallel to this, that is, the human being "punishes himself" with his own Karma; the Archons plan and "stage" the action so the individual receives beneficial lessons and can undergo important experiences.

There are people who in their past lives were extremely

rich and took advantage of the power of their money, and who in their present lives are practically beggars in order that they may themselves suffer the experiences of extreme poverty. He who had murdered a fellow man will in turn die due to the direct or indirect influence of his past action. The one who took advantage of love or passion to enslave a woman will in this life be under the domination of the female sex. Occasionally a beggar will display terrible arrogance and seem to despise the entire world, and this attitude is not just simple psychological compensation, but has deeper roots. Certainly this individual occupied a high position in his past life, and as a result, his excessive pride survived the death of his physical body.

It can be debated that if we had lived previously in other bodies, we would surely remember this, but this reasoning is infantile; when the brain is destroyed, memory is erased. Nevertheless, instinctive impulses derived from past experiences survive. For example, if an individual had been condemned for theft in his previous incarnation, he would in his present life be extremely honest, but compulsively so.

In the case of gambling we can see a direct action of the Archons of Destiny, who choose which individuals will win the greatest prizes and who will then have their lives entirely changed.

In the case of those who are already millionaires who win a substantial prize, this will only increase or reinforce the events previously decreed by the Lords of Destiny. Chance is only the visible effect of a cause unknown to us. Generally, it is not possible to establish all the causes which have provoked a certain effect, as these are entwined one with another, and we can only observe the most recent, as the present is based on the past. But with a little meditation we can, as a philosophical exercise, visualize a chain of causes which disappears into the past. It is for this reason that the Hermeticist gives great importance to small details, as these can be converted into decisive factors in a person's life. One small cause can unleash great effects.

One of the most dangerous characteristics of the Principle of Cause and Effect is the fact that Karma can project itself and affect people who are not to blame in any way for the causes set in motion by the "emitter." It is thus that an inescapable law exists in the sense that if we help a person affected by negative Karma, we will have to bear this destructive force which will cause us serious problems. It is for this reason that the Hermeticist cannot give help indiscriminately to all, as he would dissipate his strength without any benefit, and in exchange would be filled with negative vibrations, which would destroy him. Those individuals who constantly seek an audience in whom to confide the calamities they have suffered, unconsciously seek to rid themselves of the poison within them, to inject this into the ones who listen to their woes, who in turn end up in a very bad condition due to having been burdened with another's troubles.

The image of the "good samaritan" is moving in its kindness, but this individual will always be sacrificing his existence for others' benefit, while he takes on the misfortunes of those he helps. This would not be that pernicious if those who profit from his help would perhaps tomorrow turn into valuable people in aid of humanity, but the "samaritan's" help is in vain if the recipients use what they get in an absolutely selfish manner. To help deceitful louts or ruffians could eventually cause the destruction of a man who is valuable and spiritually elevated.

There is another aspect of great interest in what we are covering, and this refers to the individual who commits a concealed theft, enjoying ill-gotten gains or property he has not earned. This man enters into a contract with Nature; someday he must return or pay for what he stole. Therefore, if we are imprudent enough to help this person, we will to a great extent be responsible for the development of his life, and Nature will demand that we pay the pending debt.

All that we need or desire belongs to the common pool of Nature, which gives nothing, but sells us what we require, and it must always be paid for. Nothing is *gratis*; we even have to pay for our lives, for the moments of pleasure, for love, for serenity, for knowledge, for power, and even for the air we breathe. We do not notice this, as we consider money as the only viable instrument of payment. We are not aware that in cosmic commerce money has no value, and other things are required, such as the "golden broth" which we mentioned in previous chapters. To the "devil," for example, one soul is more valuable than all the gold in the world.

The most important thing about the Law of Cause and Effect is that the advanced Hermeticist can raise himself to the higher world of causes by a prodigious effort of will. By polarizing himself on this plane, he converts himself into a cause, and thus stops living the effects which emanate from the higher plane. From the world of causes, the Hermeticist can channel his life according to his own planning, as he has the certainty that the causes placed into movement by his spiritual power will sooner or later materialize into concrete material effects.

THE PRINCIPLE OF GENDER

The Principle of Gender states: *"Gender is in everything; everything has its Masculine and Feminine Principles; Gender manifests on all planes."*

The seventh Hermetic Principle completes the knowledge of the laws of Nature, showing us that gender is manifested in everything and that the masculine and feminine forces are present in everything. We must not make the mistake of confusing gender with sex, as sex refers only to the structure of the genital organs and the difference in adaptation between male and female. Sex is one of the many manifestations of the Principle of Gender and corresponds to the physical plane, but as we are aware, there are many planes where the *Mind* Principle exists, as does gender. Hermeticism maintains that gender has an impelling nature, and that this nature acts even in the atom, in which we find both the positive and the negative, whose mutual influence creates energy. Instead of referring to positive and negative poles, we can speak more appropriately of the masculine and feminine, the generator and the conceiver. The positive element of electricity is masculine, and the negative element is feminine.

The feminine or negative is the womb of all electrical and magnetic phenomena. The feminine energy seeks union with the masculine, and absorbs from it that which is active, thus producing a new force.

Hermetic teaching also affirms that gravity is produced

by the attraction and repulsion of masculine and feminine principles.

As stated in previous pages, analyzing our physical body, we will discover that it possesses bipolarity. Thus, man is masculine from the solar plexus down and feminine from this zone up to and including the head, while with woman, the opposite is true. In this manner we can observe that woman is cerebrally masculine, and man cerebrally feminine. The principle of conception in man is in his imagination, and in woman is in her uterus. Within our bodies, the right side is masculine or positive and the left side, negative; the right cerebral hemisphere is positive and the left, negative. It is possible, by means of the Principle of Gender, to understand the hidden significance of the mystic or religious act of joining the palms of the hands in prayer, which involves a process of generation upon opposing positive and negative.

It is through the occult law that the student of Hermeticism can create a new being, a mutant who will be conceived with superior qualities of an acutely human being. There is no other real path for spiritual evolution; all that does not involve using this secret is pure fantasy, and from it only purely subjective results will be attained.

From understanding this Law of Gender we can also realize how deceptive it is to evade problems, difficulties, and obstacles, considering them merely as hurdles, a waste of time, or irritating situations. The Hermeticist must visualize problems as the negative pole of life, that is, the force against which he must oppose his positive generative energy in order to create what he desires. If we understand this phenomenon we will achieve a completely new and different vision of the hurdles in our life, which will be nothing more than the complement needed to develop our consciousness. Consciousness, the precise quality we wish to attain, is the result of the collision between inertia and our will power, directed by an awakened intelligence. If this struggle between opposing forces did not exist, Hermetic progress would not be possible, and neither would evolution.

At this point we will reveal the great magic secret of mutation of *sapiens*, or *man of clay*, into a *Stellar Man*. This transformation is only possible if the subject enters into contact with a flesh and blood Master who will be his spiritual Father. And who will the mother be? The mother is the beast in the individual, that is, the side of himself that is of a feminine or negative polarity, spiritually speaking. It is thus that the initiate is a child of the beast and the spiritual Master. The student who is facing *a real process of initiation* (not symbolic) will find himself strongly dragged by the pendulum in an oscillation which will suddenly bring him closer to the Master, or to the beast. There will be moments when he will sense the overwhelming evidence of Hermeticism deep within himself, feeling himself raised to high planes of awareness. At other times, all will be darkness; the initiation will lose all sense and purpose, and the student will believe himself submitted to a cruel joke. Only the gradual stopping of this pendular movement will enable him to reach the stability of conscious knowledge.

The Principle of Gender shows us that it is not possible for a creation to exist without the presence of the *father* and *mother* elements, and this is valid throughout the entire Universe, including the process of initiation. This is the reason why a solitary man, no matter how much theoretical knowledge he may possess, can only reach subjective results because he lacks the other generative pole.

This is why it is necessary to find a Master, and the significance of this fact was stated previously. If a Master is not a mutant, he is then a false master, but this term is relative. Although he may be false in relation to that which is superior and optimum, he can also be very true in relation to that which is inferior. Therefore, it is necessary to clarify that although a Master is not a mutant, he can be of great help for a student. What he will not be able to offer, in this case, will be knowledge of *the absolute*, nor could he transmit the *sacred flame*, which according to fables was stolen from heaven by Prometheus. This sacred flame is not an abstraction or a symbol. It is a fact, and is the spiritual power symbolized in the acronym INRI which appears over the head of Jesus Christ. Its true Hermetic meaning is: *Inge Natura Renovatur Integrat*, but can also be read as *Jesus Nascente Renovatur Iao*, or *Igni Nitrus Roris Invenitur*. All these formulas were used by the early Rosicrucians (unknown today) and they referred precisely to the *divine fire*, the magic ferment of alchemists, which as we have already stated, "renews everything."

Nevertheless, one must not assume that it is sufficient to find a Master in order to evolve. On the contrary, the disciple will progress only to the extent that he himself handles the Principle of Gender in a superior manner, because even though a positive or active spiritual ferment is necessary, it is also nonetheless indispensable that the student himself create a mental and etheric being with the character and qualities of the initiate. This is known as *Theurgy*, a secret teaching we will study further on.

Continuing with the Principle of Gender, it is necessary to consider the tremendous positive or negative influence that marriage can have in a person's life. The influence is injurious when the union is so inharmonious that it becomes dangerously destructive, and favorable when there is true love and harmony.

The Hermetic concept of marriage is quite different from the common one. It is not necessary for there to be a marriage contract to give this union its name. We will explain this proceeding from the opposite angle: there may be a couple (and this, unfortunately, is frequent) who have entered into a legal and lawful marriage, but who absolutely lack the aptitude for achieving what we could call a *matrimonial aura*, and therefore they can be married for twenty years without forming this aura. The *matrimonial aura* is a hidden offspring, a mental child of both mates; it is a closed positive magnetic field which joins, harmonizes, and protects the couple, making the marriage truly "established" or really formed, according to the laws of Nature. It is not the laws of man which wed two people; it is only Nature which joins or separates them, according to prevailing conditions. The *matrimonial aura* is the true secret of conjugal happiness and union. When this does not exist, there is nothing, no matter how many certificates have been issued by competent authorities. Hermetically, only that which is joined by the occult bond of the bipolar orb is a marriage, which is formed solely by true and genuine love. Couples who lack this occult child of love *are not married*, they are joined solely by passion, personal convenience, loneliness, or habit.

Religions which consider marriage something indestructible and irreversible, binding the parties for life under the penalty of serious sin, urgently need to modify that commandment, for this approach means proceeding inversely, as the *sapiens* beast generally does. This approach means trying to maintain the artificial union of the family by an unnatural imposition instead of a clear and beautiful manifestation of love. Is it not preferable to teach people to truly love? In truth, if a family is not joined by genuine love, it is only a group of beasts who live together under obligation or for convenience, a situation that relates to more people than we would like. It is superfluous to say that happiness is only possible in homes where there is a real marriage, for otherwise there is only a poor imitation of an ideal situation, as there is only one tie which will keep man and wife united in a true way—love. The lack of it is the only thing that conspires against the stability of the family.

We wish to conclude this brief study of gender, suggesting that the reader try to discover for himself all that lies between the lines and meditate deeply on this subject, as the most profound secrets are revealed with this key. For our part, we are not interested in revealing too much; only enough to provide the tools for the growth and development of the initiate.

XI

THE DISCIPLES

To bring about Hermetic realization, it is not enough to find a Master, but it is necessary to have a disciple, a candidate who is converted into a true student of the mysteries of life. It is not that easy to find as people are used to the traditional concept of education or learning which maintains that all the student needs to do is study with perseverance to become a savant in a subject. It is also believed that greater or lesser advancement depends on the quantity of knowledge that the individual receives from his teacher or from the school to which he belongs. In this way, if an institution exhibits an inflated "program of Hermetic studies" or "esoteric studies," the individual would feel very inclined to believe he has found the right path. Again, it is necessary to underline the enormous difference which exists between a study program and an initiatic school. In a study program the individual is there only to learn things, which may or may not be useful, which may be real or subjective.

In any case, the individual will not obtain salvation (will not be freed from the collective soul of the species), but in any event will advance along his path of development, attaining the necessary merit to continue his progress and perhaps become free in a future incarnation.

In an initiatic school the disciple has an opportunity to reach true evolution, to free himself from the collective soul of *sapiens* and convert himself into an authentic *mutant* or *Stellar Man*. A person who has been able to enter an initiatic school will need a series of indicators or points of reference to become oriented in the work accomplished there. Otherwise, he will become prematurely disillusioned when he cannot understand the sense or contents of the disciplines and instructions. Perhaps the greatest obstacle a student may encounter is the fact that it is useless to study Hermetic theory, since his intellect is not sufficiently advanced to unveil the mysteries presented to him. However intelligent an individual may be, he will find that reason and logic are not sufficient to understand the profound truth necessary to reach a very high state of awareness in which his intellectual powers attain optimum efficiency.

We have already mentioned that a human being lives in a permanent dream-like state, interrupted only by slight sparks of awareness, and although he appears to be awake during the day, he is in reality a somnambulist with a very low state of alertness. Thus, *sapiens'* reason and logic are intellectual instruments of oneiric fantasy. This is very difficult to become aware of, because of natural obstacles to self-observation presented by the subtleties of human consciousness. For this reason, intelligence alone is not enough to become aware of events which take place in the world of waking reality. Thus, the student cannot at first rely on the strength of his reasoning. The student must learn to think with "another brain" so that "another reasoning," superior to the ordinary, can be born within him. This can only be attained through true and not symbolic initiation. True initiation induces profound and concrete changes in the student's psychological structure. Initiation, however, is a painful and difficult process, and will be successful only with the neophyte's superhuman effort. This will be explained in more detail in subsequent chapters. For the moment, we will limit ourselves to describing the conditions which a disciple must possess, and the internal and external obstacles he must overcome. In general terms, the schools do not choose their disciples from among the most intelligent candidates, but rather from those who have characteristics which make them especially fit to face the specter of their own bestiality, as in truth they must. A good guide for selection would be more or less the following:

1. To possess spiritual gold (internal content)
2. To be free from prejudices or be capable of overcoming them
3. To have consciousness of one's own insignificance
4. To ardently yearn for initiation (the complete process) as the most important thing in life
5. To practice loyalty, dedication, constancy, and faithfulness toward the School
6. To possess a flexible and agile intelligence
7. To harmonize oneself with the fundamental keynote of the School
8. To willingly comply with the instructions received
9. To be free from mental disturbances of a certain nature

We can appreciate how purity, the intellectual factor, professional titles, or social position do not count for much. What is basically sought is the individual's inner nature, and his capacity to dedicate himself to a Hermetic task which lasts not only for all this terrestrial life, but will furthermore determine his future existence. No true School wishes to waste its time with individuals who "cheat," that is, who delude themselves in their yearning for spiritual excellence and their firm determination to become converted into superior beings. The Schools prefer to dedicate their efforts to those who effectively maintain a constant line of action in their work toward initiation. It is necessary to clarify that it is only possible to become a disciple after a period of trial in the School. An individual, however, may remain forever as a simple student without ever becoming a disciple, because he does not have the required aptitude for it. There is an "easy path" and a "difficult path" which are the paths of the student and of the disciple. Each has disadvantages and privileges, and therefore no one, without an exhaustive analysis of the matter, can state that "he will never be satisfied" until he becomes a disciple.

To explain these differences, we will compare both options:

THE EASY PATH OF THE STUDENT

Obligations: Very few. These specifically refer to living a life following high moral and spiritual principles, and to practicing kindness and brotherhood. Logically, the student must also comply with the rules of the institution.

Tests to be passed: These are relatively simple, and do not demand great effort to be passed successfully.

Attainments: Dominating and channeling of one's character, overcoming complexes, inhibitions, and frustrations. Learning to handle mental power in order to channel it toward the goal of overcoming oneself or helping others. Knowledge of the mysteries of life and the fundamental causes of all that exists. Preparation for complete fulfillment in a future incarnation. In summary, the student evolves to a great extent, but does not achieve Hermetic death; he is not completely freed from the collective soul of *sapiens*.

THE DIFFICULT PATH OF THE DISCIPLE

Obligations: Tremendous and difficult to accomplish. The disciple must be willing to renounce his self during a certain period and take an oath of absolute obedience to his instructor. He must be willing to renounce everything, if this is required.

Tests to be passed: Very few individuals can endure them. In the novel *Zanoni*, one of these tests is described: the meeting with the specter on the threshold. Nevertheless, in real life this experience is less spectacular than the description in Edward Bulwer Lytton's novel, but more difficult due to its subtlety. The negative part of Nature (which could be called Satan) reacts against the disciple, who is faced with all kinds of negative reactions, as the powers of darkness attempt to prevent his arrival at Olympus.

Attainments reached in the case of triumph in the tests: After Hermetic death, the disciple is converted into a *mutant* or *Stellar Man*, an individual who has reached the peak of evolution as a terrestrial man, and who must start his evolution on a higher level. He reaches the immortality of his essence through the practice of conscious reincarnation, and crosses the veil of the Maya, reaching absolute truth. He is beyond good and evil, beyond opposites, beyond pleasure and pain; beyond happiness and misfortune; beyond life and death. These are not symbolic achievements, but are absolutely real and true. However, at this point the neophyte is impelled to ask a series of questions. The neophyte will wonder if there is an attempt to convert the initiate into a "Superman," an invincible and indestructible being who cannot become ill or die, and who does not need to eat or carry out normal biological functions. Many ask themselves, for example, why Cagliostro died in prison, deducing from this and from the countless hazards in his life that he was not a true initiate. For our part, we accept Cagliostro and the Count of Saint Germain as two of the greatest Hermetic Masters who have ever existed, and deny, at the same time, the alleged death of Cagliostro in prison. Even if this had occurred, it would not in any way make this great man any less brilliant. Appearances are generally deceptive, and Masters of the stature of a Cagliostro take great care when they reveal their true purposes in order not to suffer negative reactions from the human beast. In this case we can apply the popular saying that "those who dine with the Devil should use a long spoon." That is, those who intervene in worldly matters in order to save *sapiens* from inconvenient situations or to ease or improve their life conditions, end up being crucified by those they have tried to help.

Continuing with the false concept of "Superman," we wish to ask the reader to imagine how he would feel if he was Clark Kent, Superman of American comics, the man who arrived from the planet Krypton. At first this may seem very desirable, but after reflecting a while, it is easy to understand what a terrible punishment it would be, to be physically immortal and indestructible, illness-proof, danger-proof, immune to any attack, able to resist desires of the heart or sex, to be constantly and inflexibly virtuous and perfect. If such a being existed, he would truly be a creation of the devil, a mechanical robot, a being absolutely inhuman and unhappy, and deserving of great pity. We must remember that we learn from our failures and not from our successes, and that we appreciate things only when we are in danger of losing them. The spice of life is the lack of knowledge about what the future holds for us, constantly facing the danger of losing all we have or of failing to reach our desires. Having everything and never losing anything would be unbearable and inhuman.

The great Hermetic Masters are not free from danger, illness, or death, and this is precisely what is most beautiful, sublime, and human about their existence—the fact that being so powerful in their fight for others, they are so reluctant to use their spiritual strength for their own benefit. We know that Jesus refused to save himself when faced with the threat of crucifixion, but this does not mean that he was an impostor. On the contrary, it means that he accepted with resignation and meekness the terrible ordeal imposed on him by his Universal Father.

The great Kabbalist Eliphas Levi said that "those men (the great initiates) found it preferable to govern kings than to be kings themselves." Is it possible to understand this? It is not difficult to understand that a truly important man should prefer to pass through life unnoticed, occupying a second-rate or third-rate position, fleeing from the fame, riches, and honors which mortalize human genius.

The candidate for initiation must choose the easy or difficult path, but it should be done impartially and consciously, considering that if he chooses the path of the student, in the future he may become a disciple. If he endeavors to turn himself prematurely into a disciple, his failure may be so crushing and painful that he will become irreversibly traumatized, and in this case must await another opportunity in a future incarnation.

Whatever the choice, the student is faced with internal barriers that he must be aware of in order to have a clear idea of what is happening to him at a given moment. These barriers, among others, are: *vanity, pride, egotism, and self-sufficiency.*

When the individual has a very high degree of self-importance, this becomes the main barrier against facing Hermetic truth without prejudice; he believes he knows everything and "is above these tricks." Of course, he uses this or some similar rationalization out of ignorance of the subject, as without doubt he has never before been to a Hermetic School of Initiation, and without having lived through this experience, he can have no opinion. There are others whose contact with a school has not been felicitous, and whose pride has been seriously wounded as they were not able to overcome the ordeals they faced. Torn apart by this feeling, and in order to save their precious pride, they discredit the Teachings and the School, alleging for some reason (which they always find) that the School is deficient, useless, or dangerous.

Returning to the four main obstacles which face the candidate for initiation, it is necessary to state that vanity is not only the narcissism of the individual, but also refers to his hollow knowledge—that knowledge which has neither content nor any truly essential, profound, or transcendental significance. Vanity and pride require that a person should constantly appear before others as having power, importance, or intelligence, which without doubt he does not possess. Pride is an infantile endeavor to fight against one's own weakness, assuming a strength one lacks. Egotism leads the individual to believe that he is the center of the Universe, and that all revolves around him. On the other hand, self-sufficiency is only ignorance of what one does not know.

In summary, these defects make man exaggerate his own importance and believe himself to be superior to common mortals, looking down on all those who don't have his same educational level, social standing, or economic status. Only the experience of day-to-day living will eventually convince him that he is not as privileged as he had thought. The real harm that this situation creates regarding an individual's possibility of Hermetic evolution consists in his unconscious rejection of all he hears, except when it comes from people with an image, prestige, or fame superior to his own.

In reality there is no possibility that the candidate will authentically face Hermeticism with his intelligence until he lives the esoteric experience which Gurdjieff described as "the experience of his own nothingness," which is basically becoming aware of his own impotence to escape from the general conditions which guide one's life. This means realizing that it is not possible to attain what one desires, because things turn out differently than we expect, or simply do not occur, and moreover, undesirable events also happen. It would be more to the point to state that what Gurdjieff called "our own nothingness" is, in truth, the practical realization that one is absolutely programmed physically, instinctively, emotionally, and intellectually; that it is impossible to disrupt the program, as this cannot be destroyed or modified in its fundamental and profound structures. Thus, the more important and inflated image a man has of himself, the less likely it is that he will be able to understand Hermetic philosophy. The program rejects Hermeticism, as it is not incorporated in cultural community values, and if it were, people would blindly accept it. But such acceptance would have no value, as people would not go beyond imitation and superstition. In other words, it is important to genuinely and intrinsically recognize one's own smallness and insignificance in order to take the first steps to initiation, otherwise, it would not be the individual himself who would be a student or disciple, but the "false being," the "mask," or the "person," that is to say, the personality. Hermetically, we maintain that personality and the program are very similar, and as long as the student is not able to raise himself above his own personality, he will not come into contact with his true being, let alone attain knowledge of the truth. For the Hermeticist, "personality" has a "diabolic" sense, as it is the mechanism which keeps the *"essential I"* dormant and a prisoner.

At the beginning of his initiation, the student must endeavor to transcend his cerebral programming, even for a few minutes, for it will permit him to "see himself" to a certain extent. In order to transcend his program, he must force himself to be as impersonal as possible, leaving all previous concepts or ideas aside, as if he was a living intelligence flying through the Universe, but without a physical body. To be impersonal involves impartiality, peace, freedom from fear, and a lack of faith and "anti-faith." There is nothing more dangerous than those neophytes who are possessed with a "holy faith" or those who are dominated by blind "anti-faith." Neither can ever approach Hermeticism in a truly intelligent way.

It is necessary to insist that the neophyte must clearly understand that if he approaches a school, *it is not to be taught, since this is not the function of initiatic schools; Hermeticism is a science prohibited to Homo sapiens.* He is admitted to the School only to give him an opportunity to demonstrate the value of his internal content, that is, the power of his latent spiritual force. If this force does not exist, or is too scant, the individual is closer to the animal. This would make the leap he is trying to take completely impossible, due to the immensity of the abyss between the opposite poles: animal and man. The degree of spiritual force required indicates the magnitude of the distance an individual is from the animal condition. The neophyte is placed under very special vital conditions, and is given the tools necessary to enable him to raise his state of consciousness and have access to knowledge. The knowledge is in the School, but is not made available in the same manner as a science, a discipline, or any technique is taught; it is the disciple who must grasp this basic knowledge, which is always veiled. Thus it is necessary to "have eyes to see and ears to hear." This grasping of knowledge will only be possible if the student, with a supreme effort of consciousness, is able to penetrate the veil of allegories, parables, comparisons, and similes. Only those who are guided by their spirit or *"essential I"* will learn the truth. Those who are motivated solely by curiosity, egotism, or purely passional interests cannot reach the light of truth. This is fortunate, as there could be no greater curse than a *Stellar Man* or *Stellar Woman* who is villainous, immoral, or irresponsible; it is certain this cannot come to pass.

When *sapiens* shows his internal value, he is worthy of being helped and prepared for his subsequent and planned mutation. Gradually, Hermetic science will cease being a prohibited knowledge for him, as he will be found worthy of the high honor of knowing the *Universal science.*

Summarizing, Hermetic knowledge is only for a small elite, but anyone who is deeply moved by an authentic spiritual restlessness, may form part of this elite. Furthermore, the populace does not desire this knowledge; on the contrary, they despise it, confirming Jesus' words, "do not throw pearls before swine."

There are many who were born swine, are happy in that state, and will die swine.

It is practically certain that this Hermetic secret will

shock many people who would wish this knowledge to be freely given, and who will see in its prohibition a sign of egotism or weakness. Those who think this, should observe Nature, where abundance and mediocrity are synonymous, as superior organisms are scarce and appear only rarely and after a rigorous process of selection, as they form the elite of the species.

Although the neophyte does not arrive at an initiatic school "to be taught" as we have already stated, he must attend lectures or instructional classes. How is one to understand this paradox? It is very simple: instruction is not for teaching, but rather to destroy the disciple's cerebral program to a certain extent, so he will gather his own knowledge through a process of interior illumination. The lectures are not to be memorized or "learned," but they are the spiritual and intellectual ferment for the profound transformations which must be produced within the student.

Nevertheless, for these changes to be effective, it is necessary to know how to listen so that everything received during instruction reaches one's reasoning faculty in an integral form, as *sapiens* usually understands only what he wishes to, and rejects whatever conflicts with his self-esteem, inferior passions, or personal interests.

XII

TRUE INITIATION

True and authentic initiation is always a profound, concrete, objective, and material process. It is the barrier that can never be crossed by those who flit around from school to school, and who do not want to become free of their animal individuality; it is the path which can never be traversed by theoretical initiates, masters of symbolism, desk magicians, library rats, intellectual and rhetorical crusaders, the self-satisfied, cowards, worshipers of oneiric culture, or defenders of human mediocrity. Many famous men have used the title of initiate, but only a small minority have reached initiatic fulfillment, rising above the limits of what is generally spurious or mistaken theory. It is thus that we recognize in Gurdjieff one of the great Masters of this century, who unfortunately did not leave a Hermetic heir, perhaps because he did not consider anyone duly capable of it. The same occurred with Madame Blavatsky whose death signaled the beginning of the dissolution of the Theosophical Society.

One of the great errors committed by followers of occult and esoteric matters is to consider initiation as only an assembly of practices, knowledge, or ceremonies, ignoring the transcendental, cosmic, mystic, divine, and eternal nature of initiation. Initiation truly represents a tremendously significant act from the point of view of universal truth, as it is the transformation of *animal sapiens* into *Stellar Man*. Such an immense achievement, surpassing the highest dreams of *sapiens*, cannot be faced in the festive or frivolous spirit of an interesting adventure. This achievement should be evaluated in all its enormous dimensions as the most noble and sublime undertaking human courage can aspire to; it is the conscious abandonment of the *Homo sapiens* species to join an immensely superior species: *Stellar Man*. In the history of mankind there has never been, nor will there ever be, a feat comparable in importance to the epic of the spiritual elevation of *Homo sapiens*. However, many people talk of becoming an "initiate," the same way one becomes a physician, engineer, electronic technician, member of the Rotary Club, or a follower of the study of yoga or parapsychology. It is necessary to state that however much the student learns about esoteric theories or doctrines, if he has not passed through Hermetic death in a real way and not merely symbolically, he will never be a true initiate.

In truth, initiation is an act of renunciation and also a surgery of the soul. One should not believe that such renunciation refers only to abstaining from certain things. What it implies is the absolute sacrifice of the animal individuality. Animal egotism must disappear in order to let in spiritual impersonality. It is necessary to renounce the pleasures of the human beast, replacing them with the pleasures of the initiate, who, after attaining a perfect equilibrium, satisfies the animal and spiritual hunger in equal proportion.

Ignorant people have the satisfaction of their animal appetites as their only goal, and their productive efforts are intended mainly to gather the gold which will enable them to obtain pleasure and material benefits. Their center of gravity is located in the corporeal mass. It is the body which uses the brain, inspires emotions, and arouses passion. The body is the master, and the individual himself is the slave. When the corporeal matter decays and dies, the individual suddenly finds himself freed from his slavery. At that moment, he understands for the first time, and without any benefit, that he never had life, thoughts, feelings, or experiences of his own, and that he was only a servant who had to toil to feed and satisfy the needs of a mass of protoplasm. That life, which should have been used to evolve, to be happy, and to progress, was instead converted into the mere memory of those things he did or could not do.

In truth, the body is not the individual; the individual takes a physical body in order to acquire experience, which permits him to perfect himself and evolve. This purpose is generally frustrated or is terribly insufficient and petty. In the final inventory of his life, the individual will realize how little he gained for himself during his existence, and how much he was obliged to give, just so the *sapiens* circus could continue operating.

The initiate changes this situation completely, but far from despising the body as some pseudo-mystics do, he strengthens it, giving it further awareness and intelligence in order to humanize the beast. This spiritualized and humanized animal no longer experiences passional states, as it is subject to the individual's higher consciousness. Nevertheless, it is necessary to understand that the body itself has nothing evil or dirty about it; on the contrary, it is a perfect biological structure reflecting the master hand of the Great Creator. It is the individual himself who perverts the body and leads it to corruption. It is thus that the animals we see in a savage state are completely pure in their animal nature, and have no knowledge of perversity. If they kill, it is because of fright or the need for food, but not for the love of killing. *Sapiens* is the only bloodthirsty and impure animal, as he is neither animal nor human, but a hybrid.

We could summarize the purpose of initiation in a short sentence: *"initiation is the conversion of a programmed animal into an unprogrammed and free Stellar Man."* There is only one way to accomplish this: the destruction of the personality, since this is the individual's program. Hermetically speaking, we may consider that *sapiens* is composed of two basic forces: his cerebral biological program (personality) and his spirit or divine spark, which could be called the *"Superior I."* The program contains all the individual's robot-like elements, which connect him to the central computer of the species. The spirit is the emanation of God, or the primordial cause of life; it incarnates in a physical body to acquire experience in matter. During the initiatic process, the student must experience the death of the program, which naturally is a gradual process. Nevertheless, it should not be thought that this is merely destruction, but rather that the program dissolves upon being absorbed and transformed by the *"Superior I."* During this stage, the program loses its inherent quality, and is converted into only an assembly of data and information, which must pass through the filter of internal judgment. It is here that it loses its compulsive and dreamlike power and where it experiences a deep "pruning" and transformation. All this is possible only if certain requirements are complied with, which refer basically to the disciple's dedication and perseverance, together with a deep understanding and close union with the School and the instructor.

In order to understand this, it is necessary to have an idea of the constitution of the human being—of his spirit, body, and soul. The soul has always been an abstraction and a mystery, and all attempts to define or explain it have been distinguished by their vagueness and lack of content. Hermetic tradition tells us that the soul of *sapiens* is composed of four major systems: the procreative, digestive, circulatory, and respiratory systems, and that each one of these is in charge of an elemental intelligence which corresponds to one of the four elements.

Procreative system:	Fire
Digestive system:	Earth
Circulatory system:	Water
Respiratory system:	Air

The great Hermes Trismegistus, Master of Masters, would be horrified to see the mysteries of the sphinx unveiled. In his times, this knowledge was given only to those who had undergone many ordeals and reached certain degrees. The ancient alchemists maintained that everything in the Universe was essentially composed of four elements. This is one of the great Hermetic truths. God too is made up of the four elements, and so through his feminine aspect (Nature) he grants four virginal intelligences to *sapiens* at birth which correspond to the four elements. It must be understood that the "intelligences" we refer to are "elemental beings" with their own intelligence and consciousness according to their native element. *A fire being* takes charge of our procreative system; *an earth being* takes charge of our digestive system; *a water being* takes charge of our circulatory system; and *an air being* takes charge of our respiratory system. The initiate can put himself in mental contact with these intelligences in order to reinforce, support, or modify his work.

To avoid the reader from forming fantastic ideas regarding the intelligences of our four systems, we must clarify that they should not be imagined as human figures, but as the abstract concept of "intelligent emanations of the soul of each element." Just as God unfolds in man through the emanation of his divine spark, Nature, in its feminine side, projects itself by incorporating the elemental spark of its four "kingdoms" in man. Thus man is made up of a visible and an invisible side. The visible side corresponds to the feminine side of God; the soul, and the invisible, to the masculine side of God, that is the spirit. The Universe is similar to the example we have given, as everything that we can see, the form, structure and body of the Cosmos, is the feminine side of the Great Creator (the Universal Mother). On the other hand, the Great Father is the masculine essence that constitutes the vital nucleus, and this side remains invisible.

The innocence of a young baby is due not only to the fact that he does not yet have any knowledge of the reality of the world, but specifically to the virginal purity of his soul, that is, the ensemble of his four elements. When the infant grows, he himself will corrupt his elemental intelligences by trying, through imitation and contagion, to practice the same vices and bad habits he sees around him. Freud, by claiming that the libido is the origin of all the individual's problems, covered only the fire aspect of the soul (very cleverly, we might add, since fire is the origin of life), but he left the other three vital sources untouched. When a child smokes for the first time, he will find the taste of the cigarette very unpleasant and the smoke produces coughing, dizziness, and headaches. This is due to the fact that the intelligence of the respiratory apparatus reacts against this "aggression" and thus shows its rejection. Nevertheless, its mission is to serve the individual, and if, through an effort of his will, he continues smoking, there will come a time when the air intelligence yields and accepts the tobacco. This is its own ruination. Just like a person, it becomes corrupted and is converted into a nicotine addict. Hysteria, self-pity, depressive states, and emotional problems in general, are located in the circulatory system. Rapacity, egotism, violence, hate, envy, and jealousy reside in the digestive system, and complexes in general reside in the procreative system. The individual's behavior soils and corrupts his four intelligences, degrading his own soul and distancing him from the possibilities of spiritual evolution.

Analyzing the symbolism of the four great systems, we will discover the clear relationship that exists between the image of the crucified Christ and the *"Superior I"* enchained to the four intelligences, each one representing an extremity of the cross. The words *"I am the way"* which must be understood literally, refer precisely to the *"Superior I."*

To describe initiation through a parable, we would say that it is an endeavor to "decrucify Christ." For this, there is only one path, because if one meditates on the situation of the individual, one will reach the conclusion that there is little the individual can do, as he is programmed according to the interests of the central computer. He cannot struggle against what is inside him and which forms part of his instincts, emotions, and thoughts. His only possibility lies in the sparks of awareness generated, for some reason, when the program becomes weak. In that instant, the individual can clearly understand that there is a life superior to his own, and that when he follows the path pointed out by his teacher, he can evolve. Due to this, the student, upon starting along the path, must limit himself to fulfilling ascetic practices, which entail sacrifice and considerable effort. A sixth "I" is added to the assembly of systems, transforming it into a septenary. For this, we will call the sixth "I" the *"Volitive I,"* and our chart of the constitution of the individual will be as follows:

1. Procreative System	Fire	"Igneous I"
2. Digestive System	Earth	"Terrestrial I"
3. Circulatory System	Water	"Aqueous I"
4. Respiratory System	Air	"Aereous I"
5. Cerebral-spinal System	Ether	"Etheric I"
6. Volitive System	Astral	"Volitive I"
7. Individual Himself	Spirit	"Superior I"

The majority of people "function" only with the first four systems, which combine to form an "infrabrain" through which the individual ordinarily develops. People of a higher caliber of conceptual or intellectual capacity act partly with number five, but only with a fraction of its capacity. The capacity and power of the spinal medulla are not used or known by the common man. It should be noted that the sixth system or the *"Volitive I"* is completely unknown to *sapiens* who absolutely lacks it. On the other hand, all people have number seven, but this *"Superior I"* neither manifests itself nor intervenes in the individual's life in any way; it lives in "limbo" and is only connected to the corporeal structure by a thin thread.

It is very important to consider the fact that the *"Volitive I"* is created exclusively by man when he is converted into a true initiate, as all the other systems are the work of God, the Great Creator.

Illustrated below are the different ways the human being may be manifested.

Figure 4 of diagram 6 represents the initiate, who, upon creating his *"Volitive I"* by means of arcane theurgy, is converted into a divine being with the attributes he himself wishes to transmit to it. The *"Volitive I,"* therefore, is truly *the initiate*, who is converted into a mediator between the spirit and the *"Psychological I."* Under normal conditions, the individual cannot raise himself to divinity, nor cause divinity to descend to him. Through his *"Volitive I,"* however, (which participates in both worlds, physical and spiritual) he is able to connect, when he so desires, with his spirit, divine spark, or *"Superior I."* For this to take place, the disciple must have dominated and educated his four intelligences, placing them under the absolute control of the *"Volitive I."* Naturally, this must be preceded by the birth, growth, and maturity of the *"Volitive I."*

The first steps for the formation of the *"Volitive I"* must be along the path of sacrifice. The individual must make intense efforts and special sacrifices, beyond the usual level, which will have as their goal the formation of a volitive force and his own spiritual supremacy. The reason or purpose behind this discipline is important. If a person acted because he was impelled by ambition or obligation, this would in no way lead to the formation of his *"Volitive I,"* as he would have acted under strong compulsion, a force beyond himself (necessity or passion). In addition, the student must be perfectly clear as to what he is doing and why he is doing it, so that the being in formation will have a high degree of awareness and intelligence. For this, it is most useful to look into a mirror specially dedicated to this purpose, looking directly at the space between the eyebrows, and after a short while quietly repeat several times: *"I am will power."* The success of this exercise depends exclusively on the individual's emotional state during its execution, as well as the manner in which he pronounces and emotionally *vibrates* when saying the words: *"I am."* While emphatically saying these words, the student should internally feel "something" in the form of a strange emotion as he encounters or contemplates a sublime interior presence. If these conditions are not manifested or if the exercise is done mechanically, there will be no effect whatsoever.

After the individual has been forming his *"Volitive I"* for

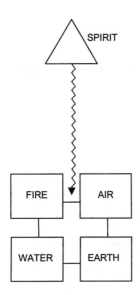

1) COMMON MAN

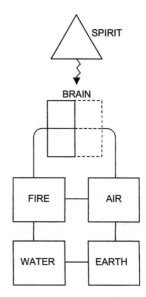

2) MAN OF HIGH CONCEPTUAL CAPACITY

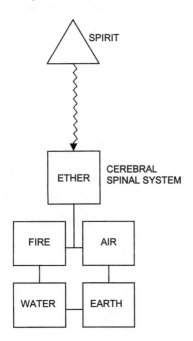

3) MAN OF HIGH CONCEPTUAL CAPACITY
WHO HAS EXCELLED THROUGH INITIATION

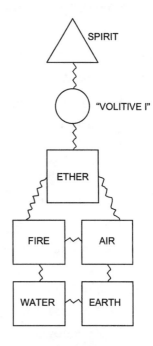

4) INITIATE

Diagram 6

some time, he will begin to note interesting changes, observing that a centripetal force has started to become a part of the directing force of the human complex. What is really occurring is that the *"Volitive I"* is converted into the supreme king of the microcosm, having above him only the *"Superior I."* When it is observed that the *"Volitive I"* has acquired certain power, the student can take the next step, which consists of trying to awaken himself, freeing himself from the universal oneiric force. In this, as in everything that refers to Hermeticism, it is necessary to reach profound understanding in order to be absolutely certain and clear as to the reason or purpose for doing certain things.

We recommend the study of a good scientific book on hypnosis in order to understand the similarity between hypnotic and somnambular sleep, which is the normal state of *sapiens*. The works of professor Anatol Milechnin are extremely useful for getting a glimpse of the mystery of sleep as it relates to what is being presented in this book.

There are five basic points that the disciple must keep before him in order to *"break"* the phenomenon of hypnotic sleep. These do not consist of an awakening technique, but are rather adopted methods of behavior that will promote awakening. These points are as follows:

1. To stop lying
2. To stop dreaming
3. To learn how to think
4. To live in the present moment
5. To activate the physical body

Point 1: TO STOP LYING

Points 1 and 2 are closely related, as we will now see. Starting with the problem of lying, it is necessary for the student to realize that he constantly lies without realizing it. When a person has lied for a long time, the time comes when he can no longer distinguish between what is false and what is true. People convince themselves of their own lies, becoming victims of their own inventions as they begin to direct their lives by standards of behavior, ideas, feelings, or instincts which do not correspond to their inner reality. What is truly serious in this matter is that the individual loses all points of reference regarding what comprises truth, and what comprises lies. He becomes used to considering as true only that which is convenient for his personal interests; everything that is in opposition to his self-esteem or in conflict with already established prejudices, he considers false.

A person lies in order to avoid difficult problems, to evade responsibility, or to avoid damage to his self-esteem. So the individual constantly lies to himself and to others, and becomes entangled in an illusory world born out of his personal fantasy. He forms concepts, ideas, judgments, aversions, and attachments that have no relation to actual events, but are only the reflection of a life full of lies and listening to lies, since everyone lies.

One of the most powerful reasons for lying is to create a good image of oneself, and to prevent others from seeing us as we really are beneath the mask of appearances. Each mask is a lie, and there are thousands in each individual's collection of disguises. It is necessary to be conscious of this phenomenon of lying, and to realize its magnitude and frequency, as well as the enormous damage it causes. One should have the goal of neither lying to oneself nor to others, and in the case of a "white lie," to be aware of telling it, and judging the need for such a lie with one's own conscience.

Point 2: TO STOP DREAMING

People are always infused with all kinds of fantastic ideas about themselves, the world, people, love, idealism, society, etc. Led by his eagerness to evade a disagreeable reality, man gives free rein to his imagination and is inclined to believe the first agreeable lie he encounters along the way. The individual projects his personal illusions onto a cold and immutable reality, and thus deceiving himself, he endeavors to contemplate reality through rose-colored glasses. "Disillusion" is a painful process and can be prolonged, depending on how much time the individual takes to realize he is living artificially and that this condition is a product of his internal dreams. Great courage is required to face reality and to destroy the mirage of a pleasant dream. On the other hand, we must consider that sooner or later dreams fade. What is dangerous for the human being is that these dreams are substituted by others, which in due course also fade. This is the life history of the human being: a succession of oneiric dreams. It is a vicious circle which is extremely difficult to break. Awakening from a broken dream, and the frustration this causes, incites a person to fabricate new and more-agreeable dreams in order to combat disillusion, loneliness, and disappointment. The lack of communication between human beings arises from the fact that all their dreams are different, and therefore, psychologically speaking, they live in different worlds.

If a person decides to seriously investigate the reason for his various acts and reactions, he will realize how his behavior is directed toward maintaining his personal fantasies. Great courage, discipline, and determination are necessary to face the truth, without any kind of adornment. Such courage is lacking in the immense majority of human beings. It is pathetic to see how people cling to their petty illusions, generally a result of their oneiric fantasies, while disdaining all that is truly valuable. Society is organized in this manner; its scale of values is so disturbed that it considers everything that enables the individual to enjoy passing pleasures as most desirable, and then condemns its members to suffer "eternally" for the price of a fleeting pleasure.

The Hermeticist proceeds to the contrary: he submits himself voluntarily to suffering, self-discipline, and privation in order to attain eternal peace and happiness. Each individual should consciously judge what could be most desirable, and on the other hand, determine if the one who seeks passing pleasure is really happy, or if he is in truth profoundly unhappy in his eternal vacuum. The majority of people have a philosophy that tells them "after this life there is no other; let us take advantage of this and enjoy ourselves as much as possible." Those who have converted this thought into their personal credo should ask themselves if they are truly satisfied and if the innumerable playthings society offers them are sufficient to quench their eternal thirst and alleviate the anguish of their loneliness.

The world of today is perfectly organized, but for what?

By observing and meditating, we will discover that everything is perfectly synchronized to maintain and feed the
"dream," and the "dreams" of *sapiens*. An individual will
cease dreaming only when he has understood and lived
what we are explaining: when he proves to his amazement
that each person lives drugged by his personal dreams,
which are transformed into the rudder which directs his life.
It is useful to analyze all the projects one has had in life,
everything that one has desired and planned to accomplish,
but which in retrospect appear as a phantasmal unreality.

Point 3: TO LEARN HOW TO THINK
It is important to completely reeducate the thinking process
in order to make it really creative, because only when this
function is accomplished can the individual think clearly.
Creative thinking is not the act of "inventing" something,
but rather consists of thinking in an unprogrammed way.
One's intelligence should be used to face each event as if it
were really new, casting prejudices to the side. This will enable the individual to create a result or form a judgment that
is truly impartial, as he has given up his habitual sources
and does not consider anything as a known fact. Described
symbolically, creative thought consists of dispensing with
the program in order to form a high level of judgment,
which is not affected in its genesis by the compulsive force of
the information stored in the cerebral computer. When people think, they do so compulsively and in spite of
themselves. This is as evident as the fact that thought is not
voluntary, for an individual cannot cease thinking when he
so desires. On the contrary, it is impossible for him to oust

ideas from his imagination or prevent unpleasant ideas from arising. The organization and security of the modern world has created conditions of life in which the individual has no need to make a great effort in order to survive. He can subsist with little effort, and in some cases practically none at all, especially when compared to the harsh struggle for life in Nature's wilderness. There is nothing which really obliges an individual to use his basic intelligence; on the contrary, he has been converted into an expert in evading or dodging all truly trying points presented to him which question his intelligence. It is much safer and more comfortable to not venture along the path of free thought, but to instead accept or adopt already established and approved systems of thought and behavior. Imitation and blind acceptance have become the easiest road to satisfy *sapiens'* ever-diminishing intellectual curiosity. Hermetically, on this subject, we speak of "dead" and "living" knowledge. "Dead" knowledge is that which is known by its specific meaning, but whose interrelation with the whole is ignored. It is a single part of knowledge and it is not known how, when, or where it fits in relation to the remaining pieces of the overall plan. In contrast, "living" knowledge is obtained in a state of superior awareness, and is always the product of perfect "mental digestion."

"Dead" knowledge is born solely from the intellect, while "living" knowledge originates in the mind. Because "living" knowledge is essentially understood by the awakened thinker, he is therefore conscious of the position which this knowledge occupies in the general context of the Universe.

Here we approach one of the most important points

which separate *sapiens* and *Stellar Man*. *Sapiens* thinks only with his brain and his intelligence is therefore limited to the intellectual-cerebral source. Further, the average person uses only a small portion of his brain for his intellectual functioning, which is furthermore located in a sort of "pre-brain" composed of the four intelligences and the unconscious, which is the ancestral soul of the animal of the species. For this reason, even on high intellectual planes, *sapiens* obeys the mandate of his animal soul, the beast. In the Bible reference is made to the number 666 as the number of the beast. Upon inverting this figure we find the number of man: 999.

The Hermeticist, however, through his initiatic work, reaches the formation of the "spiritual system," the mind, which is lacking in the average person, who usually refers to it therefore, as a symbolic abstraction of the psyche. In reality, *the mind* is the superior integration of the human faculties into a whole, directed by the *"Volitive I,"* and manifesting the *"Superior I,"* which is the spirit or the individual himself.

Sapiens, making use of his rudimentary "pre-brain," (the union of one part of his brain with the four intelligences and the unconscious) is able to make scientific discoveries thanks to the transmission of culture from generation to generation and by taking advantage of an assembly of collective experiences and knowledge. Thus, a long list of geniuses have contributed with their discoveries and investigations to raising the level of our civilization. Without discrediting the extraordinary talent of these men in any way, it must be stated that they have been only "intellectual geniuses" and as such have worked *on the smaller picture*. They have totally overlooked any relation to *the whole*, having no knowledge of the effect or reaction their work would subsequently have on *everything*.

We must necessarily classify these intellectual geniuses as "semi-sages" as they are *monoconceptual*, visualizing everything through the prism of their specialty. It is interesting to meditate on what would be the behavior, reactions, appreciation, and scale of values possessed by individuals of great intelligence who do not belong to human terrestrial culture. It would be interesting to also know the thought process of superior beings who are high above pettiness, egotism, prejudice, and *sapiens'* moral, cultural, and spiritual superstitions.

The true sages are the "geniuses of the mind"—those who are able to generate everything with their mind, those who can raise themselves over opposite poles and reconcile all that is not reconcilable, understand all paradoxes, penetrate into the essence of everything, and be aware of the hidden cause of all that is manifested as an effect. These sages are the possessors of true wisdom, the kind given to King Solomon; they are the ones who exist beyond good and evil, who know the hidden threads which connect all things. These sages demonstrate their knowledge in themselves, applying it to the control and evolution of their internal nature. They possess the "philosopher's stone" with which they produce spiritual, not physical gold; with this noble project they help sublimate the animal in *sapiens*.

Could it be possible that a group of men possess the secret of converting the entire body into a brain? Would it be possible to think with a foot, a hand, the stomach, or the lungs? The mind is something very much like this: a kind of super-brain which gathers the intellectual, emotional, in-stinctive, and physical into itself.

One might ask where the discoveries of these great brains are? To answer this, the reader needs to meditate on what he would do if he were a *super-brain*. Would his inter-ests be the same as before? Would he persist in his egotism and anthropocentrism? Would he continue being interested in temporal things or would he feel more attracted to the eternal?

In answering this, it is sufficient to consider the position and importance of the planet Earth in relation to the rest of the Universe. Consider that the *dead intelligence* of the com-mon man is the intelligence of the Earth, while the *mind* or *super-brain* is celestial intelligence. If one were an ant and suddenly changed into a human being, would one retain the interests of an ant? (Be it known however, that from the viewpoint of universal economics, the ant is just as impor-tant as man). Perhaps the highest interest of the *geniuses of the mind* does not reside in great scientific discoveries, or could it be that once aware of the "universal plan," these *ge-niuses* are not permitted to interfere with the natural development of events within an already determined span of time? To illustrate this, we recognize in Leonardo Da Vinci a great *genius of the mind*. We cannot comment on his inten-tions, which belong to the secret of his particular initiatic work. Without being aware of his motives, we cannot judge them.

In summary, *sapiens* possesses a *dead intelligence* which only permits him to be "specialized" and always within the human cultural scheme. The *Stellar Man* has a *live intelli-*

gence; he can transcend the terrestrial level and evolve his *"Superior I."* It is thus that there exists *dead knowledge* (orthodox wisdom) and a *living knowledge* (Hermetic science). One is a product of the *brain;* the other, a product of the *super-brain.* Further on, we will give instructions for the development of the *super-brain.*

Point 4: TO LIVE IN THE PRESENT MOMENT
To apply this point, it is indispensable to clearly understand the previous chapter entitled *"To Be or Not to Be?"* where we explain the absolute key which, together with unveiling the mystery of being, illustrates the methods for overcoming sleep. That key is expressed as follows: "The only reality is the present moment; there is no past or future, both are illusory" (in the present moment there is no past or future, the past existed and the future will exist). We also said that "the present is the exact point of union between the past and the future."

There is a dividing line which separates fantasy or unreality from truth or reality. This line is time. Reality is the coincidence between the steps of the human being and his companion time. It is thus that our physical body is constantly in reality; it is objective and occupies space. On the other hand, the occupant of the vehicle (the *"Superior I"*) habitually lives in unreality, that is, beyond the wall that separates reality from fantasy. The unreal is something belonging to a natural reality X, which finds itself projected into a different time from where it belongs.

For example, if a human being belongs to the reality classified as "Delta-15," which has a time similar to an X clock, but is then projected into X^2 time, he evades reality, living in a world which exists only in dimension B, which naturally his physical body has no access to, as he cannot raise his body to X^2 time. Therefore, if there are so many different velocities of time, we must ask ourselves how many realities exist? The logical reply is that there are as many realities as there are velocities of time. Nevertheless, as we are physically constrained to Delta-15 time, we must adapt ourselves to this reality. If one lives in an unreal world with respect to Delta-15 time, that is, with respect to human reality, it is the same as not existing at all, for the body would be that of a somnambulist, an empty shell without an occupying spirit or *"Superior I,"* an entity, a mere spectator of a fantastic kaleidoscope.

For example, what is the fourth dimension? It is a world that actually exists, but only for those who possess a vehicle which can manifest itself in the temporal vibration of the fourth dimension. The aphorism which says "everything is illusion" refers to this problem, which should be interpreted as follows: *"Nothing is real for the one who is in absolute reality, as all that exists has reality only for those who are on the same vibration or time, since time is velocity and velocity is vibration."* It is due to this principle that a "ghost" for us is just an illusion, and not a physical being. By "ghosts" I mean the energy remaining after a person's death.

A thought has no concrete and physical reality: we cannot weigh or see or bump into a thought. Nevertheless, for a man composed of thought-matter, thoughts would be visible and tangible. Why is it that our body cannot collide with a thought? Because it has a different speed and, therefore, a different reality.

As human beings we are the union of two forces of very different vibrations:

- Mass energy or physical body
- Mind energy or spirit

This union has only one objective: evolution. Evolution is cosmic for the great human mass, and personal for the individual. The object of having a physical body is to evolve. When the individual does not evolve due to indolence, disinterest, or personal incompetence, he does not fulfill the prime objective of his individual life, and is only open to the possibility of becoming the "sexual part" of God, being converted into an animated instrument of physical creation. He suffers greatly in this process: he has a physical body, but pays the penalty of losing *the only personal justification for having it—individual evolution.*

The body and spirit belong to very different realities, to two times which are distant or apart from each other. As a consequence, the spirit is not manifested on Earth, but remains in slavery or chained to the physical body, and must suffer the fantasies and dreams experienced by the *"Psychological I."* Not being able to become located in the Delta-15 reality, the spirit lives constantly out of the present (outside of Delta-15). It is thus that the body loses its function as a vehicle of the spirit, remaining only an instrument of the *Archons of Destiny*, with the object of becoming one more worker at the orders of his owner. It should be explained that creation is accomplished in the Universe by means of the imagination of *sapiens*, which shapes all emotional, instinctive, and intellectual states. This energy condenses in a remote future, becoming transformed into matter. This is why we can state that God is the Great Architect of the Universe and that the human mass forms his laborers' army who, as payment, receives the gift of existence.

This would not be such a terrible thing if *sapiens* had access to reality, although some think that the fact of being conscious of it and of not being able to change it, increases suffering. The only way to reach absolute reality, to destroy dreams, and earn the right to one's own evolution is *to make the body and the spirit coincide at the same doorway or temporal communication so that together they may face reality*. Upon accomplishing this, the individual lives in two worlds as he has attained knowledge of two opposite realities: that of matter and that of spirit. Both are reconciled in a third reality, the one sought by the Hermeticist: the absolute reality, which although still material, is part of that which is divine, and being divine, forms part of that which is material. This is what we call *being on this side of the dividing line* (which separates reality and fantasy), *to have one's feet on the ground and one's head in the heavens*. This is very different from profane men, with their feet on nothing and their head in oneiric fantasy.

In order to live in the present moment, the individual must have reached not only the creation of his *"Volitive I,"* but also its complete strengthening, as the *"Volitive I"* can be weak or strong. The *"Volitive I"* must oblige the *"Psychological I"* to concentrate on the present moment. This is done with adequate discipline of the imagination, a state of relaxation, and with the perfect integration of our microcosm in an internal hierarchy under the guidance of the *"Volitive I."*

It is important that our imagination should not wander, that we should overcome nervous tension, and that our entire being is under the control of the *"Volitive I."* Further on we will summarize the practical application of this, as everything is related, and if this were done in each chapter, we would have to digress many times.

Point 5: TO ACTIVATE THE PHYSICAL BODY

As the physical body represents the opposite pole from the spirit, it is obvious that it represents an "obstacle" for communication with our *"Superior I."* Nevertheless, at the same time it is necessary to "raise the vibration of our corporeal matter," which is done by making the body obey our will. To this end, let us briefly consider three principal elements:

- Food
- Breathing
- Physical Exercise

We will not discuss these points in detail, as they are not part of this chapter. We will only speak of them as some of the methods for destroying dreams. Our recommendations will be very brief, because in this case the only objective is to "activate the physical body."

Regarding food, we will only recommend abstaining from consuming dense meats "of a low vibration" such as pork, as well as practicing vegetarianism when the student must give special attention to his ascetic side in order to purify his state of consciousness. With respect to alcohol, it is necessary to be very prudent in its use, as it is a considerable organic depressor, and its effect is only noticed after some time. It acts as "super fuel" which unnecessarily wears out the organism with no advantage whatsoever. If alcohol consumption turns into a vice, it is a very dangerous element, as it breaks the individual's etheric protection or "aura." This exposes the individual to contact with demonic creations which exist on the lower astral plane (one of the vibratory planes; the lowest after the material) which is clinically known as "delirium tremens."

Breathing should be considered in relation to absorbing more oxygen, that is, by practicing complete breathing. Begin by expanding the diaphragm until completely filling the upper part of the lungs and expanding the thorax. Inhale by expanding the abdomen, projecting it forward with some force until it is slightly bulged. Continue to inhale until the lungs are filled, expanding the thorax and filling it while the abdomen is naturally flattened. Upon exhaling, the abdomen must be gently contracted to facilitate the elimination of residual air. Ten minutes of morning breathing contributes much energy toward activating the physical body.

Physical exercise is indispensable for the reactivation of our body, but it is necessary to do those exercises which make our cardiovascular system work, such as the various forms of aerobic exercises. Added to this, each person can practice calisthenics according to his age. Also, it is necessary to practice an exercise of complete immobility every morning, which should be done as follows: seated very straight on a chair, remain absolutely motionless for three minutes. Once this is perfectly carried out, continue to the second stage, which is similar to the first but starts by tensing all the muscles strongly, clenching the fists and thinking "I am awake," letting this idea fill the organism. The muscular tension must last one minute after which the muscles are completely relaxed and loose, and then complete immobility is maintained for five minutes, always with the fixed idea, "I am awake." For this exercise to be completely effective, immobility must be absolute, without moving the muscles even one millimeter. The eyes should remain open throughout the exercise.

During the process of true initiation, we have already referred to two very important stages, which are the creation of the *"Volitive I"* and the destruction of dreams. For the latter we pointed out that it is necessary to fulfill five basic disciplines:

1. To stop lying
2. To stop dreaming
3. To learn how to think
4. To live in the present moment
5. To activate the physical body

We will now approach the third stage, which is *"mental digestion."* Common man lacks a *mental stomach (mind)* and therefore cannot effectively "digest" acquired knowledge. In spite of the fact that we are speaking figuratively and symbolically, this simile closely reflects the ideal work of the intelligence, as it is equivalent to that of the stomach: to transform basic elements into "nutritional essence." No matter how much a person eats, if he does not assimilate it, the food eaten is of no use whatsoever. The same occurs with the

intelligence of *sapiens,* who has become an intellectual glutton, devouring knowledge, which becomes integrated into
the cerebral neurons without having been truly assimilated.
In short, he is a hoarder of mental food which he never uses.
Physically speaking, this is equivalent to an individual who
stores food he will never eat. There is not only corporeal
obesity but also intellectual obesity, and it is curious that
there are those who are proud of this expansion of their intellect. Man is convinced that the more he studies, the more
prepared he will be to learn the truth. It has never occurred
to him that perhaps the opposite is true. If we think about
this just a little, having understood the concept of programming, we will realize that to study more means more
program; the greater the program the less the capacity for
alertness; and less alertness means more automatism, less
humanity, more unreality and fantasy. When an individual
who lacks a "mental stomach" begins to study, the result is
always the same: intellectual inflation and reinforcement
and growth of programming. On the other hand, when the
individual who has a *mind* studies, he genuinely digests his
intellectual food and therefore a real change and evolution is
produced inside him. We have already addressed stages 1
and 2, which refer precisely to the formation of the *mind*;
therefore, if the student carefully fulfills these, he will be in a
condition to study and really assimilate knowledge.

The philosopher's stone has traditionally been the symbol of *mind*, and as such always appears as the key element
for transmutation. When a student has perfectly formed his
mind, not only will he be in a condition to transmute him-

self, but he will also be able to accomplish many other tasks of great Hermetic value.

We must point out that orthodox science has completely failed to address or even recognize the effects produced in a person who has achieved a perfect process of understanding.

Psychology knows something about understanding, but is incapable of evaluating its importance. This process, when perfectly accomplished, constitutes a *magical-alchemical operation* which produces a certain element in the body which is missing in *sapiens*, and which could be called *consciousness*. It is necessary to point out that in this stage of birth, *conscious awareness* is a material element which is present chemically in the bloodstream, and from its combustion *spiritual gold* originates, which feeds and enables our essence to grow. Alchemy represents an entirely corporeal work in which the crucible is the body itself, the fire is passion, and the lead is the raw material. Alchemical "sublimation" is the lengthy work of transmutation of *sapiens* into a *Stellar Man*. There is no prayer, no breathing exercise, no mantra, no magic formula, and no mythological Master who can offer shortcuts or a substitution for this process.

XIII

THE ORDEALS

One of the most frequent criticisms of the famous Hermetic novel *Zanoni* concerns the terrifying nature of its theme, which vividly describes the ordeals endured by Clarence Glyndon, one of the main characters. It is thought that the author, Sir Edward Bulwer Lytton, exaggerated or over-dramatized the difficulties which the neophyte encounters on the path. The fearful "specter on the threshold" is no more for the reader than the fictional symbol of abstract or subjective internal difficulties. For others, the specter is a malevolent being which actually appears before the student, submitting him to all kinds of torture.

The truth is that there are very few who understand that the terrible specter is just one of the problems the disciple encounters on the path, and that the others do not refer to situations so spectacular as those presented in *Zanoni*. Neither adepts nor Masters are represented by Zanoni and Mejnour, who were instead chosen by Lytton as prototypes to illustrate the two different paths the initiate may take upon attaining mastership.

The ordeals are mostly those of daily life rather than fantastic apparitions or magical rites. For this reason, they are even more transcendental and difficult than if they were unusual or spectacular situations. The ordeals exist and are terribly hard, and this is something that candidates for initiation must not forget. Naturally we are speaking of "true initiates" and not of those who expect to reach high degrees within the peaceful tranquility of an existence far from threatening, dangerous, or inconvenient realities. The sooner the neophyte understands that it is necessary to overcome tremendous obstacles and destroy powerful internal barriers, the easier it will be for him to recognize the importance of the initiatic process. As we have already stated, *sapiens* is programmed and depends on the *central computer of the species* and on the *collective animal soul*. It is not difficult to understand that if an individual tries to free himself from this bondage, he will face strong opposition manifested through Nature itself, which will react with great energy to bar the path of the candidate advancing toward wisdom. Thus, from the moment the individual starts on a true path free from fraud or self-deception, and when he carries out true Hermetic work on himself, all kinds of temptations, doubts, difficulties, and problems will appear in his life in order to dissuade him from persevering. This is not strange, as he is attempting to overcome his internal nature which, like all savage forces in Nature, responds with extraordinary vigor to all intent to control or dominate. To tame a savage beast is strenuous work. There is a savage beast in everyone, and no one knows how far the savagery may escalate at a given moment, in spite of culture and education. The traditional Egyptian Sphinx, which has the head, neck, and bosom of a woman and body and paws of a lion, is a symbol of the animal nature of the human being. It is she who blocks the way to the intrepid seeker of Hermetic light. Nevertheless, the Sphinx has wings to symbolize the fact that it is necessary to raise oneself through one's animal nature, and not through the strength of the spirit as many people believe. Furthermore, this corresponds exactly to the image of Jesus Christ mounted on an ass, which represents the beast that must be tamed by the *"Superior I."*

In truth, if we feel an impulse inside us to soar toward higher planes, it is not due to the spirit, but rather the beast. The beast is not bad in itself, but is only perverse in the measure in which it has taken into itself this characteristic from the common pool of human bestiality (collective unconsciousness) which forms part of the central computer of the species. To understand this, we show the spirit and the beast depicted by two triangles, one descending and the other ascending.

SPIRIT

BEAST

Diagram 7

The spirit is the celestial power, which radiates toward the Earth. It is the positive pole of life, and is attracted by the passive pole, which in this case is material terrestrial existence. The spirit is pure in itself and therefore seeks that which is unknown, the only thing which can offer an experience different to its own vibration, which is material sensations.

The beast, on the contrary, looks toward the heavens because, knowing it is impure, it struggles to reach the purity that only the divine can give it. This is why the six-pointed star called the "symbol of Solomon" is not a positive image, since it represents petrification or detention of the movement of life. It is very different when the ankh, or "symbol of life," appears in its center, for it then represents the "vital equilibrium" of creation, thus being transformed into a highly positive figure.

The fallen angels represent "spirits" or virginal divine sparks who descend to fulfill or perfect themselves through experience in matter. We recommend to the reader the inter-

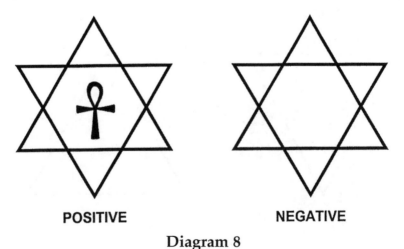

POSITIVE   NEGATIVE

Diagram 8

esting book, *The Revolt of the Angels* by Anatole France, in which the author humorously and poetically exposes the mystery of the double triangle. The existence of these two forces, one ascending and the other descending, allows us to understand in a deeper manner the superior role which the *"Volitive I"* must perform in managing spiritual energy, as well as the material force identified as the beast.

Usually, those who arrive at an initiatic school make fun of the ordeals, characterizing them as mere barriers. Nevertheless, as time passes, they are rudely shown their different faults. In spite of this, failure in some ordeals does not mean defeat, but rather a lesson that the individual must learn; and until he does so, he will remain blocked by the obstacle. The extreme difficulty of the ordeals lies in their tremendous subtlety. These ordeals are generally based on the individual's internal failures which are beneath the threshold of his awareness, and which remain unknown to him. This is similar to what occurs with a person's defects; generally, he is completely incapable of observing them.

The first steps taken by an individual who enters a Hermetic school are decisive, as he is prone to be guided by false and capricious impressions, arising primarily from a projection of his internal problems. Many times, the individual looks upon the school as an entity which is trying to use or pressure him in order to obtain something from him. He craves salvation or a guide to success, but at the same time he does not want to let himself be saved easily, and he wishes to show that he is not easy to convince or handle. The individual does not realize that he himself is the only one interested in his own salvation (freedom from being used by Nature) and if he does not free himself, no one will come to his rescue. Until he understands his real situation in the world, he will lack the necessary motivation to fight for his own existence, as this is what he is striving for after all. The only possibility of success resides in being able to visualize his true position in life before Nature and destiny, and in his ultimate use of the "*Volitive I*" as an instrument for fulfillment.

We have seen the most incredible things happen to sincere students. Sudden riches or love are often sufficient to make him stray from his path. Other times, his loved ones turn into his worst enemies as far as initiation is concerned; these loved ones are undoubtedly controlled by the central computer of the species. This is very much like some apprentices of sorcery who try to dominate Nature, but end up as its slaves. The difficulties which the student must face just to reach the meeting place of the brotherhood on time, sometimes take on tragicomic overtones. The oddest things occur solely to prevent him from reaching the meeting, and the problem is that it is the individual who is "sabotaging" himself. The ass is a symbolic animal in Hermetic Art. It represents the negative animal nature of the individual; its basic keynote is stupidity, inertia, laziness, negligence, and irresponsibility. It is due to this that when an individual makes a harmful mistake, it is said figuratively that he should not "think as an ass" or rather that "the ass should not be allowed to think for him." Hermeticism also speaks of the "path of the ass" to describe those who, after so much effort and hardship, and after covering so much ground, always remain in the same place. In ancient times, asses were used to bring up water for irrigation from springs or wells, and the animal walked many miles per day, but because this was in a circle, he always remained in the same place. Hermetic teaching states that only after conquering the ass is it possible to conquer the Sphinx and soar on its wings to cosmic space. The Sphinx is the vehicle of the *Stellar Man*.

Regarding the candidate's gender, it is necessary to state that for men the ordeals are mainly expressed through instinct, along with all the related psychological and material situations and conditions. On the other hand, the women's weak point is situated in their emotional nature. It is due to this that the admission of women into "initiatic schools" has been traditionally prohibited, and this is the reason why the Freemasons only admit women on "ladies' nights." In ancient times when women belonged to initiatic orders, many brotherhoods were destroyed when one of the female members, under the influence of passionate love, revealed the secrets of the order to enemy organizations.

The Freemasons were originally a Hermetic brotherhood formed by high initiates as a preparatory school for other higher-level work. Nevertheless, with the symbolic death of Hiram, Freemasonry lost the secret of the rites and symbols such as the true meaning of the passwords. Hermetic tradition was extinguished and there remains only the unknown language of the symbols. The light that existed has lost its Hermetic meaning, and only the philosophical significance remains. The brothers have fallen "asleep" with the passage of time, perhaps sung to sleep by their pride in having thirty-three degrees of Masonic splendor. However, their symbols, inspired from ancient rites, are truly beautiful. Without a doubt, entering into Freemasonry will morally, culturally, and philosophically benefit any clear-minded person. But between entering Freemasonry and becoming truly *twice born*, there is a world of difference.

It must be pointed out that true Schools of Initiation have never banned the entry of women into their ranks, and that women may also work in the Temple.

The ordeals the candidate for initiation faces may be internal or material. Material ordeals concern concrete situations, which arise from the reactions of Nature. Remember that Nature is internal as well as external, and tremendous internal conflicts are therefore produced. Two interesting events make a profound impression on the disciple during the process of initiation. One is the gradual vision the candidate acquires of himself, seeing himself as he really is without subterfuge, idealization, or hypocrisy. Another is the gradual contemplation of the truth, the world, and its people. In the first case, the student suffers a profound *shock* upon seeing himself as he really is for the first time. This vision opens two paths to him: he can either accept or reject his true nature. If he rejects his true nature, instead of breaking through the shell of his isolation from reality, the individual, terrorized by the naked truth, builds up an impenetrable and indestructible shell of iron. There are many illusions (in the sense of that which is illusory) that the individual must overcome in order to evolve. This is carefully stated in the well-known and beautiful book *Light on the Path* by Mabel Collins:

> Before the eyes can see, they must be incapable of tears.
> Before the ear can hear, it must have lost its sensitiveness.
> Before the voice can speak in the presence of the Masters, it

must have lost the power to wound. Before the soul can stand in the presence of the Masters, its feet must be washed in the blood of the heart.

Life's truths are so terrible in their nakedness, that for a disciple to endure them in a well-balanced manner, he must have adequately prepared himself. It must be realized that Nature is completely cold and could not care less about the kindness of a monk or the perversions of an assassin. Within her bosom Nature conceives equally wheat and hemlock, healing herbs and poisonous plants. Neither the greatest idealism nor the most despicable evil alter the immutability of the laws of Nature. There are truths that are so dangerous, they are truly like "a razor's edge," for if the student still retains the seed of egotism or evil, the vision of these mysteries will traumatize him to such an extent that he will never return to normality. Herein lies a great similarity with the case of our neophyte in *Zanoni*, although reality is always more deadly and less spectacular than the theme of a novel. Many have gone insane upon glimpsing a truth which was too unbearable for those who have not been able to overcome their baser passions. Truth is only attained by the absolute nakedness of the innocent purity of those who "become little children." Truth is a double-edged sword: it raises up the pure and destroys the passional.

In an Initiatic School, hundreds of different situations arise which test the integrity, purity, and decisions of the student. These tests range from loss of confidence in the School and the Master to a feeling of being used or cheated in one manner or another. Each individual reveals his internal failings through his doubts and conflicts. Thus, the one who has no honor firmly believes that they will oblige him to lose his honor; the one who is not free believes he will lose his freedom of choice; an immoral individual believes he would be obliged to violate moral rules; and a thief would complain of "losing his integrity."

Many feel they are passed over and believe there is favoritism and prejudice, or believe they are not being taught enough. Others, especially the unfeeling egoists, accuse their companions of "having lost all sensitivity." In brief, in a School, a series of vital situations is reproduced, much like in a laboratory, so the student can consciously observe the behavior of others and also take note of his own. In this setting it is also possible for the School to profoundly understand the student in order to better help him. Naturally, for this work to bear fruit it must be authentic, that is, the student must not pretend at any time, but must be honest and sincere, and his reactions must be absolutely authentic. It must be pointed out that each ordeal that is successfully overcome raises the disciple to higher states of awareness, allowing him to understand that which was previously incomprehensible.

XIV

THE OBSTACLES

In contrast to the ordeals, obstacles are not Nature's reactions but ordinary barriers, which all people have to face in order to evolve. The absolute rule of dreams over *sapiens* must be understood, and that if *sapiens* wants to evolve, he must necessarily awaken. If he does not awaken, he will remain static.

To awaken is difficult to do, as *sapiens* is submitted to a cosmic hypnotic influence which is the universal energy of creation; and if this were not enough, each individual, when he does not like the reality of life or is not satisfied with himself, *dreams of himself and the world in a manner ideal for himself.* Hermetically, we call this foolish romanticism, to differentiate it from the idealism of the poets. *Romanticism* is the ingredient which enables the human being to accept his dreams as an expression of reality, and his life is limited to attempting to satisfy his own fantasies. Let it be understood that we refer to an inferior and destructive type of romanticism, although people cannot differentiate this from its higher counterpart.

In general the individual has the following obstacles along the way:

AN ERRONEOUS CONCEPT OF HERMETICISM OR ESOTERICISM AS A WHOLE

People's beliefs in this area swing between two extremes: those who consider esotericism as something superstitious, evil, or diabolical, and those who blindly believe. The latter speak occult jargon and say that *"it is necessary to unfold on the astral plane, to open the third eye, or awaken the Kundalini,"* and due to their tremendous naïveté are sincerely convinced of the truth of their own words.

THE DIFFICULTY OF SEEING ONESELF OBJECTIVELY

Each person wears the banner of the qualities he most appreciates in himself.

A person cannot avoid projecting his own image to others, and judging everything according to his own concepts rather than in a free and experiential manner. It is as if each day a person digested part of the world, only to afterwards vomit all that did not correspond to his image of what is *pleasant, true,* or *positive.* In his self-projection, man has created a God in his image and likeness, one he imagines as a *kindly old man with a white beard.*

DISINTEREST IN LEARNING THE TRUTH

People do not want the truth because they are not interested in it. They prefer to sleep peacefully, even if it means tomorrow they will be devoured by Nature, a presentiment which exists in all human beings from childhood.

CONFORMING WITH THE "FLOCK"

This conduct gives the individual the false sensation that *all is well* simply because he is *doing what everyone else does and accepts.* For the same reason, he does not dare to decide anything for himself, least of all to study or accomplish something not approved by "official science." In this respect it would be interesting to verify whether hypnotism was any less effective before being accepted by science, and whether its acceptance, in truth, made it more *respectable* and effective. Following along this line, we see that in most cases *respectability* and *morals* only reflect the degree of conformity with the flock.

BEING DEPENDENT ON THE PASSIONS

Passions express the individual's baser animal tendencies, which exist alongside superior animal tendencies. The baser tendencies are manifested in the appetite of the corporeal mass, which seeks its own satisfaction without considering the higher interests of the individual whatsoever. Indolence, inertia, laziness, apathy, bitterness, resentment, jealousy, envy, and lust, to name a few, manipulate man as a puppet, and he will be unable to free himself from this situation. Each state of passion takes control of the body including its psychological components at a given moment, and the individual completely forgets his previous resolutions.

PROJECTION OF PSYCHOLOGICAL PROBLEMS
ONTO THE TEACHINGS

It often happens that people seek Hermetic Teaching not to evolve spiritually, but to compensate for their yearning for power or their inferiority complexes. People frequently project their unconscious traumas, fears, ambitions, and desires onto the Teaching in order to extract from it the same "food" they derive from these problems. They in turn use the new knowledge they receive in order to fortify their process of psychological rationalization.

FEAR OF FREEDOM

We know that *sapiens* fears freedom with the force of an irrational anguish. Deep down inside himself he knows that the Hermetic path will inexorably lead him toward freedom or *salvation*. But, does the individual really wish to be free? Generally, the greater percentage of the *sapiens* species prefers mediocre slavery to the most glorious and brilliant freedom. It is for this reason that people search in life for something to become enslaved to, as they cannot stand the sensation of liberty. There are those who "chain themselves to a stone" even if they know that this rock will drag them into the abyss of the sea.

What has been discussed here is a brief summary of the obstacles to advancement encountered along the path to spiritual supremacy.

XV

INITIATIC PRACTICES

DEVELOPMENT OF THE SUPER-BRAIN

Our brain alone is not equal to the task of discovering the truth and attaining spiritual evolution; it is necessary to form *the mind,* a super-brain which will enable us to reach the condition of a *Stellar Man.* The following is a brief summary of the elements needed to form a super-brain:

1. The four intelligences (the soul of man): water, air, earth, and fire
2. The "Volitive I"
3. The Mind
4. Three basic objectives:
   a) The forming of the "Volitive I"
   b) Awakening
   c) Mental digestion
5. Three superior objectives:
   a) Deprogramming
   b) Initiatory death
   c) Rebirth

6. Three supreme objectives:
   a) Evolution
   b) To be converted into a *Stellar Man*
   c) To transcend *Maya* (cosmic illusion)

It is not possible to insist enough on the fundamental requirement that the student must have a Hermetic Master who has already traveled the path the disciple wishes to follow. Only those who have consciously reincarnated are able to do without a Master, or, if possible, have *many Masters* who will *refresh the memory* of the reincarnated. The one who has consciously reincarnated certainly knows this, but this happens infrequently.

The indications given here are of an elemental character, and their object is to shed light on the path of the student toward the truth, to guide him in his goals. Only a genuine Master is able to transmit to the disciple the spiritual flame, the magical ferment which becomes his occult power as an initiate. This is not a poetic abstraction, but something material, a concrete process which takes place between the Master and the disciple. Naturally this power does not free the student from his ascetic disciplines; on the contrary, it obliges him to undertake them with greater perseverance.

EDUCATION OF THE FOUR INTELLIGENCES

To educate the four intelligences, the student must consider them to be the seat of his bad habits and vices, and he must proceed to cleanse them of all that is negative, giving them awareness and intelligence, according to the model of desired behavior.

INTELLIGENCE OF THE DIGESTIVE SYSTEM
(Earth Element)

The earth element encompasses all corporeal matter, but its seat is in the stomach. Its key word is *absorption*. To educate this intelligence it is necessary to submit its functions, to a certain extent, to the control of will, the *"Volitive I."*

The digestive system must be thought of as an intelligent being with which we can communicate, to which we can speak, and control. For this the following formula is used:

"You, intelligence of my digestive system, I order you to blindly obey me in all I say. I give you awareness and intelligence so you may perfectly fulfill your biological functions. From this moment, my will shall be your will, as I am your god, master, and owner whom you must respect and obey. When you are fed, it will be because it is my will and when you fast, it will be because I want no food."

This formula must be repeated several times, endeavoring to penetrate into the hidden forces of the digestive system.

Periodically it is necessary to fast for an entire day, and upon initiating this one must say:

"You, intelligence of my digestive system, will abstain from all food for 'x' amount of hours, as this is my will and I order you to blindly obey this mandate."

If the student suffers from any hepatic ailment or any type of digestive disorder, he must try to cure it by reinforcing the intelligence of his digestive system with all his will power. The reader will need to try to discover the cryptic sense of these instructions, as occult laws prohibit saying more than necessary.

INTELLIGENCE OF THE REPRODUCTIVE SYSTEM
(Fire Element)

The fire element is located in the sex, which is the seat of the instinctive center. Its key word is *irradiation*. For the education of this intelligence, the previous formula should be used. This formula does not vary for any of the other systems. Only the name and function of the corresponding element is changed. It is necessary to regulate the sexual function, submitting it to one's will power in order to have sexual relations only when the *"Volitive I"* permits it, and at no other time. We must remember that this system is the seat of the libido, a fact we can make use of to extricate all the complexes we may have by working on this center of activity. For this it is necessary to make the respective intelligence reason, so that it may abandon its infantile activity and proceed in a more mature manner. This should be complemented by the practice of controlling the imagination, which we will refer to under the respiratory system.

INTELLIGENCE OF THE CIRCULATORY SYSTEM
(Water Element)

The water element resides in our circulatory system, the seat of the emotions. Its key word is *unification*. As in the above cases, the formula already described for educating this intelligence is also used. Together with this formula, it is necessary to practice rigorous emotional hygiene to prevent the heart from receiving harmful or destructive emotions.

This is achieved gradually, through the *"Volitive I."* Furthermore, daily concentration on the heart (the brain of this system) should be practiced in order to create a state of profound peace and perfect submission of the emotions to the will.

INTELLIGENCE OF THE RESPIRATORY SYSTEM
(Air Element)

The air element resides in our respiratory system, the seat of the imagination. Its key word is *vitalization*. We must work with the known formula and further establish an adequate control of the imagination. It is necessary, at all costs, to suppress any morbid imagination, only letting positive, harmonious, balanced, and higher thoughts enter. The spoken word must be educated, cleansing the language and always accomplishing that which is affirmed out loud. The student who affirms something verbally and does not keep his word is converted into a plaything of Nature, and it will be very difficult for him to accomplish his personal projects.

Through breathing, we have access to the world of vibrations and by sharpening our sense of smell, it is possible to capture any kind of vibration through the inhalation and retention of breath.

We must insist on the fact that there are many secret keys in these instructions, but whether or not they are discovered is left to the interest and discernment of the reader.

For instance, and as an exercise, think about what occurs with the union of the elements of air (respiratory system) and fire (reproductive system) or, water (circulatory system) and earth (digestive system).

XVI

THE "VOLITIVE I"

We have already explained how the *"Volitive I"* is created, but we have not indicated the means of giving it
strength and power, which are in general as follows:

- Domination and sublimation of one's desires
- Charging one's psychic battery
- Economizing one's energy
- Action directed by will

Desires are one of the principal sources of energy (or energetic loss) in *sapiens*. If we listen to our internal world we
will realize that desire forms an integral part of our lives and
that desire acts with an astounding potency and persistence.
This implies that a great quantity of energy is lost, since desire uses up time and energy when our magnetic strength is
projected elsewhere. Nevertheless, if we control and guide
our desires, they can be converted into a source of extraordinary potency. Desire must never be a crazy or fleeting whim

for the Hermeticist, but an act of intelligence and method. When a desire is not satisfied, a powerful force vibrates within the individual, but as soon as he obtains what he wants, this power is extinguished and a vacuum is produced. There are those who pursue a desire intensely for a long time, and finally attain fulfillment, but far from making them happy, this fulfillment of the desire causes a state of deep emptiness, laxness, and disappointment. This occurs when the fuel which motivated the individual runs out, as desire provides the power which carries us toward fulfillment. We have already said that each person has "x" amount of energy at his disposal during his life, and can distribute it among many things or concentrate it on a few. Applying this concept to the subject we are addressing, it does not mean repressing or frustrating desires, but permitting their existence only if reason considers them just and convenient, and allowing them to materialize when, how, and where the "Volitive I" dictates.

We could also apply this to the principle of penitence, but from a different point of view. For example, we could sacrifice one thing we greatly desire in order to obtain another of greater spiritual or moral value. This could also be applied to vices, denying satisfaction of them through will power in order to obtain what we want. For example, a person may say, "I will not smoke because . . . (stating what he desires to obtain)." This affirmation should be mentally repeated every time the individual desires to smoke.

One of the desires it is necessary to suppress in order to channel this force toward higher purposes is that of telling others certain things we have learned *exclusively* or in secret, in order to impress them or to raise our self-esteem. This does not mean that we should not tell anything, but do so only after a time, only if in truth we want to, and not in order to make ourselves important. It should also be stated that it is more difficult to accomplish projects that become publicly known than when we endeavor to keep them secret.

The "psychic battery's" charge is the nervous and psychological tone produced by the magnetism which people accumulate and project; some in very small doses, and others with great potency. Magnetism is accumulated through conscious breathing and all practices of self-control. In fact, the more *magnetic* an individual is, the more possibility he has of being a success in life.

At the same time, it must be understood that the "*Volitive I*" concretely exists in the form of a strong magnetic field which must be constantly revitalized, as all action absorbs energy.

It is necessary to remember that it is indispensable to economize the energy that has been concentrated, as the "*Volitive I*" requires fuel; it is continuously expending strength just like any other living being.

A series of bad habits and conflicts brings about a great expenditure of energy within the human being. Impatience, emotional conflict, unnecessary haste, mental rumination, the sense of guilt, anger, unnecessary or exaggerated laments, different kinds of frustrations, fear, disorder, and indolence all rob energy from the "*Volitive I.*" The Hermeticist must establish discipline and internal order at all costs in order to match his conduct with the purposes he wishes to achieve.

In relation to "action directed by will," the difference between "to desire" and "to want" should be very clear. The worn out axiom "to want is power" has fallen into disrepute, not because it is false or exaggerated, but because no one has ever been able to explain how one has to want in order to obtain that which is desired. Jesus taught his disciples that "if you have the faith of a mustard seed you will move mountains." On the surface this has nothing to do with will, but deeper analysis will show that Jesus was not talking of ordinary faith, as ordinary faith is not enough to *move mountains*. In truth, he referred to *Hermetic faith*, which consists of two basic forces:

1. To want
2. Reasoned belief

To want is the masculine power of the *"Volitive I,"* and reasoned belief is the feminine energy of feelings. In order to want intelligently, the word "want" must be joined to the rest of the words which form the magicians' acrostic, that is to know, to dare, to want, and to keep silent, with which the following combinations may be formed:

To know how to want	To want to know	To dare to know
To know how to dare	To want to dare	To dare to want
To know how to keep silent	To want to be silent	To dare to be silent
To know how to know	To want to want	To dare to dare

In order to know how to want, a person must be very clear as to what he desires to obtain, and must give the objective a high place in his scale of values in order to obtain adequate motivation from where the power to want is acquired.

One must also practice the four Hermetic "commandments," which are:

- Love
- Hope
- Knowledge
- Peace

LOVE

By means of love, God, the Supreme Intelligence, transmits his creative essence to us. It is not only the attraction between the sexes; it is a power born from the spirit which is directed toward all that carries the divine essence. Love that is passional is not love but only a selfish possessive force, which fights to retain an instrument of pleasure. To clarify the true meaning of love, it is necessary to meditate on the axiom, "love, and do what you want."

HOPE

Hope is the womb which collects the seed, which it develops and gives form to. It is the counterpart of sex. It is the feminine soul in man and masculine soul in woman. Through it we conceive and create. It is the etheric double which has an opposite gender from that of the physical body; man's double is feminine, and woman's is masculine. This is where the feminine part of man and the masculine part of woman is found, and from which it is necessary to detach oneself, changing its polarity.

KNOWLEDGE

Knowledge for the Hermeticist is like the compass for the navigator, for Hermetic science is the knowledge of the laws of Nature. The possession of knowledge places the student on a higher step than one who lacks such knowledge. One must know Nature thoroughly, and thereby control all. One should meditate on the axiom which says *"the magician reigns in heaven and rules in hell"* (to rule in hell means having sufficient power to avoid being destroyed by satanic forces).

PEACE

The student must fight to establish harmony between the brain, heart, and sex, and thus attain the union of the *"Superior I"* with the soul. This is the only way to end the internal conflicts which develop within the human being. When the individual's will grants or denies his body the satisfaction of desires or needs in a completely conscious manner, he will become the king of his physical body and will live in deep peace; and with the power of peace, everything will be harmonious and happy. *He will be king of the Universe, as he will be in harmony with the laws of Nature.*

The power of peace is acquired only by the will to maintain control of the imagination. Impure and uncontrolled imagination is the primary source of restlessness and anxiety. One can only enjoy peace and serenity by controlling the imagination, but nevertheless, there is no peace without love. It is for this reason that it is necessary to overcome egotism, which is the opposite vibration of love.

REASONED BELIEF

Reasoned belief comes from applying Hermetic theory to vital situations. Observation of the action of natural laws and practical verification of the Teaching, confers on the disciple blind belief in himself and in Hermeticism. This is not done through faith, but through absolute certainty of the logical and material verification of everything that he has learned in the Hermetic School.

MIND

We have already pointed out that *Homo sapiens* lacks *mind*, merely possessing a brain and intelligence. We could state that *cerebral* intelligence is unconscious intelligence without any internal sense, while *mental* intelligence has the character of being conscious. The former is oneiric, and the latter awakened. In order to give an elementary idea of the basic material the individual possesses in a latent state, which can form his mind, we refer to the three vital sources:

1. Brain: Intelligence
2. Heart: Feelings
3. Sex: Instinct

Normally the individual *works* with one of these centers predominating, or with a mixture of two of them. For proper Hermetic effects to be realized, the individual must learn to *function* in the following way:

Example No. 1:

1. Brain: Intelligence

We may distinguish three possibilities, or three different vibratory forces. These are:

- The intelligence of the intelligence
- The feeling of the intelligence
- The instinct of the intelligence

2. Heart: Feelings

There are also three possibilities:

- The feeling of the feelings
- The intelligence of the feelings
- The instinct of the feelings

3. Sex: Instinct

Also as above, there are three possibilities:

- The instinct of the instinct
- The feelings of the instinct
- The intelligence of the instinct

These nine possibilities form the number of man, and as man is triple, we may state this in the following manner:

Man: 999

Beast: 666 (the nine inverted)

It is thus that the number of the beast is manifested in *sapiens* in the following manner:

Example No. 2:

1. Brain: Intelligence

- The dream of intelligence (brain)
- The fanaticism of intelligence (heart)
- The bestiality of the intelligence (sex)

2. Heart: Feelings

- The fanaticism of feelings (heart)
- The dream of feelings (brain)
- The bestiality of feelings (sex)

3. Sex: Instinct
   - The bestiality of instinct (sex)
   - The fanaticism of instinct (heart)
   - The dream of instinct (brain)

When the human being "thinks with the number 666" there is no possibility of reaching the knowledge of truth. He is, however, able to perfectly execute marvelous works of good and evil. Furthermore, the works will be programmed and therefore can be tremendously dangerous for the human species and the individual himself. People always believe that good brings forth goodness, and vice versa, but in practice this is not always true.

In Example No. 1, it is hoped that the student should reach integral thought in which there is a perfect equilibrium between intelligence, feelings, and instinct. The formation of the *"Volitive I,"* in addition to the different disciplines the student must accomplish, will gradually lead to the formation of a magnetic bipolar spheroid which extends from the head to the sex, the center point being the spinal column.

This magnetic field is actually present in the Hermeticist and is the seat of his higher awareness; it is a force which resists dissolution by death, and it is through this magnetic field that the individual exists and thinks, even without a physical body. Observe the similarity between this and our planet Earth.

Summarizing the concept of what *mind* is, we can affirm that:

(a) Mind is the "*Volitive I.* "
(b) Mind is a magnetic bipolar spheroid, which is formed within the Hermeticist.
(c) Mind is the "philosopher's stone."
(d) Mind is the whole body.
(e) Mind is the super-brain.
(f) Mind is celestial intelligence.
(g) Mind is the integration of the superior faculties latent in the human being.

The naïve reader will probably ask how it is possible that *mind* is a magnetic sphere, if in point (d) it is said that "it is the whole body." The answer is simple as the one does not contradict the other.

The *mind* or *super-brain* is what permits the *Stellar Man* to reach true wisdom; that which within the individual is "beyond good or evil"; the part of man which reaches eternity. The semi-sage, on the contrary, only accumulates knowledge (*dead* or unconscious knowledge, which is only useful for recognition in the world of *sapiens*) and uses his intelligence for temporal and limited aims. When common men think, they do so with their brain; the Hermeticist thinks with the *mind*.

THREE BASIC OBJECTIVES

As we have already pointed out, these three objectives are awakening, mental digestion, and the formation of the "*Volitive I.*" We have already spoken sufficiently on these points, but must again emphasize mental digestion as the most important part of *processing* the information we acquire through study. When we learn perfect mental digestion, a

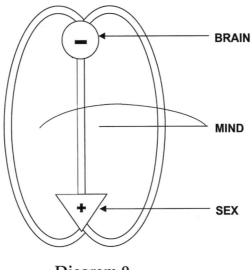

Diagram 9

new world is opened before our astonished eyes, as we thus discover the real sense of written or verbal information, and the genuine meaning of art, music, and other forms of human expression. This capacity of penetration which is reached through the *mind* is so extensive, that no matter what book we read, no matter what we do at a given moment, we will always extract wise and beneficial lessons from our situations, as we will have learned *to read the open book of Nature*. Animals, plants, birds, and even stones will speak to us in silent language, but we will understand perfectly. Further, through the process of understanding, we will be in a permanent transformation into beings who are wiser and more conscious. This will enable us to help our fellow men, not by charity, donation, or politics, but in a superior way, teaching them to live wisely, teaching them to think and decide for themselves, showing them the advantage of taking their lives in their hands and being saved by their own efforts. Because the age of the Messiah has passed, the one who does not save himself condemns himself. Only the individual who is able to form his mind can appreciate the transcendental importance of this fact.

THREE SUPERIOR OBJECTIVES

We have pointed out three superior objectives: deprogramming, initiatory death, and rebirth. The three form part of one process and represent different degrees of it. *Programming* is the assembly of mechanical and automatic circuits, which rule the biological and psychological side of *sapiens*.

Naturally, we do not wish to interfere with biological functions except as an effort to correct some anomaly; we only seek the individual's psychological liberation, and for this it is necessary to reeducate the motor capacity.

We will explain very generally and simply what constitutes the basis of deprogramming: to exchange automatic circuits for conscious circuits. *The individual is deprogrammed by submitting to the relearning of what it means to be awake.* To understand this, it is necessary to bear in mind that mechanical circuits are also formed within the human being thanks to learning. It is thus that at a given moment the child starts to walk without any effort, due to the automation of the circuit, which has been formed by the repetition of voluntary movement. However, we maintain that the low level of alertness in which *sapiens* lives gives all learning an oneiric character; that is, he does not incorporate a superior state of awareness within himself. Therefore, the learning is generally of a *mechanical* character and reinforces the individual's program, progressively reducing his level of awareness and making the possibility of his awakening to greater alertness even more remote. Paradoxically, the more a human being learns, the "less human" he will become, as the potency and reach of his mechanical circuits will increase, making him more and more like a robot. This, as we have already stated, invariably annuls genuine intelligence and leads to absolute slavery or dependence on the program. IQ tests only determine *how well trained the individual's intelligence is*, along with the agility, coordination, and speed by which the neuronal information is synthesized. Such qualities bring to mind the general characteristics of a computer. If perfect robots existed which could both design and apply intelligence tests, they would certainly obtain outstanding performance, but they would only measure mechanical intelligence. Nevertheless, these robots could apply their extraordinary "intellectual" capacity to accomplish functions much more rapidly and efficiently than *sapiens*.

Hermetically, we consider the human being a perfect robot. Therefore, we deny that his intelligence genuinely corresponds to what should be the superior intellect of a truly awakened and conscious human being.

The deprogramming of the individual is obtained gradually by means of an apprenticeship in a state of superior alertness, and gives birth to true intelligence, which leads to "living knowledge," as opposed to the "dead knowledge" of *sapiens*.

Hermetic observations from the most remote ages have established that *sapiens* does not necessarily die when his spirit leaves his body as is the usual process, but in many cases the body continues to live as a veritable *zombie*, in spite of the fact that the spirit has moved on to a better life. A person can live 30 or 40 years under these conditions, leading an apparently normal life. The terrifying thing is that no one realizes this; no one knows that he is greeting, speaking to, or living with an authentic *living cadaver*. From the Hermetic point of view, a cadaver is not a physical body in which the biological life has ended, but is the body without a spirit, as this spirit is the individual himself, the true "I," the real individual behind the *person*. If people cannot recognize a cadaver, it is not at all surprising that they are not aware that they themselves and their fellow men *do not truly think* but that *something thinks for them*. This *something*, which is the source of their ideas, is also converted into the rudder and compass of their existence. We already know that this *something that thinks* is the central computer of the species and the individual is freed from it when he becomes deprogrammed.

Returning to eternal paradoxes, let us consider the enormous contradiction of the fact that an individual's professional preparation limits him intellectually. Instead of expanding the scope of his intelligence, only his cultural, technical, or professional program is furthered.

No university student is prepared to withdraw from the power of suggestion imposed by the prestige and authority of professors, enhanced by the university's imposing image. Thus the student blindly accepts all he is taught, and imitates the behavioral model of the prestigious professors. On the other hand, something absolutely different occurs with the self-taught, who, intellectually speaking, are generally on a much higher level than those who graduate from a university, as their programming is weaker. From the Hermetic point of view we should always prefer self-taught knowledge to that acquired from professors, at least until present educational systems are modified.

Referring once again to deprogramming, we must point out that there is one stage which the disciple is able to cover by himself, and another more advanced and rapidly progressing stage which can only be passed through with the help of a Master or instructor. The disciple's part refers basically to reeducation of motor skills, an effort to give awareness to movements. This can be practiced in ten-minute intervals and repeated as many times a day as desired. It is necessary to move slowly, thinking about and feeling each of the movements being made. Moving slowly should be understood as "moving a little slower than is habitual." This means practicing a deliberate motor action. The consequence of this is an immediate elevation in the level of awareness, placing the student in the "present moment." It is necessary to reflect on the fact that there is nothing which gives a stronger sensation of existing than the act of moving within a space. Walking should be done consciously, moving the hands, arms, head, trunk, and eyes while thinking and feeling.

Together with this exercise, one should meditate daily on the difference between the "I" and "John Doe." That is, person X should think that he is not X, and look at X only as a puppet or vehicle of the "I." It must be observed how X has feelings, ideas, impulses, and fears, which in reality "are not his," but in fact are absolutely foreign to his "I." This practice must be perfected until two absolutely separate beings with perfectly defined boundaries appear, until the practitioner is able to state with complete certainty: "I am not X," and be absolutely convinced of this.

Another discipline that may be practiced by the student consists of controlling the five senses until he is able to see or not see at will, hear or not hear at will, thus successively placing his senses under the control of his will. This exercise is extremely important but we will not elaborate on its benefits, since only those who assiduously practice will learn the secret.

Regarding the part which must be accomplished with the help of a Master, we will only state that the Master can progressively annul the disciple's circuits so that the disciple may rise above all that is mechanical. This is however, a long and delicate task, which may only be known to the person who has arrived at such an experience. The culmination of this stage is *initiatic death*. This is the dissolution of the *personality* in the Hermetic sense, where personality is a synonym for the program. During this period, and until the rebirth is complete, the disciple really ceases to exist, psychologically speaking, living during the time it takes for rebirth with very basic elemental circuits which will not form an obstacle to his evolution.

After his rebirth he will be called the "twice born," and in this manner we understand the esoteric symbol of the birth of Jesus, as it is said that his mother was a virgin. Likewise, we may say that the reborn "is not born of woman."

Once Hermetic rebirth has occurred, the individual starts to live an absolutely new existence, that is of an individual who has been deprogrammed and *freed from the central computer of the species*. For the first time, he has genuine self-determination and autonomy; his thoughts belong to himself; his intelligence has risen to a higher level, and he has been freed from the cosmic-oneiric influence.

Likewise, his soul has been cleansed, becoming again as pure and innocent as a child's. This, and only this, is true heaven, which can be found within the individual. God, who is supposed to be in heaven, and into whose lap it is believed that those of faith will arrive, is in truth the *"Superior I" or Divine Spark*, before whose luminosity the individual feels intimidated and at the same time transported to a condition of supreme peace and love. The angels in their heavenly choir raise paeans in honor of one who died in the world of the beast to be reborn into the world of men. One cycle has ended and another begun: the ascension of man to semigod.

THREE SUPREME OBJECTIVES

We have pointed out three supreme objectives: evolution, conversion into a *Stellar Man*, and transcending Maya.

As we already know, evolution means the growth of our spiritual essence, freeing it from the tyranny of the beast. Our spirit should grow in *size* and *quality*. We will illustrate an evolutionary process in this simple diagram.

In the first figure of Diagram 10, the spiritual essence is represented by the small dark point in the center, and the large circle represents *the rest*. In the second figure, we see the growth of the center point in relation to *the rest*, which symbolizes an evolutionary process.

Here we wish to point out a profound difference between the Western Hermetic path and the goals sought by Yoga,

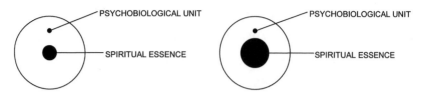

Diagram 10

where it is intended that the individual should be *integrated into Nirvana*, that is, reintegrated into the cosmic egg. As a matter of fact, we could call Yoga the path of the egg, and Hermeticism the path of the spermatozoid. Through an enormous effort, the yogi reaches dissolution of his essential individuality which has taken so long to form. It is thus that he never reincarnates and joins the cosmic egg, awaiting a new wave of life. It is appropriate to ask what happens when this new wave of life arrives after eons of time. Nothing is eternal, and when one who has been freed from reincarnation awakens from his eternal sleep, he is obliged to reincarnate. Thus everything begins again.

On the other hand, the Hermetic path is the conscious evolution of the spiritual individuality. It pursues the indefinite growth of the individual's spiritual essence, so that always conscious of his own identity, the individual evolves until his body as we know it is not sufficient to contain his enormous spiritual power. At this point, his evolution continues in celestial bodies, such as the planet Earth or others. It is completely impossible to conceive of the life of one of these beings and to imagine how they think, talk, feel, and move. In any event, it is useful to observe that a celestial sphere possesses a body basically the same as represented in the two figures, that is, the essence corresponds to the nu-

cleus and the rest to the physical body. Likewise, we can surmise the important difference which may exist, for example,
between the sun and a planet of the solar system.

To clarify what a *Stellar Man* is, it should be said that he is
an individual who was a *sapiens* in the near or remote past.
Through his own effort he was able to provoke a genetic and
functional-psychological mutation in himself, which established the basis for his transition to the other extreme of the
evolutionary spectrum. One of the poles of this spectrum is
represented by *Homo sapiens* and the other by the *Stellar
Man*, the name given to Hermeticists who have reached a
high level of consciousness. A *Stellar Man* is not necessarily a
Hermetic Master of wisdom, as this is a difficult specialty; but
he is a man who, having surpassed his *terraqueous* condition,
is fit to continue the study of the great mysteries of the Universe and to choose his future destiny.

There are many "masters" who have accomplished great
things and have outstanding knowledge, but who are not
Stellar Men. On the contrary, when a *Stellar Man* reaches Hermetic mastery he will always be a "Master of Masters."

With respect to the specialization a Hermeticist may follow when he is advanced along his path, only two of the
most important possibilities will be mentioned, following
the theme of *Zanoni*. These refer precisely to the path of
Zanoni and to the path of Mejnour. The path of Zanoni is
that of high politics, of those leaders who march at the head
of the history of mankind; or better stated, are the creators of
history and leaders of civilization. The path of Mejnour is
that of a *Master of wisdom*, which is the best known. It needs
to be said that these individuals are very scarce, and there

are but few in the world, as the extreme difficulty of their task permits only a few with the necessary spiritual strength to choose this path. Even though gullible people see "masters" everywhere, they are very scarce and are more carefully hidden than is believed. Those who show themselves do so only for purposes of initiation.

Some of these Masters, but certainly not all, *transcend* Maya, or the universal principle of illusion. This means that they live above the *disguised appearance of reality* and that the most important events for the human race mean no more to them than the *ebb and flow of Maya*, an illusion created only to be destroyed and infinitely and repeatedly reformed, as the tide which incessantly fluctuates, always repeating the same cycle with practically imperceptible change. With the supreme calm of absolute reality, they imperturbably contemplate the *circus* of human life, as Mejnour did in the novel *Zanoni*.

It is fitting to meditate on the controversy which arose between two *mythological* Masters, Cagliostro and the Count of Saint Germain. As is well known, Cagliostro was one of the fomenters of the French Revolution, and the celebrated episode of Marie Antoinette's necklace was directly provoked by Cagliostro through Madame de la Motte to unleash the revolutionary process. The Count of Saint Germain, on the contrary, was in favor of maintaining the royalty, and believed that the revolution was not necessary. What is interesting is the philosophical stand taken by each of them. Cagliostro maintained that the revolution would bring about an extraordinary evolutionary advance in the world. Saint Germain argued that there was no hurry for the evolution of the human masses, and that it would be the same if this evolution were slow or fast, as evolution is always cyclical; one cycle ends and another commences.

In order to understand what it means to transcend Maya, we must recall the Principle of Mentalism: "The Universe is mental; the only essential reality is mind: the Universe is a mental creation and we live in the mind of God. . . . All is infinite, eternal, immutable, and unknowable; all that which is finite, movable, and transformable cannot be the All, and as nothing exists beyond this, all that is finite must in reality be nothing."

To transcend Maya means being fully and totally conscious that all that is finite, movable, and transformable is illusory. It means to be able, in time, to project our consciousness toward the infinite, immutable, and eternal, that is to say, toward God.

XVII

THE LIFE AND POWERS OF THE STELLAR MAN

If we had the opportunity to meet and speak to a *Stellar Man*, we probably would not find him appreciably different from any other man. There is nothing more laughable than the physical appearance that some *mystics* pretend to find in the great initiates. Looking at pictures of legendary Masters such as Jesus, Koot Humi, Morya, Serapis Bey, or others, some people expect to see extraordinary physical beauty as if the Masters were angels incarnate. This shows exactly how people idealize these men whose physical appearance is in reality no different from any other man. The only things which expose them to the eyes of those who can see is the aura of strength and power which surrounds them, their brilliant eyes, their shining faces, and the harmonious vibration they project. There is an interesting description of the Rosicrucians by Henri Durville in his book *History of Secret Science*, which demonstrates this point. In their era the

Rosicrucians were the most important Hermetic Order, the seedbed of the *Stellar Man*. Nevertheless, true Rosicrucians do not easily reveal themselves, and those who identify themselves as such and endeavor to demonstrate so by touch or passwords are generally only vulgar imitators who have usurped the sacred name. There are Rosicrucians and "rosicrucians," and the initiate or student can only recognize the authentic members through internal and not external signs. Here are the comments by Durville on Rosicrucians:

> Their existence, although historically uncertain, is surrounded by prestige that forces acceptance and wins admiration. They speak of mankind as infinitely beneath them; their pride is great although their exterior may be humble. They love poverty and declare that for them this is obligatory, although they may possess great wealth. They keep themselves apart from human affection and do not submit to it except as a convenient obligation which is imposed by their living in the world. They are very courteous to women, although incapable of affection and they consider women to be inferior beings. Externally they are unaffected and deferential, but the confidence in themselves which fills their hearts is not radiated except before the infinity of the heavens. They are the sincerest people in the world but granite is soft in comparison with their impenetrability. Compared to these adepts, kings are poor, at their side the wisest are stupid; they never take a step toward fame, which they despise, and if they should become famous, it is in spite of themselves; they seek no honors as no human glory attracts them. Their great desire is to walk unrecognized through the world; due to this, they are impassive in the face of mankind and responsive to whatever befalls them; self-impelled, self-enlightened by themselves

in everything; but willing to do good as their strength permits. What measure can be applied to this immense exaltation? Critical concepts vanish before this. The state of these occult philosophies is the sublime or the absurd. Not being able to understand their souls or their objective, the world declares that one and the other are futile.

This portrait is far from being attractive or agreeable, but it shows the idea that *sapiens* has of *Stellar Man*. Hermeticism of which we speak in this book, sustains that the Hermetic initiate can acquire the following privileges along his or her path of initiation:

1. Freedom from complexes and base passions
2. Freedom from the central computer of the species and becoming a truly awakened man
3. Absolute mental clarity and emotional equilibrium
4. Knowledge of the occult forces of Nature (the nature which is unknown)
5. Entrance into the elite of the truly wise; the true sage is a sage of the mind and not of the intellect
6. Victory over the eventualities of life
7. To know and to find oneself
8. To grasp the secret of happiness and love
9. Emotional, instinctive, and cerebral deprogramming
10. Freedom from the collective unconscious or animal soul
11. Union with one's inner divinity
12. Knowledge of transcendental truth and *the only truth*, becoming converted into a *sage of the mind*
13. Freedom from futile pain and suffering
14. Conscious reincarnation by means of an *avatar*
15. Knowledge of the occult causes of all that exists
16. Power over vibrations and the secret of transmutations

17. To achieve the status of *Stellar Man* or *Stellar Woman* by means of genetic and psychological mutation
18. Freedom from Maya

These powers place the Hermeticist on a much higher level than the ordinary and common man, and for this reason it is hard to really know a Hermetic Master, even though we may be his close friend and he tells us his most secret thoughts and feelings. From our position, it will be impossible to adequately interpret or evaluate these Masters, and probably we will arrive at conclusions absolutely opposite to the truth.

One must take into account the purely *spiritual* condition of the *Stellar Man*. All his higher faculties are of a spiritual nature, and are the opposite of the worshippers or practitioners of astral magic who need not have awakened, nor least of all become deprogrammed, in order to carry out their *spells*. It is necessary to issue a warning that a great percentage of those practicing *magic* fall completely into *black magic*, which we can define in one of its aspects as the *use and projection of the body's mass energy without having previously been deprogrammed*. All sorcerers' apprentices are generally men who are asleep and programmed. These are people who in their oneiric state have had the opportunity, for whatever reason, to gain access to Hermetic theory. This theory is generally then used to satisfy their base passions or to live the agreeable fiction of passing for *extremely evolved* and powerful beings. At times, behind these personages, there is the sincerity of one who deceives himself and lives in the illusion of a subjective world created especially for him.

"Black magic" is usually not that which kills and destroys, but rather that which causes chaos and anarchy. Its worshipers are used by the beast, from which they have not been freed, and they are used for its own dark designs.

It is easy to understand that *magical* and *spiritual* are two absolutely different things, and one never reaches the spiritual by way of the *magical*. On the other hand, there is no individual who is truly spiritual who has no access to the *magical*. *Magic without spirituality is always black magic.* To understand this, we must remember that *spirituality* does not mean *adopting* a spiritual attitude of purity, meekness, and love; it means, as we have already stated, *succeeding in having the spirit manifest through one's own brain.*

For this reason, we must necessarily consider parapsychology as the joining of phenomena involving the projection of energy, and which have absolutely nothing to do with spirituality. It is not necessary to be spiritual to become a medium or to have premonitions. On the contrary, these phenomena take place in the lower astral realm and are related to the animal and passional part of the human being.

Returning to the spiritual powers of the Hermeticist, we must state that his higher qualities do not let him escape or elude material reality; on the contrary, he must respect the laws of the All, as no one can go against the laws. From the moment he takes life in a material body, he must feed, sleep, rest, and entertain himself the same as any other person; he must suffer the same problems as any biological organism in a hostile environment. Books on pseudo-occultism have given the wrong impression because they depict the initiate as a fabulous being who needs no food or sleep and who spends most of his time on the astral plane.

Spiritual perfection is confused with the material, forgetting that perfection in matter does not exist, since matter is subject to constant transformation. Nevertheless, the Hermetic initiate possesses the secret of transmutation, and can, under certain circumstances, create or transform vital situations in order to alleviate problems which afflict him, or to help other people with their difficulties.

The *Stellar Man* is the possessor of truth. Many people are irritated when someone claims to possess absolute truth, deeming this an act of egocentrism and profound arrogance. Imagine for a moment that someone could actually have access to absolute truth. Should this man keep silent forever and hide his knowledge? Or would it be his duty to help those who also desire to attain knowledge of the truth?

With full knowledge of the truth, we affirm that the Stellar Man possesses absolute truth and that no one can reach the absolute without first being converted into a Stellar Man. Therefore, only *Stellar Men* know absolute truth. This occurs not because a special person, human or divine, has revealed the truth to them, but because the special cerebral and intellectual forms they have attained through genetic and psychological mutation have enabled them to become aware of the naked truth which under the trance-like conditions in which *sapiens* lives, cannot be seen. It is necessary to understand that *sapiens* does not possess the *organ of truth*, but rather the *organ of illusion and lies*. Some great Masters affirm that when man lived in Paradise, he knew the truth, although he could not take advantage of this knowledge since he did not evolve. When God punished man by driving him out of Eden, he injected into him the *organ of illusion* so that he could reach the truth only by means of a titanic effort of will and intelligence and not by divine grace. This means that man can reach knowledge of truth and further evolve as he now has a physical body subject to transformation.

Now, the fact that *Stellar Man* possesses absolute truth does not remotely mean he knows everything. In fact, he is aware of all that he does not know. But he has the *fundamental science*, which makes it possible to reach the knowledge of all he desires, if he dedicates sufficient time to this effort.

To possess absolute truth means to have risen above the universal plan, reaching union with *the All* who creates and sustains the universal illusion. *The absolute is that which never changes and always remains identical in its intrinsic nature.* Specifically, Hermetic truths do not change in themselves; it is only necessary to know how to apply them differently in situations which are always changing.

There are three types of truth:

- Absolute cosmic truth: knowledge of the mysteries of Nature; knowledge of the seven Hermetic Principles
- Specific absolute truth: absolute truth relative to a specific problem or situation
- Relative truth: truth in the illusory world and a lie in relation to absolute truth

It is from the point of view of relative truth that the well-known aphorism arose which says that "nothing is truth or a lie; all is according to the color of the glass through which it is viewed."

The *Stellar Man* is happy. His happiness, however, is not based on material things, although he makes use of all that Nature offers. His happiness is based on the perfection, beauty, harmony, and stability of his internal world. The world is full of unhappy people, who seek to satisfy their *internal hunger* but do not know how to attain it.

Each individual requires special food for his spirit, which is the only thing that will truly satisfy him; but generally his ignorance leads him to seek one of the following paths:

1. Those who constantly satisfy their beast without feeding the spirit
2. The ascetics who renounce worldly pleasures moved by internal convictions or impelled by their complexes, they devote themselves to a spiritual search but do not obtain the happiness yearned for
3. Those who try to maintain a balance between the above two points, but who end up enslaved to the Law of the Pendulum, which forces them alternatively from one path to another

The *Stellar Man* reaches a perfect internal equilibrium and equally satisfies his spiritual and bestial hunger; he feeds his beast and his spirit, thus maintaining perfect stability. His beast is not perverse as mentioned in other chapters, but is a pure and natural beast.

The *Stellar Man* is humble. He is perfectly aware of the enormous magnitude of his ignorance, and when he compares himself with the immensity that surrounds him, he is awed by his own smallness.

The *Stellar Man* loves all living creatures. His consciousness is in everything and everything is within him. This feeling of total unity makes him deeply aware of human nature, and when he learns the deepest motives of men, he finds it difficult to blame them for their mistakes. No one is capable of giving more love than he is, for loving is giving, and the *Stellar Man* is like a radiant sun. Like a giant star, he manufactures energy in himself via the transformation of matter. This is an extension of the Hermetic concept of "as above, so below."

The *Stellar Man* is just and impartial. He possesses *internal judgment*, which enables him to always think impersonally, to judge without any personal bias, and without considering his personal convenience. A true sage is always just.

The *Stellar Man* lacks passions. All his instinctive, emotional, and intellectual manifestations are active, that is, genuinely self-generated. He receives stimuli and makes use of them, but this does not oblige him to feel certain things or to become enslaved. He takes pleasure from what he enjoys.

The *Stellar Man* is above death. If his physical body dies, the same does not happen to his *spiritual individuality* which survives this destruction and takes possession of another physical body, either returning to the material womb or *taking charge* of an already grown body. This permits him to consciously reincarnate, becoming an *avatar*.

The *Stellar Man* constantly renews himself. Every so often he modifies his standards of behavior to the point that someone observing him could state that *"he has no standards of behavior."* He knows the mystery of the Phoenix which is reborn from its own ashes, and when the time comes, kills itself, then being luminously reborn. This mysterious process occurs several times in the life of a *Stellar Man* within the same physical body.

The *Stellar Man* is absolutely indifferent to the opinions of others. He is not at all concerned about the image he projects. Furthermore, he knows that under certain circumstances it is preferable to show a *bad image* as there will then be no possibility of being idolized; in this way, he comes to know who his most sincere friends really are. He is friendly, but only with those who possess internal substance; he will not tolerate superficiality, except if there are special qualities in a latent state.

The *Stellar Man* is beyond good and evil, and therefore his opinion of the events in the world and its people differs considerably from the usual ones. At times he is very hard on those who have committed an error, which may appear insignificant, and on other occasions treats with kindness those who in our opinion deserve the worst punishment. No one knows his reasons, but his attitude is certainly never the result of a whim.

The *Stellar Man* lives in the world of causes. By being in contact with the higher plane of causes, he himself places the causes he desires into motion in order to manifest concrete effects in his own life or in the lives of others. The common man must wait for things *to happen*, for the thing he calls *chance* to favor him. When this does not happen, he must be resigned to live with the effects of causes he is completely unaware of.

The *Stellar Man* is truly human. His spiritual powers do not make him shun life, and he generally complies with his civil duties and earns his living as does any other person. If he marries, he always tries to raise his companion to his level, but if this is not possible, is able to live in peace, harmony, and love.

The *Stellar Man* has no political ideology. He is a humanist whose desire is for all human beings to attain spiritual evolution. Observe the difference between *revolution* and *evolution*. *Revolution* indicates rotation, a cyclical repetition. Everything changes, but with the passage of time, everything returns to what it was in the beginning. *Evolution*, on the other hand, means an ascending spiral, where a profound transformation that is not superficial takes place. The *Stellar Man* rejects all that impedes the individual's freedom, but does not condone the irresponsible use of freedom. He believes that the individual himself must deserve to be free, and should not expect it as a gift from society or God.

The *Stellar Man* may become ill and die like any other person, as his physical body is also subject to the law of material transformation. Nevertheless, if he so desires, in the majority of cases, he can transmute illness into health in a progressive and gradual manner. The greatest danger for him lies in the negative attitudes taken by other people he has helped at some time, and whose *Karma* he has absorbed, as this provokes a real *illness of mental origin*, which is extremely difficult to cure. Recall that Jesus could not heal himself in spite of being the savior of mankind.

The *Stellar Man* is not a hermit who keeps himself apart from the ups and downs of life. Far from being insensitive, he lives more intensely than most people. Nevertheless, he can choose to be harder than a rock or a diamond, or on the contrary, love with all his being. Emotionally speaking, he has exquisite sensitivity because his awareness encompasses a range of vibrations infinitely wider than that of the ordinary man. It is as if he could play a piano with an immense keyboard with thousands of different notes.

The *Stellar Man* is introverted, but not selfishly so; his introversion is due to the extraordinary richness of his internal world. His consciousness is so rich that it is painful for him to leave that veritable heaven to perform in this material world. This is especially painful for the *Master of Hermetic wisdom*, or for the one who has assumed the responsibility of transmitting knowledge, for every authentic Master is, in a certain manner, crucified, symbolic of Christ. There is a Hermetic-Rosicrucian axiom which says that "it is necessary to decrucify Christ (the *'Superior I'*) to crucify the heart (emotional egotism)." No one knows the sacrifice it entails for an individual who has reached heaven to descend once again into the dark world of mud. However, this action obeys the true wisdom of the Polarity Principle, for if the individual were to be permanently in heaven, he would eventually degenerate as his virtue would encounter no obstacle. It is for this reason that the *Stellar Man* lives in heaven but has his feet on the earth. As we have already stated, he is an *inhabitant of two worlds*; he lives simultaneously in heaven and on earth; he is human and divine.

The *Stellar Man* knows the secrets of universal magnetism, and this permits him to vitalize himself and project his consciousness to his surroundings.

Every highly developed Hermetic initiate has a tremendous magnetic irradiation which surrounds his body like a sphere of energy, and is the extension of his mental power.

This sphere of magnetic energy occupies a space and corresponds in size to the initiate's spiritual development. It is said that Jesus Christ possessed a powerful magnetic sphere that engulfed the entire Earth, and that this had an enormous influence on the human race.

This teaching makes it possible to understand why "God is everywhere," as his irradiation fills the entire universe.

The *Stellar Man* practices the secret of the *evolutionary circle*. We have already referred to the *circle of the ass*, the long road walked by the *human beast* who always remains in the same place. This circuit gives him no benefit or evolution. On the contrary, the "evolutionary circle" consists of the wise handling of the Polarity Principle, where the initiate oscillates between Earth and heaven, alternately polarizing and depolarizing himself. In this way, a perfect equilibrium is maintained, achieving the wisdom of one who accustoms himself neither to the light nor darkness. His long journeys always take him to the starting point, but with considerable evolution. As an example of this, we will cite the process so beautifully described by Herman Hesse in *Siddhartha*, where the protagonist fights tirelessly for a long time in order to become separated from the human horde and attain his own individuality. But once he does this, he must suffer all kinds of trials and diverse experiences to finally reach a union with the whole. But what a difference, what an infinite abyss separates the Siddhartha in the beginning from the sage at the end: evolution had been completed. If we had to put this in a single aphorism, we would say that the sincerest desire of one who has fallen is to reach heaven, and naturally, the strongest impulse of one who has reached heaven is to descend to earth. Again we must meditate on the *Revolt of the Angels* by Anatole France.

The *Stellar Man* has his own morals. Celestial morals are different from the morals of terrestrial man. Celestial morals are absolute and invariable within the flexibility of internal judgment, while terrestrial morals accommodate themselves to the customs of the dominant culture. If one day a cannibalistic culture should be dominant, cannibalism would be considered perfectly moral and correct, and, furthermore, perhaps those who did not conform to it would be punished.

When we state that the morals of the *Stellar Man* do not vary, we do not mean they are rigid. In spite of constant transformation they remain intact in their essential nature. On the other hand, the Hermeticist considers many of *sapiens'* attitudes as immoral. Irresponsibility, abuse of power, emotional blackmail, apathy, hypocrisy, blind conformism, self-pity, cerebral programming through the media, and glorification and applause are only a few of the immoral attitudes and customs of *sapiens*. Hermetic ethics are on an infinitely higher level than the accommodating rules of conduct of the common man.

The power of the *Stellar Man* does not emanate from his *third eye*, nor from *chakras* or the *Kundalini*. Nor does he possess parapsychological abilities. As we have already stated, Hermeticism maintains that parapsychological qualities merely represent the *displacement and projection of mass energy;* therefore, the more bestial the individual, the better chance of success he has. For this reason parapsychological qualities *work better* when the individual is experiencing strong instinctive or emotionally passionate states, which intensify or multiply the radiation of mass energy. There is no spiritual merit in this; it is only *unconscious sorcery*. The power of the Hermeticist emanates from a spiritual force, from purity, the domination of his passions, from the sublimation of his animal energy, and from the rectitude of his intentions.

The *Stellar Man* may have great material problems in his earthly life, as his enormous difference in level from other people makes them instinctively look at him with a lack of confidence and fear upon perceiving a strange power they cannot classify. Persecution and economic failure may turn into serious obstacles for the Hermeticist, whose "kingdom is not of this world" and whose skills are not outstanding on this earth where social and economic success are for those who possess a specific psychological makeup. Nevertheless, in spite of the fact that the Hermeticist can fail in some things, this experience will never oppress him, and if he strives sufficiently, he will always end up as a conqueror.

The *Stellar Man* does good works, but "is careful to whom." He helps to the limit of his strength, but only for those who, in his estimation, truly merit help. He believes that helping those who lack merit means to truly harm them. If the support offered is wasted or not fully utilized, he helps two or three more times, but then no more.

The *Stellar Man* can be a difficult person to understand, or the most agreeable person in the world. As he is used to living in a world of lies, hypocrisy, cheating, and falseness, it is a shock to some individuals who are friendly with a *Stellar Man*, that he is absolutely genuine, natural, and authentic, without hidden corners or attitudes of any kind. His sincerity may be unbearable for those who hide beneath the countless masks of the personality. The following phrase explains the natural simplicity of the actions of the *Stellar Man*, "*when he eats, he eats; when he thinks, he thinks; when he speaks, he speaks; and when he rests, he rests.*"

He is not a perfect being and does not aspire to be one; as we have already explained, he endeavors to reach only *relative perfection*, as absolute perfection does not exist.

However, after his mutation into a *Stellar Man* is accomplished, he has ended his ascension to Mount Olympus, and is one more inhabitant of the sacred mountain, a semigod who does not as yet desire absolute divinity. Nevertheless, his studies of the mysteries of the Universe never cease, for they can never be completely known.

It may be thought that this path is much too individualistic for an era in which the world is moving faster each day toward collective structures. For those with this view, it needs to be pointed out that if a person does not first acquire his own *individuality*, he is really only an appendage of the masses; he is nothing more than one of the elements forming a circuit which in turn is part of the great machine.

We understand that there are individuals who have personally failed, and endeavor to fuse their undesirable "I" with that of the collective of the mass. But there is also an opportunity to emancipate and develop a *"Superior I"* to reach complete fulfillment and maturity. To understand this, it is necessary to differentiate between an individual whose egotism leads him to blind individualism that is dangerous to society, and one who has become an individual and has a very clear sense of his duty toward mankind. Only one who has reached freedom can have a true *collective consciousness,* while at the same time retaining full freedom and autonomy without handing over his brain to any conqueror. What a difference there is between being incorporated into mankind because of an inability to be free, and joining up with humanity after having attained freedom!

It is interesting to consider that *sapiens* fears freedom, since this involves the only thing an animal within a flock cannot possess: intelligent individuality. For this same reason *sapiens* endeavors to join movements which do not demand any thinking or decision-making. Conversely, the Hermetic path obliges the individual to take the responsibility of his life into his own hands, instead of transferring it to social groups.

From the philosophical point of view, *one who has not first achieved his own individual existence can do nothing for the world and its people.* One who *is not,* has nothing to give. On the contrary, when the Hermeticist has reached his complete individual stature, he is in condition to help others in the only truly efficient way: teaching them to live wisely.

XVIII

GENERAL OVERVIEW

Through the study of Hermeticism we can see how *sapiens* loses the best in his life by not being able to obtain really lasting values for himself. The happiness he seeks slips from his hands and only the passing joy of a moment of pleasure remains. Understanding of this phenomenon generally converts the individual into a materialistic cynic whose main belief is that "things must be enjoyed while it is possible as after this life there is no other." This really is the goal most sought after by people: "to have a good time." Nevertheless, little by little, with experience and as the years go by, the individual realizes that he has not attained happiness, for even if he has had a good time, those moments have been followed by others of pain, suffering, and internal emptiness. Generally, people think they are lacking something specific in their lives which will make them happy, and that when they obtain it, they will be happy. When they obtain their desires and continue to be as unhappy as before, they become more materialistic and unfeeling every day, or deliver themselves over to an unreal philosophical or religious mysticism.

There is nothing more daunting than taking stock of what has been gained in life, beyond subsistence, suffering, enjoyment, or what one has done for his fellow men. The naïve person can easily fill the credit column with his professional titles, his material possessions, wealth, family, or knowledge obtained. Nevertheless, the cold reality is that *the individual is not the owner of anything, unless he is certain that what he possesses will endure.* Under ordinary circumstances he can only make a list of the things life has given him to handle, and even in this case he does not know when this mandate will expire.

In truth, the individual only gets out of life, for himself, what he can keep indefinitely, beyond death. Obtaining something for oneself means having a purpose in life; it means taking possession of something intimate and personal, which is, after all, the fruit of life.

Everyone should ask himself, "What have I obtained from life? Is it sufficient just to go along with what life brings? Do I really possess what I believe I have obtained, or will it vanish tomorrow like a soap bubble?"

Many may think that this kind of reasoning is very selfish, but we must consider that gaining nothing for oneself is just as foolish, or more so, than excessive selfishness. To give everything away for the air we breathe and for the food and well-being necessary to keep the body alive may be very romantic and poetic, but is extremely inconvenient, as this represents eternal slavery. Eternal in this case is meant in the cosmic sense of time, which compared to the terrestrial, is really unending. This can be verified from dreams, for during an instant of time, the individual has access to cosmic time, and it is for this reason that in thirty terrestrial seconds one may dream the summary of a whole lifetime, from birth to death. This same concept can also be applied to the "eternal torment of the fires of hell."

Many people laugh at Hermeticism, occultism, and all things esoteric, but generally none of them have had any direct experience in the matter, and only speak from hearsay or prejudice. Some are intellectually proud and use their reasoning to discredit Hermeticism. It is hoped that those who reason that way are absolutely and completely certain of their reasoning, and do not fall into any of the following categories of flawed critical thinking:

- Those who believe themselves awake, but are really dreaming
- Those who blindly imitate, placing implicit faith in other people, systems, or institutions to avoid thinking for themselves
- Those whose passions take the place of reason; they draw a line in advance, and will accept no reason of their own or of others that is not within this line, but leaning towards what flatters their state of mind, vanity, or interest
- Those that adore their own ideas as sacred images; our ideas have belonged to us from time immemorial and we are unaware of how these ideas are subtly insinuated into our brain. They never allow anyone to contradict or discredit them.

We must not forget that the main part of the individual's reasoning generally consists of finding a reason to continue believing what he already believes.

Others will blindly deny their possible dependence on a *central computer*, arguing that they *do as they please*. They do not realize that they desire what the central computer makes them desire. It is sufficient to analyze individual motivation in depth to understand that everything takes place under internal or external pressure. Ideas, feelings, impulses, or actions are always compulsive; they are never born from an act of superior and free reasoning.

The usual reason for upholding the idea of one's own freedom consists in the argument of showing a long list of all things accomplished in life. Nevertheless, it should be asked, were these things done by our own desires, or were we obliged to do them in spite of ourselves? Did we desire a certain thing, or were we obliged to desire it?

There are a few very simple reflections, which should lead any individual who meditates on them to reach the conclusion that *sapiens'* scale of values is tremendously distorted. Here are some of these reflections:

- Science does not bring true happiness to the human being; it only provides comfort, pleasure, and technology.
- Intelligence does not develop or form *content* in a person.
- The internal nature of the human being has not appreciably evolved during the course of history.
- Man has no knowledge of the greater portion of his internal nature.
- The human species has no one with whom to compare itself, only animals; therefore, they have no point of reference for their own worth or their real position in the cosmic scale.

Each person must reach his own conclusions on these thoughts.

It is necessary to consider that Hermeticism is not solely dedicated to showing *how bad sapiens* is, or *how insignificant* he is, but that it has a well-defined plan for the human race. Pointing out the real position of *sapiens* as a *small animal of little importance* in the face of universal grandeur, and whose only value is that he possesses the divine spark, has a creative and not a destructive objective. We attempt to encourage a person, through reflection, to see the unbarred cell in which he lives, as this is the only way that the desire to escape will be born in him. While an individual believes that *all is well* and that he himself *is very well*, there will be no possibility of real evolution. This is the reason why many mystics suddenly feel spiritual restlessness after having gone through tremendously painful experiences which came as a positive *shock*, awakening them from their somnambulistic lethargy. The object of suffering is to awaken the individual's consciousness. Nevertheless, there are many so deeply asleep that suffering only further brutalizes them, and is absolutely unproductive.

There are many who have a purely devotional attitude toward Hermeticism, thinking that it is sufficient to be *very spiritual* to progress along the path, and that these *spiritual* individuals (according to their own opinion) will be the best prepared to ascend to higher levels. They believe that progress is attained by a kind of *contact* with heaven or with the *occult powers*, and that it is sufficient to sacrifice oneself by serving mankind in order to obtain everything.

In truth, the great *disadvantage* of Hermeticism lies in the fact that it is the path of pure intelligence, and if the student does not develop his intelligence and awareness to the required levels, no evolution is possible. Another enormous obstacle for people is that it is necessary to work very hard as Hermeticism is the path of *self-salvation*, and out of laziness and indolence, one does not wish to save himself. People prefer to be *saved by Christ* even if this should only be a figment of their deluded brains; or to be saved by *magic* or by the crew of *flying saucers*. One of the reasons people do not make a decision to save themselves is because they have no idea what they have to be saved from, believing that on earth, everything is just as it seems.

Professional occultists or eternal students of esotericism live in the hopes of one day finding someone who will open their *third eye*, for example, in the belief that therein resides all magical secrets. For them we would say that the third eye only gives them a vision of the human being's energy projections without even remotely offering them any spiritual progress or advancement. Furthermore, we must mention the purely symbolic nature of the supposed *operation* of the opening of the *third eye*, under which Lobsang Rampa hid the true mystery of what the Hindus call *Maya Virrupa*, whose most approximate translation is the *path of illusion*.

The fabulous unicorn, the mythical animal with a horn on its forehead, represents what we are referring to. One who wants to act with his third eye must develop a *horn* in the middle of his forehead.

Much has been made of *unfolding* in the belief that control of this indicates a higher degree of spiritual evolution. Nothing is farther from the truth; it is easy to unfold with an extract of *cannabis indica* without any spiritual merit whatsoever. Unfolding is no more than a dangerous exercise and is extremely fatiguing. We must add that it has never been known if the *visions* that the operator sees when unfolded, or with his third eye, are really true or only mirages of cosmic ether. The eternal aphorism *"as above, so below"* confirms this fact. If we can so frequently deceive ourselves in the physical world using the senses we freely control, there is even more likelihood to deceive ourselves upon using such difficult and restricted faculties.

The real importance of unfolding is something we have spoken little about, and which could be called *Hermetic unfolding*. This consists of being *conscious simultaneously on two planes*: physical and spiritual, in heaven and on earth. It is thus that the Hermeticist rises above himself upon becoming divided into two persons, both of which simultaneously have "their eyes open." It is said that in this way the Hermeticist obtains the power of powers, which is uniting earth with heaven. Of this state we will describe just one phenomenon which is very curious and incomprehensible to the ordinary individual, and that is to simultaneously perceive two extremes. If this can be understood, the individual will be *sad and happy at the same time, simultaneously. Pleasure and pain, serenity and agitation, attraction and repulsion, and life and death are experienced at the same time.* It must not be believed that this experience produces an average without differentiation. On the contrary, this gives absolute understanding and experience of each of these states without the negative repercussions which good or evil extremes may produce.

When we mention this, it is not with the intention that this should be easily understood, but rather "sensed."

Admirers of Yoga give tremendous importance to Kundalini and the Chakras, believing them to be the fundamental pillar of spiritual fulfillment. The truth is that no benefit would be gained by a person through this touted *awakening* of Kundalini, except perhaps an intense creative euphoria that has nothing to do with spiritual progress.

We must understand that true evolution cannot be improvised in any way, and that no one in the Universe can attain it without a slow, sustained, and vigorous process of self-fulfillment.

There are those who pursue *magical powers* such as clairvoyance with tremendous perseverance, without stopping to think whether it is really beneficial to them or not. As an example, one of the easiest things to attain is what is commonly called *second sight*. For this we will give the method, although we honestly trust that no one will use it. To attain *second sight* it is sufficient to become a *medium* and endeavor to develop mediumistic faculties, easily done by means of the collective suggestion which takes place during seances. Upon becoming a medium, the individual becomes clairvoyant very rapidly, as he is possessed by what we may call *controlling spirits* of a lower nature. Traditionally, in classic occultism these are called *astral shells*; they are the bestial principles of individuals which survive for some time after death, and which need to absorb and feed on magnetic energy from living beings, producing a type of vampirism. The medium is taken over by these "astral shells" and they project into his imagination all that they themselves have seen in the "world of the dead." However, they charge a high price for their work, as they absorb the energy of the medium who is left exhausted, generally ending up contracting leukemia or some other ailment which science cannot cure.

There was an interesting case of an ex-medium who managed to infiltrate a new group of people who did not believe in spiritualism. He related to them his spectacular visions during which there appeared prehistoric beings who spoke to him. In a short while, five or six of the group were *seeing* things similar to this, for the first time in their lives. This is an example of *magnetic contagion*.

Many who have attained power or great riches scoff at spiritual things, alleging that there is nothing their money cannot buy, despising the philosopher, believing he has something *to sell*. Protected by their wealth, they believe they have attained the pinnacle of their ambitions. Unfortunately, they do not understand that beyond a certain limit there is nothing their money can buy, not even material pleasures, and that the effort of retaining their possessions consumes all their energy.

How many modern Croesus types are unable to acquire a new stomach at any price, one that will enable them to again enjoy gastronomic pleasures; or perhaps are unable to restore their worn out sexual energy in order to possess the woman they desire? It is ironic that they cannot enjoy what the most humble laborer is able to have.

One of the comforting things in life is to contemplate the exceptions to this rule, as in the case of those who use their wealth for truly significant social work, and for which they will most certainly receive a prize from the Lords of Destiny in a future reincarnation. It is true that by means of good works the sins of the individual are forgiven. It is necessary to clarify that, for the Hermeticist, sin as it is commonly known does not exist; there is the Law of Cause and Effect, and the occult judges who judge and punish people according to their individual responsibility, group them into four categories:

- The illiterate human masses
- The middle class
- The great scientists, outstanding professionals, philosophers, and leaders
- The initiates

The occult judges punish the individual according to his responsibility. They consider the responsibility of the first category to be practically nil; that of the second category slightly higher; the third has a lot of responsibility; and the fourth, the initiates, are considered absolutely responsible. Therefore, should they stray from the correct path, they receive the worst possible punishment, as they have acted with their eyes open. This penalty may even be the violent physical elimination of the individual or being *demoted* in future incarnations.

It is necessary to point out that *Hermetic science*, like all that exists, may be used for good or evil. In itself it is neutral, as it is beyond good or evil, but some of its rules may become known and used erroneously. It is for this reason that *white magic* and *black magic* are always differentiated as we have already mentioned in previous pages, and that in their manifestations, one is constructive and the other destructive. Speaking of *black magicians* reminds one of a tale like *A Thousand and One Nights*. The truth is that there are *black magicians* in the worst sense of the word, who are in reality the most ferocious enemies of the *Stellar Men*, moving all kinds of forces and people in order to attack them. In contrast to *stellar*, we could perhaps correctly call them *abysmal*.

Many of these *black magicians* know the strangest secrets to resist death. Alexandra David-Neel relates in one of her books on Tibet the horrible case of some indescribably ancient priests who stayed alive by feeding on live men who had to die slowly in a special sarcophagus, on top of the remains of others who had died before in that same place. In reality, they had to slowly rot to death, but for the spell to be successful, this had to be done willingly, being convinced by the priests of the extraordinary and decisive spiritual merit of a supreme confrontation with death.

Count Dracula is not a simple fantasy. Hermetic tradition maintains that these beings really exist and that many of them live hundreds of years by drinking fresh blood extracted from humans, obtaining the vitality necessary to restore their own system. It is a fact that many people practice unconscious vampirism at another level and absorb the energy of others. It is thus that "machismo" and "matriarchy" are merely forms of unconscious emotional vampirism.

Within the realm of this subject it is interesting to consider certain businessmen, who, guided by animal instinct, vampirize their competitors whom they gradually absorb until they are ruined and destroyed. Vampirism is such an extensive subject that we expect to cover it more in detail in a future book.

The world is unaware of the terrible battles waged between stellar and abysmal men. Just as with most truly important things, they remain hidden beneath absolutely different appearances.

With respect to the future of mankind, we maintain that the best hope of salvation lies in the possibility of scientifically establishing our theory of *people's levels of consciousness*. Perhaps in the near future important advances and discoveries will occur in the field of measurement of yet undiscovered cerebral rhythms. The most important of these is the *rhythm of superior awareness*, which appears in people possessing a high level of awareness, the result of Hermetic work upon themselves. The day this discovery becomes a scientific reality, human beings must undoubtedly be grouped according to "levels of consciousness." Social and intellectual classes will disappear to give way to degrees of awareness. It is probable that in this way a scale of one to ten will be established in which 1 would represent the highest state of awareness among people, and 10, the lowest. It is understood that those possessing the higher levels would be the group which would guide mankind. They would absolutely guarantee a world free from wars, delinquency, and poverty, with an equal opportunity for all, as everyone would be able to climb the scale of awareness and some day reach level one. Nevertheless, for this system to be justified and accepted by people, it would necessarily have to carry much more weight and scientific authority than the current system of measuring human intelligence. It would have to be the obvious result of an absolutely clear scientific verification of the theory of levels of awareness, and the basis of it would have to be made known in simple language so that the entire world could understand it.

We guarantee that this discovery would be the greatest that man has ever invented during his existence on earth, the only discovery capable of guaranteeing the future and happiness of the human race to a certain extent.

However, at first this would cause tremendous problems among the *disqualified* people. We would be very surprised to find that the majority of individuals who previously were known as superior beings due to their great intelligence would be classified under number 5 after measuring their level of awareness. Men who previously were great leaders might be relegated to the lowest categories upon verifying, without any doubt, their absolute lack of a state of superior alertness and *internal judgment*, which is the very condition from which a high level of consciousness is derived.

On the other hand, simple men, with minimal culture and a very *elemental* intelligence would possibly occupy the highest positions. In the last instance, this cerebral examination to determine the level of awareness would establish the degree of the individual's *spiritual age*, translated into concepts of *evolution, wisdom, and spiritual perfection.*

It is thus that the world could be governed by an *Advisory Committee of Spiritual Ancients*, true sages, possessors of a high level of awareness and very clear *internal judgment.*

Many people believe, based on ancient prophecies or interpretation of supposed messages contained in the pyramids or ancient documents, that the world will come to an end in the near future, as a result of a great catastrophe, possibly of stellar origin. Disregarding the truth or error of these prophecies, we consider the human being as the great determining factor of these phenomena. Thus, as Sodom and Gomorrah were destroyed because of the extreme perversion of their inhabitants, the planet Earth is influenced in its interstellar relations by mankind's mental, emotional, instinctive, and psychological states. The behavior and character of people influence, to a very important extent, the climate, vegetable and animal life, and telluric phenomena.

Any catastrophe predicted for the near future could be annulled by a decisive or important upheaval in the behavior and spiritual life of the human being.

In this respect, as in any circumstance which pretends to predict the future, the Hermeticist is more interested in creating the future than in predicting it.

We hope that in the nearest possible future, the scientific measurement of "levels of consciousness" will become a reality for humanity, thus signifying a new dawn for Mankind.

Other books published by John Baines can be ordered through the publisher:

_____	*The Secret Science*	ISBN 1-882692-01-2	$12.95
_____	*The Stellar Man*	ISBN 1-882692-04-7	$13.95
_____	*The Science of Love*	ISBN 1-882692-00-4	$12.95
_____	*HypsoConsciousness*	ISBN 1-882692-02-0	$9.95
_____	*Morals for the 21st Century*	ISBN 1-882692-03-9	$18.95

Books are also available in
Spanish, Bulgarian, Russian, Italian, Latvian, German, and Portuguese.

Use this page for ordering:

THE JOHN BAINES COLLECTION
P.O. Box 8556, F.D.R. Station
New York, NY 10150
JBI@bway.net

Please send me the above title(s).

I am enclosing a check for $ _____

(Please add $3.50 shipping for $ _____
1–4 titles within the USA and $12.00
for shipping outside of the USA.)

TOTAL $ _____

We also accept MasterCard, Visa, and American Express:

Card Number: _____

Expiration Date: _____

Signature: _____

Mr/Mrs/Ms: _____

Address: _____

City/State/Zip: _____

E-mail: _____

Prices and availability subject to change without notice.